Susan H. Mung

THE INTERNATIONAL BUSINESS COMMUNICATIONS DESK REFERENCE

- foreign words and phrases
- currencies
- exchange rates
- time zones
- business holidays
- metric weights and measures
- country and city codes
- customs regulations
- postal codes and abbreviations
- and more

amacom

American Management Association

New York • Atlanta • Boston • Chicago • Kansas City • San Francisco • Washington, D.C.
Brussels • Toronto • Mexico City

This publication is designed to provide accurate and authoritative
information in regard to the subject matter covered. It is sold with the
understanding that the publisher is not engaged in rendering legal,
accounting, or other professional service. If legal advice or other expert
assistance is required, the services of a competent professional person
should be sought.

Library of Congress Cataloging-in-Publication Data

Munger, Susan H.
    The international business communications desk reference   /   Susan H.
Munger.
        p.   cm.
    Includes index.
    ISBN 0-8144-7786-0
    1. Business communications—Handbooks, manuals, etc.
    2. Communications in international trade—Handbooks, manuals, etc.
    I. Title.
    HF5718.M83   1993
    651.7—dc20   93-6944
                                                                                                              CIP

Printing number

10 9 8 7 6 5 4 3 2 1

Contents

Introduction

Major changes around the world are affecting business everywhere. In the United States, small and medium-sized companies are seeking new markets in other countries as never before. In the countries of the former USSR, people in all walks of life are eager to exchange ideas and goods with the rest of the world. In China stock exchanges have been established and Special Enterprise Zones are thriving centers for export and import between China and the rest of the world. The North American Free Trade Agreement eases trade between Canada, Mexico, and the United States. Trade barriers between the countries of western Europe are being removed.

Change provides new sales opportunities for companies with useful products and services to sell. Whether you are a new player or have been in the field for some time, the *International Business Communications Desk Reference* is a tool to help you communicate effectively. A guide to written and spoken communications, it contains practical information for writing letters, sending packages and faxes, and making telephone calls quickly, efficiently, and correctly to seventy-three countries. The countries are the United States' top fifty trading partners (importers and exporters) as compiled by the International Trade Administration of the U.S. Department of Commerce, the more stable eastern European countries, and the countries of the former USSR (see the list below).

A WORD ON LANGUAGES

You will find English equivalents for selected useful words, abbreviations, and phrases in French, German, Italian, Japanese, Portuguese, and Spanish. Be aware that not all languages use the same alphabet. The Roman alphabet is used in most Western languages, although some do not use all the letters and some have several additional ones, for example, Ø in Scandinavian languages and ß in German.

Other alphabets include the Greek alphabet and the Cyrillic alphabet, which is used in Russian and other Slavic languages. Japanese, Chinese, Hebrew, Arabic, and South Asian languages all use yet other writing systems. When words in other alphabets are transliterated or Romanized to be readable to English users, variations in spelling, use of punctuation, and capitalization occur. For example, the capital city of China may be written as Peking, Peiping, or, as preferred today, Beijing. To take another example, since Arabic does not distinguish between capital and lowercase letters, transliterated Arabic names may be inconsistent, understandably, in capitalization and lower casing.

HOW TO USE THIS DESK REFERENCE

This desk reference provides answers to specific questions that arise when sending and receiving international communications. Although it cannot possibly answer every question it can give the reader insight into the diversity of ways of communicating and suggest possible sources for answers. Simply by being aware of the variety of practices a person gains confidence about asking questions.

The following describes major topics covered in each Part of the *International Business Communications Desk Reference.*

Part 1, Addresses This includes a multilingual glossary of words and abbreviations commonly used in addresses. The section "How to Read Addresses" shows typical addresses by country to illustrate placement of street numbers and postal codes, use of state and province names.

Part 2, Business Words, Phrases, Abbreviations This includes a multilingual glossary for words and abbreviations indicating type of business organization, such as corporation; titles, such as partner; and department, such as sales.

Part 3, Dates and Numbers The various ways of writing dates and numbers are explained. The names of the days and months are given in English, French, German, Italian, Japanese, Portuguese, and Spanish.

Part 4, Personal Names This describes various customs regarding placement of given name and surname as well as guidelines for correct pronunciation, forms of address, and typing accents.

Part 5, Letter Writing Advice is offered on slang, jargon, spelling, British versus American English. Sample letters are provided with and without salutation, with reference numbers, and other useful notations.

Part 6, Mailing Letters and Packages This part compares the public postal system to private services, describes classes of international mail, explains how to fill out customs forms.

Part 7, Shipping Terms and Documents The Shipper's Export License (SED), Certificate of Origin (CO), and other documents are explained; also shipping terms, such as Cost and Freight and Delivered Ex Quay.

Part 8, Measures This explains U.S. Customary, British Imperial, and metric systems of measures. There are conversion tables and definitions of terms.

Part 9, Currency Foreign currency symbols, notes, and coins are listed along with an explanation of how to calculate currency exchange and where to buy foreign currency.

Part 10, Time Considerations This describes 12-hour and 24-hour time, lists business and banking hours and business holidays. Seven tables show the time in seventy-three countries when it is 9 a.m., 12 noon, and 5 p.m. in Greenwich Mean Time, and U.S. Eastern, Central, Mountain, Pacific, Alaskan, and Hawaiian time.

Part 11, International Telephone Calls International direct dialing and international access codes are explained; country and city codes are listed.

Part 12, International Telexes and Faxes This part explains the difference between these two methods of communication and when one may be preferred.

Part 13, Translation and Interpretation This describes what to look for in a business translation service and what steps are involved in translating written and spoken words.

Part 14, Sources of Information This is a bibliography of directories and reference books useful for international business people.

Part 15, Country Information Capital city, language, area, population size, and predominant religion are provided.

Cross References

In order to make this desk reference as user friendly as possible, the reader is often referred to other pages for related information. For example, the part on international telephoning has cross references to pages where time differences and business hours are listed by country. The reader calling another time zone can quickly obtain the necessary information to ensure that the call is made during business hours for the receiver.

Using Common Sense

Commonsense rules apply when conducting international business as they do when conducting local and national business. Communications, whether written or spoken, should be made promptly and politely in a simple, direct, unambiguous style. Legitimate information that has been requested should be provided. When communicating with people you do not know well, be formal, at least during initial contacts. This means using surnames rather than given names, avoiding joke-telling and slang.

International communications take longer than domestic ones. Overnight delivery of letters and packages often is not possible. When people observe different holidays and business hours, combined with time differences, advance planning becomes necessary, not only when sending letters and packages but also when telephoning and sending faxes. Responses will be slower.

A sense of humor, patience, an open mind and willingness to plan ahead are crucial to success in international communications. Remember that not everyone speaks the same language. While communication may take longer, the spirit of cooperation that develops makes the experience rewarding.

LIST OF COUNTRIES

Algeria	Germany	Philippines
Angola	Guatemala	Poland
Argentina	Hong Kong	Portugal
Armenia	Hungary	Romania
Australia	India	Russia
Austria	Indonesia	Saudi Arabia
Azerbaijan	Ireland	Singapore
Belarus	Israel	Slovakia, Republic of
Belgium	Italy	South Africa
Brazil	Japan	Spain
Bulgaria	Kazakhstan	Sweden
Canada	Korea, Republic of	Switzerland
Chile	Kyrgystan	Taiwan
China	Latvia	Tajikistan
Colombia	Lithuania	Thailand
Costa Rica	Luxembourg	Turkey
Czech Republic	Malaysia	Turkmenistan
Denmark	Mexico	Ukraine
Dominican Republic	Moldova	United Arab Emirates
Ecuador	Netherlands	United Kingdom
Egypt	New Zealand	United States
Estonia	Nigeria	Uzbekistan
Finland	Norway	Venezuela
France	Pakistan	
Georgia	Peru	

INTERNATIONAL ORGANIZATIONS

Following is a list of some important organizations for international business.

AID United States Agency for International Development.

ASEAN Association of Southeast Asian Nations. Members (in 1992) included Brunei Darussalam, Indonesia, Malaysia, Philippines, Singapore, Thailand.

Benelux Economic Union Economic treaty signed by Belgium, the Netherlands, and Luxembourg in 1958.

BLEU Belgo-Luxembourg Economic Union.

Caribbean Basin Initiative (CBI) Promotes economic development and political stability among twenty-two Central American and Caribbean countries. Its members enjoy duty-free entry to the United States for a wide variety of products.

CARICOM Caribbean Community and Common Market. Members are thirteen countries in the Caribbean.

CBI See Caribbean Basin Initiative.

Central American Common Market Includes Costa Rica, El Salvador, Guatemala, Honduras, Nicaragua.

Commonwealth of Nations A voluntary association of fifty independent states, including the United Kingdom and most of its former dependencies. Ireland and South Africa are not members.

DOC United States Department of Commerce.

EC European Community. The twelve members are Belgium, Denmark, France, Germany, Greece, Ireland, Italy, Luxembourg, Netherlands, Portugal, Spain, United Kingdom. By the beginning of 1993, the members removed many barriers to free trade, movement of capital and of people. Under consideration are plans for a common currency, foreign policy, and defense.

EEA European Economic Area.

EEC European Economic Community. One of the three communities in the European Community (EC). Also known as the Common Market.

EFTA European Free Trade Association. Member countries are Austria, Finland, Iceland, Liechtenstein, Norway, Sweden, and Switzerland.

European Community See EC.

European Economic Community See EEC.

European Free Trade Association See EFTA.

EXIMBANK The Export-Import Bank of the United States, founded in 1934 to promote U.S. exports. The Eximbank offers financing and export insurance programs for goods of U.S. origin. Its programs may be accessed through commercial banks.

IEP International Economic Policy. Refers to a division of the U.S. Department of Commerce that collects information on business and economic conditions around the world and provides up-to-date information on regulations for exporting from the United States. It maintains desk officers by country.

International Trade Administration See ITA.

ITA International Trade Administration. Within the U.S. Department of Commerce, ITA is responsible for development of the export market. Has offices throughout the United States and in more than sixty other countries. It has three branches: the Trade Development Division; the International Economic Policy Division; and the U.S. and Foreign Commercial Service (US&FCS), with field offices in the U.S. and abroad.

Latin American Free Trade Association Members are Argentina, Bolivia, Brazil, Chile, Colombia, Ecuador, Mexico, Paraguay, Peru, Uruguay, Venezuela.

League of Arab States (The Arab League) Its members are Algeria, Bahrain, Djibouti, Egypt, Iraq, Jordan, Kuwait, Lebanon, Libya, Mauritania, Morocco, Oman, the Palestine Liberation Organization, Qatar, Saudi Arabia, Somalia, Sudan, Syria, Tunisia, United Arab Emirates, Yemen.

OAU Organization of African Unity. Its members are fifty African nations.

OECD Organization of Economic Cooperation and Development. Its members include leading Western industrialized countries. The Group of Seven and the Group of Ten are subgroups of the OECD.

OPEC Organization of Petroleum Exporting Countries. Its members are Algeria, Ecuador, Gabon, Indonesia, Iran, Iraq, Kuwait, Libya, Nigeria, Qatar, Saudi Arabia, United Arab Emirates, Venezuela.

Organization of African Unity See OAU.

SBA Small Business Administration, an agency of the United States federal government, with many offices around the country.

Part 1

Addresses

WORDS AND ABBREVIATIONS IN ADDRESSES

Sometimes words are similar in two languages but do not mean the same thing. An *allee* in Germany is a rather grand road, something like an avenue, usually with a parklike divider in the center. An *alley* in the United States is a short narrow back street, often closed at one end, not at all grand.

Often words used in addresses reflect a geographic feature of the area (such as "knoll" or "creek"), the location of a historic building (such as "rampart" or "forge"), or the shape of the road (such as "crescent"). The meaning of these words should not always be taken literally. The creek may be hard to find, the rampart long ago torn down.

In the United States, the ground floor of a building is called the first floor, or the ground floor. In many other parts of the world the first floor is the floor above the ground floor.

Abbreviations

Space limitations on mailing labels often require the use of abbreviations. In the United States, abbreviations in addresses (state names, St for street, and so on) are widely used and quite standardized. Increasingly, periods are not used with these abbreviations in keeping with the style used elsewhere. In other countries, including many in South America, abbreviations are not so widely used and may not be standardized. Not all Spanish-speaking countries use the same words and abbreviations in addresses. In some countries of South America you will see the abbreviation A.A. for *apartado aereo* meaning "post office box," but not in other countries and not in Spain. Be alert to these differences to avoid using an abbreviation incorrectly.

☞ See pages 12–17 for words and abbreviations that commonly appear in addresses. Check them to understand an unfamiliar address, to address a package or envelope, or to prepare a mailing list.

☞ See Part 2, pages 51–56, for words, phrases, and abbreviations that often appear in a company name and on business stationery.

☞ See pages 18–38 for how to read addresses.

☞ See pages 38–45 for names and abbreviations of states, regions, provinces.

Compounds

The word meaning "street" may be attached to the street name. For example, in Finnish the word *katu* means "street," so if you send a letter to Kalevankatu do not write "Kalevankatu Street."

Here are some examples of compounds in German:

strasse: *Sophienstrasse* (Sophien Street), *Marienstr* (Marien Street), *Max-Huber-Str* (Max Huber Street)
allee: *Brahmsallee* (Brahms Avenue)
platz: *Wienerplatz* (Vienna Square)
weg: *Oberbuschweg* (Oberbusch Way)

The German alphabet has a special character, ß, which is often written as "ss" in the Roman alphabet (the alphabet this book uses). Two examples of where this character might appear: *straße* for *strasse* (meaning "street"); *schloß* for *schloss* (meaning "castle").

MULTILINGUAL GLOSSARY OF ADDRESS TERMS

This multilingual glossary contains commonly used words and phrases found in addresses.
Fr = French, Gr = German, It = Italian, Pt = Portuguese, Sp = Spanish.

A.A. (Sp) Abbreviation for *apartado aereo*, post office box. Has nothing to do with airmail or the airport.

À droite (Fr) Right, on the right.

À gauche (Fr) Left, on the left.

Ag. Hs. (South Africa) Agricultural holdings.

Alameda (Sp) Promenade.

Allee (Gr) Avenue.

Aly Abbreviation for alley.

Andar (Pt) Floor. *10° andar* means 10th floor.

Apartado See *Apdo.*

Apartado aereo See *A.A.*

Apdo (Sp) Abbreviation for *apartado*, post office box.

Apt Abbreviation for apartment.

Aptdo See *Apdo.*

Arc Abbreviation for arcade.

Au rez de chaussée (Fr) Ground floor.

Autop See *Autopista.*

Autopista (Sp) Highway.

Av (Sp) Abbreviation for *avenida*, avenue.

Ave Abbreviation for avenue (English, Fr) or *avenida* (Sp, Pt).

B or **Bol** (Russian) Abbreviation for *bolshoi*, meaning great, grand.

Baixos (Catalan, spoken in Barcelona, Spain) Ground floor.

Bajo (Sp) Ground floor.

Banchi (Japanese) Small district within a Japanese city.

Bandar (Malaysian) Town.

Bch Abbreviation for beach.

Bei (Chinese) North.

Bez (Gr) Abbreviation for *Bezirk*, district.

Bezirk See *Bez.*

Bg Abbreviation for burg.

Bis (Fr, Sp) Literally meaning twice. In an address it means something like half. A street address of *Calle Bot 4 bis* would refer to the building between *Calle Bot 4* and *Calle Bot 5*. Possibly the building *Calle Bot 4 bis* is newer than the ones on either side. By using *bis* it is not necessary to renumber the rest of the buildings on the street.

Bldg Abbreviation for building.

Blf Abbreviation for bluff.

Blk Abbreviation for block.

Blv (Turkish) Abbreviation for *bulvar*, boulevard.

Blvd (English, Fr) Abbreviation for boulevard, or *bulevard* (Bulgarian, Romanian).

Bôite postale See *BP*.

Boul (Fr, Canadian) Abbreviation for *boulevard.*

BP (Fr) Abbreviation for *bôite postale*, post box.

Br Abbreviation for branch.

Brg Abbreviation for bridge.

Brk Abbreviation for brook.

Bt (Malaysian) Abbreviation for *bukit*, hill.

Btm Abbreviation for bottom.

Bukit See *Bt.*

Bul (Russian) Abbreviation for *bulvar*, boulevard.

Bulevard See *Blvd.*

Bulvar See *Bul* and *Blv.*

Byp Abbreviation for bypass.

Byu Abbreviation for bayou.

C (It) Abbreviation for *corso*, avenue, large street.

C/ (Sp) Abbreviation for *calle*, street. Do not confuse with the symbol c/o, which means "in care of."

Cad (Turkish) Abbreviation for *caddesi*, avenue.

Cadde (Turkish) Avenue.

Caddesi See *Cad.*

Caixa postal (Pt) See *CP.*

Calata (It) Quay.

Calle (Sp) Street.

Camino (Sp) See *Cno.*

C.A.P. (It) Abbreviation for term for postal code.

Carrera (Sp., Catalan) Highroad.

Carretera (Sp) Highway.

Case Postale (Fr) Post office box.

Casilla, casilla de correos (Sp) Post office box.

C.C. See *Casilla, casilla de correos.*

C.C.C. (Sp) Abbreviation for *casilla de correo central*, mail box in central post office.

Cd (Sp) Abbreviation for *ciudad*, city.

CEDEX (Fr) An acronym for *Courrier d'Entreprise a Distribution Exceptionnelle*, a device used in business addresses in France in addition to the postal code.

Cheng (Chinese) City.

Chmbr(s) Abbreviation for chamber(s).

Cho (Japanese) A subdistrict within a *ku* (the largest district) in a Japanese city.

Chome (Japanese) The smallest district within a Japanese city, usually only a few blocks in area.

Cir Abbreviation for circle.

Circus A place where a number of roads come together; similar to circle.

Ciudad (Sp) See *Cd.*

Cl Abbreviation for close (or courtyard).

Clb Abbreviation for club.

Clfs Abbreviation for cliffs.

Cno (Sp) Abbreviation for *camino*, road, highway.

Conm (Sp) Abbreviation for *conmutador*, switchboard, main telephone number.

Conmutador See *Conm.*

Cor Abbreviation for corner.

Correo (Sp) Post office.

Corso See *C.*

Cp Abbreviation for camp.

CP (It) Abbreviation for *casetta postale*, post box, or *caixa postal* (Pt).

Cpe Abbreviation for cape.

Cra (Sp) Abbreviation for *carrera.*

Cres Abbreviation for crescent.

Crk Abbreviation for creek.

Crse Abbreviation for course.

Cswy Abbreviation for causeway, a road built over water.

Ct Abbreviaton for court.

Ctr Abbreviaton for center.

Cv Abbreviaton for cove.

Cyn Abbreviaton for canyon.

Dajie (Chinese) Street, road.

Dalu (Chinese) Road, street.

Dao (Chinese) Street, road.

Dcha (Sp) Abbreviation for *derecha*, right.

Dept Abbreviation for department.

Derecha See *Dcha*.

Diagonal (Sp) Referring to a street that runs diagonally.

Dist Abbreviation for district.

Div Abbreviation for division.

Dl Abbreviation for dale.

Dm Abbreviation for dam.

Dong (Chinese) East.

Dong (Korean) A smaller subsection within a city.

Dr Abbreviation for drive.

Duan (Chinese) Section of a street.

Dv Abbreviation for divide.

E Abbreviation for east.

Edif (Sp) Abbreviation for *edificio*, building.

Edificio See *Edif*.

Edo (Sp) Abbreviation for *estado*, state.

En face (Fr) Facing, opposite.

Esq (Sp) Abbreviation for *esquina*, corner, angle. When following an American's name, indicates the person is a lawyer, as in James Wilson, Esq.

Esquina See *Esq*.

Est (Fr, It) East.

Est Abbreviation for estate.

Este (Sp, Pt) East.

Estrada (Pt) Road, highway.

Étage (Fr) Floor. *3e étage* means third floor.

Expy Abbreviation for expressway.

Ext Abbreviation for extension or extended.

Fl Abbreviation for floor.

Fld Abbreviation for field.

Fls Abbreviation for falls.

Flt Abbreviation for flats (flat land).

Frd Abbreviation for ford.

Frg Abbreviation for forge.

Frk Abbreviation for fork.

Frst Abbreviation for forest.

Fry Abbreviation for ferry.

Ft Abbreviation for fort.

Fty Abbreviation for factory.

F'way Abbreviation for farmway.

Fwy Abbreviation for freeway.

Galleria (It) Gallery, arcade.

Gata (Swedish) Street.

Gdns Abbreviation for gardens.

Ginko (Japanese) Bank.

Gln Abbreviation for glen.

Gongyuan (Chinese) Park.

Grn Abbreviation for green, square.

Grns Abbreviation for gardens.

Grv Abbreviation for grove.

Gtwy Abbreviation for gateway.

Hbr Abbreviation for harbor.

Hl Abbreviation for hill.

Hls Abbreviation for hills.

Holw Abbreviation for hollow.

Hou (Chinese) Back.

Hq Abbreviation for headquarters.

Hse Abbreviation for house.

Hts Abbreviation for heights.

Hutong (Chinese) Lane.

Hvn Abbreviation for haven.

Hwy Abbreviation for highway.

I Abbreviation used in the United States for a numbered interstate highway, as in Interstate 95, or I-95.

Inlt Abbreviation for inlet.

Interstate See I.

Is Abbreviation for island.

Isl Abbreviation for isle.

Iss Abbreviation for islands.

Izda (Sp) Abbreviation for *izquierda*, left.

Jalan See *Jl*.

Jct Abbreviation for junction.

Jiao (Chinese) Suburb.

Jie (Chinese) Street, road.

Jl or **Jln** (Malay, Indonesian) Abbreviation for *jalan*, street.

Junc Abbreviation for junction.

Kampong See *Kg*.

Katu (Finnish) Street. Often attached to end of street name, as in *Aallonkatu.*

Kg (Malay) Abbreviation for *kampong*, village.

Km Abbreviation for kilometer. Used with a number to indicate location on a road.

Knls Abbreviation for knolls.

Kom (Russian) Abbreviation for *komnata*, room.

Komnata See *Kom.*

Kor (Russian) Abbreviation for *koridor*, corridor.

Kou (Chinese) Intersection.

Ku (Japanese, Korean) A large division, like a ward or borough, within a city, as in Minato-ku or Chiyoda-ku in Tokyo.

Kv (Russian) Abbreviation for *kvartira*, apartment.

Kvartira See *Kv.*

Ky Abbreviation for key.

Largo (It) Square.

Lcks Abbreviation for locks.

Ldg Abbreviation for lodge.

Lebuh (Malay) Street.

Lf Abbreviation for loaf.

Lgt Abbreviation for light.

Lk Abbreviation for lake.

Ln Abbreviation for lane.

Lndg Abbreviation for landing.

Loja (Pt) Ground floor.

Long (Chinese) Lane.

Lor (Malay) Abbreviation for *lorong*, lane, course.

Lorong See *Lor.*

Lu (Chinese) Street, road.

Machi (Japanese) A subdistrict within a *ku* (the largest district within a Japanese city).

Malu (Chinese) Street, road.

Mans Abbreviation for mansion.

Mdws Abbreviation for meadows.

Mews A small street behind a residential street traditionally containing private stables for town houses.

Mey (Turkish) Abbreviation for *meydan*, square.

Meydan See *Mey.*

Ml Abbreviation for mill.

Mn Abbreviation for manor.

Mnr Abbreviation for manor.

Most (Russian) bridge.

Ms Abbreviation for milestone.

Msn Abbreviation for mission.

Mt Abbreviation for mount.

Mtn Abbreviation for mountain.

N Abbreviation for north.

Nab (Russian) Abbreviation for *naberezhnaya*, embankment.

Naberezhnaya See *Nab.*

Nám (Czech) Abbreviation for *námestí*, square.

Námestí See *Nám.*

Nan (Chinese) South.

Nck Abbreviation for neck.

NE Abbreviation for northeast.

Nei (Chinese) Inside.

Nord (Fr, It, Gr) North.

Norte (Sp, Pt) North.

NW Abbreviation for northwest.

Occidente (Sp) West.

Oeste (Sp, Pt) West.

Ofc or **Off** Abbreviation for office.

Orch Abbreviation for orchard.

Oriente (Sp) East.

Ost (Gr) East.

Ouest (Fr) West.

Ovest (It) West.

pA Abbreviation for *per Adresse*, care of.

Paseo (Sp) A boulevard or promenade.

Pcia (Sp) Abbreviation for *provincia*, province.

Pejabat pos (Malay) Post office.

Per (Russian) Abbreviation for *pereulok*, alley.

Per Adresse See *pA.*

Pereulok See *Per.*

Piazza (It) Square.

Piso (Sp) Floor. *1° piso* means first floor.

Pk Abbreviation for park.

Pkwy Abbreviation for parkway.

Pky Abbreviation for parkway.

Pl (English, Fr) Abbreviation for place, square. Or *platz* (Gr), *plaza* (Sp), *plac* (Polish), *ploshchad'* (Russian), *ploshtad* (Bulgarian).

PL (Russian) Abbreviation for *posti lokero*, post office box.

Plac See Pl.

Plass (Norwegian) Place.

Plaza See Pl or Plz.

Pln Abbreviation for plain.

Ploshchad' See Pl.

Ploshtad See Pl.

Plz Abbreviation for *plaza*.

PMB Private mail bag.

Pnes Abbreviation for pines.

PO Post office.

POB Abbreviation for post office box.

Pohj (Russian) Abbreviation for *pohjois*, northern.

Pohjois See *Pohj*.

Posbus (Afrikaans) Post office box.

Postafiók (Hungarian) Post box.

Postahivatal (Hungarian) Post office.

Postboks (Danish, Norwegian) Post box.

Postbus (Dutch) Post box.

Postf (Gr) Abbreviation for *postfach*, post box.

Postfach See *Postf*.

Posti lokero See *PL*.

Pr Abbreviation for prairie.

Pr (Russian) Abbreviation for *prospekt*, avenue or square.

Praça (Pt) Plaza, place.

Praisanee (Thai) Post office.

Prospekt See *Pr*.

Proyezd (Russian) Passage.

Prt Abbreviation for port.

Pt Abbreviation for point.

Pto (Sp) Abbreviation for *puerto*, port.

Puerto See *Pto*.

Qian (Chinese) Front.

Qiao (Chinese) Bridge.

Qu (Chinese) District.

R Abbreviation for rural.

R (Sp) Abbreviation for *ruta*, route.

Rad Abbreviation for radial.

Rd Abbreviation for road.

RD Abbreviation for rural delivery. Was used in the U.S. before 1992 for locations in rural or country areas in contrast to city or suburban areas. See RR.

Rdg Abbreviation for ridge.

Rez de chaussée (Fr) Ground floor.

Riv Abbreviation for river.

Rm Abbreviation for room.

Rnch Abbreviation for ranch.

Rpds Abbreviation for rapids.

RR Abbreviation for rural route. Currently in use in U.S. See RD.

Rst Abbreviation for rest.

Rt Abbreviation for route.

Rua (Pt) Street.

Ruta See *R* (Sp).

S Abbreviation for south.

Sala (Pt) Room.

Santa See *Sta*.

Santo See *Sto*.

SE Abbreviation for southeast.

Sec Abbreviation for section.

Sect Abbreviation for sector.

Section (Taiwan) Referring to a section of a street that is very long.

Shan (Chinese) Mountain.

Shi (Chinese) Market.

Shi (Korean) City.

Shls Abbreviation for shoals.

Shosse (Russian) Highway.

Shr Abbreviation for shore.

Siège (Fr) Offices.

SlHs (South Africa) Small holdings.

Smt Abbreviation for summit.

S/Ofc Abbreviation for site office.

Sok (Turkish) Abbreviation for *sokak*, street.

Sokak See *Sok*.

Spg Abbreviation for spring.

Sq Abbreviation for square.

Sr (Russian) Abbreviation for *sredny*, middle.

SR Abbreviation for state route.

Sredny See *Sr.*

SS Abbreviation for saints or *santissimo* (It) (most holy).

St Abbreviation for street or saint.

Sta (Sp, It) Abbreviation for *santa,* saint.

Sta Abbreviation for station.

Ste (Fr) Abbreviation for *sainte,* saint.

Ste Abbreviation for suite.

Stn Abbreviation for station.

Sto (Sp, It) Abbreviation for *santo,* saint.

Str (Gr) Abbreviation for *strasse,* street. Or *strada* (It), *straat* (Dutch), *straede* (Danish), *straeti* (Icelandic), *stradă* (Romanian).

Str (Russian) Abbreviation for *stroenie,* building.

Straat See *Str* (first entry).

Strada, Stradă See *Str* (first entry).

Stradale (It) Street.

Straede See *Str* (first entry).

Straeti See *Str* (first entry).

Strasse See *Str* (first entry).

Strm Abbreviation for *stream.*

Stroenie See *Str* (second entry).

Subd Abbreviation for subdivision.

Sud (Fr, It) South.

Süden (Gr) South.

Sul (Pt) South.

Sur (Sp) South.

SW Abbreviation for southwest.

Tanjong See *Tg.*

Tel Abbreviation for telephone number.

Telefono (Sp) Telephone.

Ter Abbreviation for terrace.

Ter (Hungarian) Square, room.

Tg (Malay) Abbreviation for *tanjong,* cape.

Tiao (Chinese) Lane.

Torre (Sp) Tower. Used in a building name, such as Torre La Limpia.

Tpke Abbreviation for turnpike.

Trl Abbreviation for trail.

Tsp (South Africa) Abbreviation for township.

Tunl Abbreviation for tunnel.

Tupik (Russian) Cul-de-sac.

U (Hungarian) Abbreviation for *utca,* street.

Ul Abbreviation for *ulice* (Czech), street. Or *ulica* (Polish, Serbocroatian, Slovak, Slovene), *ulitsa* (Russian, Bulgarian), *ulită* (Romanian).

Ulica See *Ul.*

Ulice See *Ul.*

Ulită See *Ul.*

Ulitsa See *Ul.*

Un Abbreviation for union.

Upp Abbreviation for upper.

Ut (Hungarian) Avenue.

Utca (Hungarian) Street.

V (It) Abbreviation for *via,* street.

Val (Russian) Rampart.

Via see *V.*

Via Abbreviation for viaduct.

Viale (It) Avenue.

Vis Abbreviation for vista.

Vl Abbreviation for ville.

Vlg Abbreviation for village.

Vly Abbreviation for valley.

Vs Abbreviation for vista.

Vw Abbreviation for view.

W Abbreviation for west.

Wai (Chinese) Outside.

Weg (Gr.) Road, way.

Wls Abbreviation for wells.

W/Site Abbreviation for work site.

Xi (Chinese) West.

Xiaojie (Chinese) Street, road.

Xing Abbreviation for crossing.

Yol (Turkish) Road.

Yubin-kyoku (Japanese) Post office.

Zheng, Zhong (Chinese) Main, central.

How to Read Addresses

Addresses can be difficult to read. No universally recognized format for placement of the elements prevails. Although each postal system provides information on the format it prefers, these formats are often not used.

In countries without postal codes or where they are not used widely, an address may be long and descriptive. Building names and area names within a city may be important parts of the address. When in doubt, use more rather than less in the mailing address, even though it may not fit easily into a small space.

Order of Elements

The postal code may precede or follow the city or regional name. The street number may precede or follow the street name. In directories and advertisements, on business cards and stationery, the parts of the address may appear in different order. The city may appear above the street. Telephone, telex, and fax numbers could appear in the middle of the address, between the street address and the city.

Some countries put the smallest unit first (a company or individual name) and the largest (city name) last, a style common in the United States and Europe. Others reverse the order, going from largest to smallest, as is the custom in Japan. (Unless writing in Japanese characters, however, use the smallest-to-largest order.)

Two Addresses in One

Sometimes a company listing includes two addresses. One is the box number in a post office for mail sent through the national postal system. The other is the street address used when customers visit the company and when mail is delivered by private courier services like Federal Express and UPS, which do not deliver to post office boxes.

If the company building is located in a different city from the post office, you might see two cities named (one may be a suburb of the other). In this case, the name of the city where the post office is located may be written in capital letters. The postal code will be shown for the post office address.

Languages

In some countries two or more languages are widely spoken. For these situations, the following list of addresses includes at least several of the major languages of business of the country (only in the Roman alphabet, however). Once you recognize words and abbreviations for standard address elements, such as *street* and *post office box*, you can decipher addresses more easily.

☞ See pages 12–17 for a list of words and abbreviations in addresses.
☞ See Part 15, pages 239–246, for languages spoken in each country.

Box Numbers

Some addresses show a box number with or without a street address. If there is no street address, the box is most likely in a post office and could be written either Box 123 or P.O. Box 123.

If the address includes a street address, the box may be a mailbox located in an office complex or on a rural route. In that case, it would be incorrect to write it as P.O. Box.

Street Names

Street names can be quite long when commemorating a person or event, such as this one in Paris commemorating the 8th of May, 1945:

> *280, rue du 8-mai-1945*

Or they may be named after famous military or religious figures. When titles are abbreviated they make the address more difficult to understand. Here are examples of South American street names abbreviated and spelled out in full:

> *Av. Pte. Figueroa Alcorte*
> *(Avenida Presidente Figueroa Alcorte)*
> *Av. Libertador Gral. San Martín*
> *(Avenida Libertador General San Martín)*

Other Spanish abbreviations of military titles include *Cnel.* (*Coronel* for Colonel), *Cte.* (*Comandante* for Commander), *Mcal.* (*Mariscal* for Marshal).

In French, it is not customary to capitalize words like *rue* (meaning "street"), *place, boulevard: rue de Galliera, blvd St-Germain.*

Postal Codes

Postal codes (or ZIP codes in the United States) are used in many countries. In some, they have been assigned to larger cities only or have been assigned but are not widely used. The postal code might be a useful clue to the fact that a town is near a larger city or in a certain region.

Sometimes addresses in larger cities include both a national postal code and a number or letter designating part of the city.

Although the postal code is usually sufficient, people use the other out of habit and as an added assurance.

Postal Code Directories

If you plan to do a lot of mailing to one country, obtain a postal code directory from the postal service of that nation. These can help you find the geographic location for the various postal codes and also the post office's preferred ordering of the address. Many post offices use optical character scanning equipment that works best when the address is in a certain format. You may be able to get your mail delivered faster and cheaper if you use this format.

☞ See pages 87–94 for more information on postal codes and other postal requirements for Canada, Germany, the United Kingdom, and the United States.

European Postal Codes

Some European countries place a letter or letters before the numbers in the postal code. (The letters correspond to the letters used on vehicle license plates.) It is not necessary to use the letter, but if you do not use it, be sure to include the country's name in the address. Mail sent within Europe might not use the country name as long as the country letter is used. The letter is usually followed by a hyphen and then the postal code, for example, F-80100. The countries and letters used are:

Austria A	Germany D	Norway N
Belgium B	Hungary H	Romania R
Denmark DK	Iceland IS	San Marino I
Finland SF	Italy I	Sweden S
France F	Liechtenstein FL	Switzerland CH

Name of Country

The names of countries in the list below are the ones used when mailing *from* the United States. That is, write the country's name as Germany, not Deutschland, on a letter to be mailed from the United States.

As a rule, the country name should not be abbreviated in a mailing address ("USA" being a notable exception). Sometimes abbreviations are not recognizable to everyone, especially those who are not from the country. An example might be R.A. for the Republic of Argentina, which is the official name of the country. More examples of abbreviations are given in the list below. It is not necessary to use the official name. For example, Argentina is sufficient; you do not have to write Republic of Argentina.

☞ See Part 15 for official names of countries.

☞ See pages 46–48 for place names that are known by different names in different languages (e.g., Germany and Deutschland).

Names of Regions

Regional names—provinces, states, counties, parishes, and so on—are often abbreviated in addresses. They are not always necessary if the city is well known but may be very important when the location is small, not well known, or when there is another place with the same name in a different region of the country.

☞ See pages 38–45 for regional names and abbreviations by country.

Names of Intercity Districts

Large cities often are divided into districts, boroughs, wards, or zones and these may have names that are commonly used, such as Brooklyn, one of the five boroughs of New York City. It is not necessary to include the borough name in a New York City address as long as the correct ZIP code is used. In Tokyo and Mexico City it is important to include the correct district name. Telephone directories are good places to find the names of localities surrounding a large city.

☞ See page 39 for a list of metropolitan areas of Canadian cities.

☞ See page 43 for a list of *delegaciones* of Mexico City.

Sample Addresses by Country

Here are sample addresses for more than seventy countries showing the customary placement of typical elements. Although the company, organization, or government agency name is real, the address should not be used because it may not be up-to-date.

Algeria

Halliburton Limited	←company name
33 Blvd. Mohammoud V	←number and street name
Algiers	←city
Algeria	←country

Angola

Sociedad Nacional de Combustiveis de Angola	←company name
Box 1316	←box number
Luanda	←city
Angola	←country

Argentina

Frigorifico La Pampa	←company name
Av. Pedro de Mendoza 347	←street name and number
1156 Bs.As.	←postal code and city
Argentina	←country

Bodegas Valentin Bianchi S.A.	←company name
Comandante Torres 500	←street name and number
5600 San Rafael (Mza)	←postal code, city, province
Argentina	←country

Buenos Aires is the name of the capital city and also of the province in which it is located. Bs.As. is an abbreviation for Buenos Aires.

Names of provinces are often used in Argentinian addresses. (Mza) shown in the second address is the abbreviaton for the province of Mendoza. In Argentina the country name may be written as Républic de Argentina, Rép. Argentina, R.A., or Arg.

Armenia

Armenian Chamber of Commerce	←company name
39, Alaverdyana Street	←number and street name
375010 Yerevan	←postal code and city
Armenia	←country

Australia

D W Thorpe Pty Ltd	←company name
20-24 Stokes Street	←number and street name
Port Melbourne, Victoria 3207	←city, state, postal code
Australia	←country

State names are used in Australian addresses, such as Victoria in this example.

Austria

OMV Aktiengesellschaft	←company name
Otto Wagner-Platz 5	←street name and number
A-1090 Vienna	←postal code and city
Austria	←country

In Austria the country is referred to as Österreich.

Azerbaijan

Azerbaijan Chamber of Commerce	←company name
31-33 Kommunisticheskay St.	←number and street name
370601 Baku	←postal code and city
Azerbaijan	←country

Belarus

Belarus Chamber of Commerce	←company name
14, Masherova Pr.	←number and street name
220622 Minsk	←postal code and city
Belarus	←country

Belgium

Kompass Belgium NV	←company name
Molièrelaan 256	←street name and number
B-1060 Brussel	←postal code and city
Belgium	←country

Office Belge du	
Commerce Extérieur	←company name
Boulevard Emile Jacqmain 162	←street name and number
B-1210 Bruxelles	←postal code and city
Belgium	←country

The first address above is in Dutch and the second address is in French. Both are in the capital city known as Brussels (English), Brussel (Dutch), or Bruxelles (French). In Belgium the country is referred to as Belgique by the French-speaking population and België by the Dutch-speaking population.

Brazil

American Chamber of	
Commerce in Brazil	←company name
Praça Pio X, 15-5° andar	←street name and number, and floor
20040 Rio de Janeiro, RJ	←postal code, city, state
Brazil	←country

Cia Siderurgica Belgo-Mineira	←company name
Av Carandai, 1115	←street name and number
Belo Horizonte, MG 30134	←city, state, postal code
Brazil	←country

State names often appear in Brazilian addresses, as shown in abbreviated form above. The postal code may be placed before or after the city name. In Brazil the country name is spelled Brasil.

Bulgaria

Balkancarpodem Co.	←company name
48, Kliment Ohridski Blvd	←number and street name
BG-1040 Sofia	←postal code and city
Bulgaria	←country

Canada

Federal Express Canada Ltd	←company name
32 Keefer Court	←number and street name
Hamilton, ON L8E 4V4	←city, province, postal code
Canada	←country

Caisse Populaire St-Stanislas	←company name
1350 Rue Gilford	←number and street name
Montreal, PQ H2J 1R7	←city, province, postal code
Canada	←country

Names of provinces are used in Canadian addresses, as shown in abbreviated form above: ON for Ontario and PQ for the Province of Quebec.

☞ See pages 88–89 for more on Canadian postal requirements and postal codes.

Chile

Amcham-Chile	←company name
Vespucio Sur 80	←street name and number
Santiago	←city
Chile	←country

Chile does not have postal codes.

China

Quanzin Knitwear Fty	←company name
102 Liwan Lu	←number and street name
Guangzhou 510425	←city and postal code
Guangdong	←province
China	←country

Beijing Machine Tool I/E Corp. No. 1	←company name
4 Jianguomenwai Dajie	←number and street name
Beijing 100022	←city and postal code
P.R. China	←country

Province names are used in Chinese addresses except for Beijing. *Dajie* and *Lu* mean "street" or "road." In the first address, *Fty* is the abbreviation for factory. In the second address, I/E is an abbreviation for Import/Export. The country name might be shown as the People's Republic of China, P.R.C., or P.R. China.

Colombia

Empresa Colombiana del Petroles	←company name
Carrera 13, No. 3624	←street name and number
Apartada Aereo 5938	←post office box
Bogotá	←city
Colombia	←country

Colombia has no postal codes. *Apartado Aereo* means "post office box."

Costa Rica

Guanacaste Tours	←company name
Aptdo. 55-5000	←post office box
Liberia	←city
Guanacaste	←province
Costa Rica	←country

Aptdo. is the abbreviation for *Apartado*, meaning "post office box."

Czech Republic

Chamber of Commerce
   of Czech Republic   ←company name
38, Argentinska   ←number and street name
CS-17005 Prague   ←postal code and city
Czech Republic   ←country

Denmark

Hernovs Forlag   ←company name
Bredgade 14-16   ←street name and number
DK-1260 Copenhagen K   ←postal code and city
Denmark   ←country

A/S Farvefoto   ←company name
Postboks 2120   ←post office box
1015 Copenhagen K   ←postal code and city
Denmark   ←country

In Denmark the country is referred to as Danmark.

Dominican Republic

J. M. Franco & Cia, C. por A.   ←company name
C/. El Conde No. 301   ←street name and number
Santo Domingo   ←city
Dominican Republic   ←country

C/. does not mean "in care of" (c/o), which it resembles, but *calle*, meaning "street." The capital city of Santo Domingo is sometimes abbreviated Sto Dom. In the Dominican Republic the country is referred to as Republica Dominicana, abbreviated Rep.Dom. or R.D.

Ecuador

Camera de Comercio de Guayaquil ←company name
Avenida Olmeda 410   ←street name and number
Guayaquil   ←city
Ecuador   ←country

There are no postal codes in Ecuador.

Egypt

Egyptian General Petroleum Corp. ←company name
Box 2130   ←post office box
Cairo   ←city
Egypt   ←country

Estonia

Estonian Chamber of Commerce   ←company name
17, Toomkooli St.   ←number and street name
200001 Tallinn   ←postal code and city
Estonia   ←country

Finland

Rakennuskirja Oy	←company name
Runeberginkatu 5	←street name and number
SF-00100 Helsinki	←postal code and city
Finland	←country

Katu in Runeberginkatu means "street." In Finland the country is known as Suomi.

France

Editions Alpina	←company name
60, rue Mazarines	←number and street name
F-75006 Paris	←postal code and city
France	←country

Editions Charles-Lavauzelle SA	←company name
BP 8	←post box number
F-87350 Panazol	←postal code and city
France	←country

Aerospatiale	←company name
37 Boulevard de Montmorency	←number and street name
75781 Paris CEDEX 16	←postal code and city
France	←country

In French business addresses you will often see the word CEDEX, which refers to a device used in addition to the postal code to facilitate delivery.

Georgia

Georgian Chamber of Commerce	←company name
11 Charchavadze Pr.	←number and street name
380079 Tblisi	←postal code and city
Georgia	←country

Germany

F A Ackermanns Kunstverlag	←company name
Wienerplatz 7-8	←street name and number
D-8000 Munich 80	←postal code, city, city code
Germany	←country

Arani-Verlag GmbH	←company name
Kurfürstendamm 126	←street name and number
Postfach 310829	←post box and number
D-1000 Berlin 31	←postal code, city, city code
Germany	←country

In 1990 West Germany (the Federal Republic of Germany) and East Germany (the German Democratic Republic) were unified. In Germany the country is known as Deutschland.

☞ See page 89 on how to distinguish between addresses in eastern Germany and western Germany.

Guatemala

Camara de Comercio de Guatemala ←company name
10a Calle 3-80, Zona 1 ←number and street name
Guatemala City 01001 ←city and postal code
Guatemala ←country

Hong Kong

Expo Management Ltd. ←company name
1713 Sun Hung Kai Centre ←building complex
30 Harbour Road ←number and street name
Hong Kong ←country

AVP Exposition Company ←company name
1201 Nan Fung Centre ←building complex
264-298 Castle Peak Road ←number and street name
New Territories
Hong Kong ←country

Hong Kong has no postal code.

Hong Kong is a British crown colony. In 1997 Hong Kong will cease to be a British Crown Colony and will become a Special Administrative Region of China.

The territory is comprised basically of three entities: Hong Kong Island, including the port city of Hong Kong; the Kowloon Peninsula (referred to as Kowloon); and the New Territories. Most business is conducted on Hong Kong Island and in Kowloon, but many factories operate in the New Territories.

Hungary

Tankönyvkiadó Vállalat ←company name

H-1055 BUDAPEST V ←postal code, city, city code
Szalay u 10-14 ←street name and number
Póstafiók 20 ←post box

Hungary ←country

Hungarian addresses are written as shown above with the city name above the street name and with extra space above and below. The letter *u* is the abbreviation for *utca*, meaning "street."

India

Oil and Natural Gas Commission ←company name
Kailash, 6th floor
26 Kasturba Ghandi Marg ←number and street name
New Delhi 110 001 ←city and postal code
India ←country

Not all addresses in India have postal codes.

Indonesia

Eresco PT   ←company name
Jl Hasanudin No 9   ←street name and number
Bandung   ←city
Indonesia   ←country

Jl is the abbreviation for *jalan*, street. Postal codes exist in Indonesia but often are not used.

Ireland

C J Fallon   ←company name
P.O. Box 1054   ←post box
Dublin 20   ←city, postal code
Ireland   ←country

Postal codes are used in Dublin only. County names often appear in Irish addresses.

Ireland is an independent country, also referred to as Eire or the Republic of Ireland. Northern Ireland, occupying the northeast corner of the island, is part of the United Kingdom.

Israel

Israel National Oil Co. Ltd   ←company name
6, Kaufman Street   ←number and street name
Tel-Aviv 61500   ←city and postal code
Israel   ←country

Italy

Ermanno Albertelli Editore   ←company name
Via S Sonnino 34   ←street name and number
I-43100 Parma   ←postal code and city
Italy   ←country

Salvini Marmi   ←company name
v. Repùbblica   ←street
25080 Prevalle (Brescia)   ←postal code, city, province
Italy   ←country

Italy is divided into regions and provinces. The name of the province may be included in the address, following the name of the city: Romano di Lombardia (Bergamo). The city of Romano di Lombardia is in the province of Bergamo. If the name of the city is the same as the name of the province, as is the case with Torino, then it is not necessary to repeat the name.

In the first address above, no province name is included because Parma is the name of both the city and the province. In the second address, the city (Prevalle) and the province (Brescia) are included.

Japan

The Japan Times, Ltd	←company name
5-4 Shibaura 4-Chome	←building numbers, district, subdistrict
Minato-ku	←district
Tokyo 108	←city and postal code
Japan	←country

Osaka Nishi Mazda Co., Ltd	←company name
2-7-7, Shonai-Takaramachi	← chome and building numbers, district
Toyonaka City, Osaka 561	←city, prefecture, postal code
Japan	←country

Japanese addresses are arranged differently from Western addresses. In Japanese they are written with the largest unit first and smallest last, but when written in the Roman alphabet (as in this book) they are written in customary western fashion with the smallest unit at the top.

Over the centuries, Tokyo developed from a group of villages, which is reflected in the ordering of units in the address today. The city is divided into 23 districts *(ku)*, for example, Minato-ku. These are divided into subdistricts *(cho* and *machi)*, for example, Shibaura. Next is the block *(chome)* number and then the number of the building or group of buildings. Often the word *chome* is dropped and the number placed before the building number, for example, 4-5-4 Shibaura.

Prefecture names may appear in Japanese addresses. When a city and prefecture have the same name, the suffix *shi* is added to the city name or *ken* is added to the prefecture. For example, Okayama-shi and Okayama-ken.

Kazakhstan

Kazakhintorg	←company name
111, Gogola St.	←number and street name
480006 Alma Ata	←postal code and city
Kazakhstan	←country

Korea, Republic of (South Korea)

Hwimoon Publishing Co.	←company name
30 Kyunji-dong, Chongno-ku	←smaller district, larger district
Seoul 110	←city and postal code
Republic of Korea	←country

The word *ku* refers to a large section within the city, and *dong* refers to a smaller section within the *ku*. The postal code has five digits but the first three are sufficient for large cities.

Republic of Korea is South Korea. The Democratic People's Republic is North Korea.

Kyrgyzstan

Kyrgyzstan Chamber of Commerce   ←company name
205, Kirova St.   ←number and street name
720000 Bishkek   ←postal code and city
Kyrgyzstan   ←country

Latvia

Latvian Chamber of Commerce   ←company name
21, Lenina St.   ←number and street name
226189 Riga   ←postal code and city
Latvia   ←country

Lithuania

Lithuanian Chamber of Commerce   ←company name
31, Algirdo St.   ←number and street name
232600 Vilnius   ←postal code and city
Lithuania   ←country

Luxembourg

Arbed SA   ←company name
Avenue de la Liberté   ←street name
19, Luxembourg   ←postal code and city
Luxembourg   ←country

Malaysia

Berita Publishing Sdn Bhd   ←company name
22 Jalan Liku   ←number and street name
59100 Kuala Lumpur   ←city and postal code
Malaysia   ←country

Far East Oilwell Services
  Sdn. Bhd.   ←company name
P.O. Box 383   ←post box
Miri, Sarawak 98007   ←city, state, postal code
Malaysia   ←country

State names often appear in Malaysian addresses. In the second address Miri is a city in the state of Sarawak.

Mexico

Société Générale   ←company name
Paseo de la Reforma No. 382-401   ←street name and number
Juárez   ←delegation name
06600 México, D.F.   ←postal code, city, state
Mexico   ←country

Halliburton de Mexico S.A. de C.V.   ←company name
Km. 10.4 Carretera a Reforma   ←location on highway
Reforma, Chis.   ←city and state
Mexico   ←country

Banco Del Atlantico, S.N.C.	←company name
Av. Hidalgo No. 128	←street name and number
Del. Coyoacán	←delegation name
04000 Mexico, D.F.	←postal code, city, state
Mexico	←country

State names often appear in Mexican addresses. The second address is in the state of Chiapas (Chis.). The office is located at the 10.4 kilometer point on the Carretera a Reforma.

Mexico City, which is in the Distrito Federal (D.F.), is divided into *delegaciones* (districts or wards). In the first address above, the *delegacione* is Juárez, which might also be written Del. Benito Juárez. In the third address, the *delegacione* is Coyoacán.

☞ See page 43 for names of all the delegations in Mexico City.

Mexico City is often referred to simply as Mexico, as in the first and third addresses.

Moldova

Chiparusul	←company name
Str. Puskin 22	←street name and number
277612 Kishinev	←postal code and city
Moldova	←country

The Netherlands

Uitgeverij Contact BV	←company name
Keizersgracht 486	←street name and number
1017 EH Amsterdam	←postal code and city
The Netherlands	←country

The Dutch postal code consists of four numbers followed by two letters, typed in capitals. Although also known as Holland, the country should be referred to as the Netherlands.

New Zealand

Mallinson Rendel Publishers Ltd	←company name
5A Grass St.	←number and street name
Oriental Bay, P.O. Box 9409	←area within Wellington
Wellington	←city
New Zealand	←country

Golden Press	←company name
Private Bag	←private mail bag
Rosebank	←suburb of Auckland
Auckland 7	←city and postal code
New Zealand	←country

Nigeria

Aniema	←company name
14, Alhaji Karimu Street	←number and street name
P.O. Box 2656	←post box
Apapa	←city
Lagos State	←state
Nigeria	←country

State names often appear in Nigerian addresses. Lagos is the name of the capital city of Nigeria and of a state.

Norway

Gyldendal Norsk Forlag	←company name
Sehestedsgt 4	←street name and number
Postboks 6860 St Olavs Plass	←p.o. box address
N-0130 Oslo 1	←postal code, city, city zone
Norway	←country

In Norway the country is known as Norge.

Pakistan

Daily Beopar	←company name
118 Bombay Hotel	
I.I. Chundrigar Road	←street name
Karachi	←city
Pakistan	←country

Peru

American Chamber of Commerce in Peru	←company name
Avenida Ricardo Palma 836	←street name and number
Miraflores	←name of suburb
Lima 18	←city and postal code
Peru	←country

Philippines

Asics Industries	←company name
37 J.P. Rizal St., Arty Subd.	←number, street name, subdivision
Valenzuela, M.M. 1405	←town within Metro Manila and postal code
Philippines	←country

Asian Wood Product and Devt. Corporation	←company name
113 G. Angeles St., Mapulang Lupa	←number, street name, district
Valenzuela, M.M. 1405	←town within Metro Manila and postal code
Philippines	←country

Asiaworld Commercial	←company name
203 Biak na Bato cor. Mauban Str.	←number and street name
Quezon City, M.M. 1115	←city within Metro Manila and postal code
Philippines	←country

Manila addresses often include districts, cities, towns, and subdivisions (Subd.) within Metro Manila (M.M.). In the first address above, Valenzuela is a town within Metro Manila. In the second address, Mapulang Lupa is a district within Valenzuela within Metro Manila. In the third, Quezon City is within Metro Manila.

There are more than 70 provinces in the Philippines. It is not necessary to use the province name with major cities. Not all provinces have postal codes.

Poland

Spółdzielnia Wydawnicza 'Czytelnik'	←company name
ul Wiejska 12a	←street name and number
00-490 Warsaw	←postal code and city
Poland	←country

Kompass Poland	←company name
1, Jasna St	←number and street name
PL 00-031 Warsaw	←postal code and city
Poland	←country

Ul is the abbreviation for *ulica*, street.

Portugal

Petroleos de Portugal EP	←company name
Rua das Flores No. 7	←street name and number
Box 2539	←mail box
1200 Lisboa	←postal code and city
Portugal	←country

Romania

Chamber of Commerce and Industry of Romania	←company name
P.O. Box 1-875	←post office box
R-79502 Bucharest	←postal code and city
Romania	←country

Russia

Tekhnopromexport	←company name
18/1 Ovchinnikovskaya Nab	←number and street name
113324 Moscow	←postal code and city
Russia	←country

Saudi Arabia

Saudi Arabian American Oil Co.	←company name
Box 5000	←post office box
Dhahran 31311	←city and postal code
Saudi Arabia	←country

Singapore

Singapore Trade Development Board	←company name
1 Maritime Square #10-40	←location within building complex
World Trade Centre	←building complex
Telok Blangah Road	←street name
Singapore 0409	←city and postal code
Republic of Singapore	←country

The Board is on the tenth floor in suite 40. World Trade Centres, located in many countries, often occupy several buildings. Singapore City, or simply Singapore, is the capital of the Republic of Singapore.

Slovakia, Republic of

Rol' nické noviny	←company name
Martanovicova 25	←street name
819 11 Bratislava	←postal code and city
Republic of Slovakia	←country

South Africa

Ernst & Young	←company name
Dividend House	←building name
1 Prieska Road	←number and street name
Sybrand Park	←suburb
Cape Town	←city
P.O. Box 51	←mailing address
Athlone 7760	←suburb and postal code
Cape Town	←city
South Africa	←country

Both mailing address and office location are shown above. The postal code is used only for Athlone because mail should be sent to the P.O. box there. If you have to use the Sybrand Park address for mail, you must use that suburb's postal code. The mailing address can be shortened to P.O. Box 51, Athlone 7760, South Africa. Cape Town, the more well-known name, is not needed as long as the postal code is used.

Spain

Editorial Casals SA	←company name
Calle Caspe 79	←street name and number
08013 Barcelona	←postal code and city
Spain	←country

Direccion General De Tributos	←company name
C/ Alcalá, n.º5	←street name and number
28014 Madrid	←postal code and city
Spain	←country

C/ in the second address above is the abbreviation for *calle*, street. In Spain the country is referred to as España.

Sweden

Skandinaviska Enskilda Banken	←company name
Kungsträdgardsgatan 8	←street name and number
S-106 40 STOCKHOLM	←postal code and city
Sweden	←country

Gatan means "street." In Sweden the country is referred to as Sverige.

Switzerland

Baudedarf AG	←company name
Postfach 65	←post office box
8050 Zurich	←postal code and city
Switzerland	←country

Matériaux de construction SA	←company name
Case postale 340	←post office box
2001 Neuchâtel	←postal code and city
Switzerland	←country

Farmacia Elvetica	←company name
via Milano 10	←street name and number
Casella postale	←post box
6830 Chiasso 3	←postal code and city
Switzerland	←country

In the first and second addresses, the post office box has its own postal code. In the third address, it does not have its own postal code.

In Switzerland the country is referred to as Schweiz (in German), Suisse (in French), or Svizzera (in Italian).

Taiwan

Huang, Chang and Associates	←company name
Suite 302	
54-5 Chung Shan N. Road, Sec. 3	←street number, name , section
Taipei	←city
Taiwan, ROC	←country

Linking Publishing Company, Ltd.	←company name
555 Chunghsiao East Road, Sec. 4	←number and street name
Taipei (10516)	←city and postal code
Taiwan, ROC	←country

Section, or Sec., refers to a section of a long road. In Taiwan, the country may be referred to as the Republic of China (or R.O.C.). In the People's Republic of China, Taiwan is referred to as a province of China.

Tajikistan

Tajikistan Chamber of Commerce	←company name
21 Mzayeva St.	←number and street name
734012 Dushanbe	←postal code and city
Tajikistan	←country

Thailand

Department of Mineral Resources	←company name
Ministry of Industry	
Rama VI Road	←street name
Bangkok 10400	←city and postal code
Thailand	←country

Turkey

Turkish Petroleum Refineries Corporation	←company name
Box 211-212	←post office box
41002 Izmit, Kocaeli	←postal code, city, province
Turkey	←country

In the address above, the city of Izmit is in the province of Kocaeli.

Turkmenistan

Edebiyet ve Sungat	←company name
ul. Atabayeva 20	←street name and number
744604 Ashkabad	←postal code and city
Turkmenistan	←country

Ukraine

Ukrainian Chamber of Commerce	←company name
336, Zhitomirskaya St.	←number and street name
252025 Kiev	←postal code and city
Ukraine	←country

United Arab Emirates

Abu Dhabi National Oil Co.	←company name
Box 898	←post office box
Abu Dhabi	←name of emirate
United Arab Emirates	←country

Abu Dhabi is one of the seven emirates in the UAE.

☞ See page 246 for the other six.

United Kingdom

The Association for Information Management	←company name
Information House	←building name
26-27 Boswell Street	←number and street name
London WC1N 3JZ	←city and postal code
Great Britain	←country

Automobile Association   ←company name
Fanum House   ←building name
Basingstoke, Hampshire RG21 2EA   ←city, county, postal code
Great Britain   ←country

Building names are often used in the address. The postal codes can be confusing because the placement of letters and numbers is not uniform. The letter l ("ell") can be mistaken for the number 1 and vice versa. Postal codes are not used in the Channel Islands.

☞ See pages 90–93 for more information on British postal codes, use of county names, and other mailing information.

United States

Washington/Baltimore Regional
  Association   ←company name
1129 20th Street, N.W., Suite 202   ←number and street name
Washington, DC 20036   ←city, district, postal code
USA   ←country

U.S. Small Business Administration   ←company name
26 Federal Plaza, Room 3100   ←number and street name
New York, NY 10278   ←city, state, postal code
USA   ←country

California Export Finance Office   ←company name
107 South Broadway, Suite 8039   ←number and street name
Los Angeles, CA 90012   ←city, state, postal code
USA   ←country

State names always follow city names in U.S. addresses. The capital city of Washington is in the District of Columbia (D.C.). The city of Georgetown is also in the District of Columbia.

New York City has five boroughs: Manhattan, Brooklyn, Queens, Bronx, and Staten Island. It is not necessary to use the borough name if you use the ZIP code (postal code). Some ZIP codes have an additional four digits after the five-digit number, separated by a hyphen.

Uzbekistan

Uzbekistan Chamber of Commerce   ←company name
700017 Tashkent   ←postal code and city
Uzbekistan   ←country

Venezuela

Venezuelan-American Chamber of
  Commerce and Industry   ←company name
Torre Credival, Piso 10   ←building name and floor
2da Avenida de Campo Alegre   ←number and street name
Apartado 5181   ←postal box
Caracas 1010   ←city and postal code
Venezuela   ←country

Edificio La Limpia	←company name
Calle Guaicaipro	←street name
Avenida Chacao	←street name
Altamira - Caracas	←parroquia and city
Venezuela	←country

Building names often appear, as in both addresses above. In the second address, the building (La Limpia) is on the corner of Calle Guaicaipro and Avenida Chacao. Caracas, the capital city, is divided into areas called *parroquias*, such as Altamira.

Postal codes are often not used. The state name is necessary only for addresses in small towns. MBO is an abbreviation for the city of Maracaibo.

NAMES OF PROVINCES, STATES, REGIONS

Most countries are divided into regions known by a variety of terms, including states, provinces, prefectures, counties, regions, districts, republics, cantons, governorates, departments, territories, parishes, and municipalities. It is important to use these names when addressing letters and packages when a city or town is not well known, or when several cities in the country have the same name.

A package addressed to Chicago, United States, would probably be sent to Chicago, Illinois, but one addressed to Springfield might go to Springfield, Illinois, or Springfield, Massachusetts. Correct use of postal codes solves the problem.

Argentina

Argentina has a federal district, twenty-two provinces, and a national territory (Tierra del Fuego), listed with their capitals. The federal district is the city of Buenos Aires, which is within the province of Buenos Aires.

Buenos Aires (Buenos Aires)
Catamarca (Catamarca)
Chaco (Resistencia)
Chubut (Rawson)
Córdoba (Córdoba)
Corrientes (Corrientes)
Entre Ríos (Paraná)
Formosa (Formosa)
Jujuy (Jujuy))
La Pampa (Santa Rosa)

La Rioja (La Rioja)
Mendoza (Mendoza)
Misiones (Posada)
Neuquén (Neuquén)
Río Negro (Viedma)
Salta (Salta)
San Juan (San Juan)
San Luis (San Luis)
Santa Cruz (Río Gallegos)
Santa Fe (Santa Fe)
Santiago del Estero (Santiago del Estero)
Tierra del Fuego (Ushuaia)
Tucumán (San Miguel de Tucumán)

Australia

Australia has six states and two territories, listed with capitals and abbreviations.

Australian Capital Territory
  (Canberra) ACT
New South Wales (Sidney) NSW
Northern Territory (Darwin) NT
Queensland (Brisbane) QLD
South Australia (Adelaide) SA
Tasmania (Hobart) TAS
Victoria (Melbourne) VIC
Western Australia (Perth) WA

Brazil

Brazil has twenty-seven states, listed with capitals and abbreviations.

Acre (Rio Branco) AC
Alagoas (Maceió) AL
Amapá (Macapá) AP
Amazonas (Manaus) AM
Bahia (Salvador) BA
Ceará (Fortaleza) CE
Distrito Federal (Brasília) DF
Espirito Santo (Vitória) ES
Goiás (Goiana) GO
Maranhão (São Luís) MA
Mato Grosso (Cuiabá) MT
Mato Grosso do Sul
  (Campo Grande) MS
Minas Gerais (Belo Horizonte) MG
Pará (Belém) PA
Paraíba (João Pessoa) PB
Paraná (Curitiba) PR
Pernambuco (Recife) PE
Piauí (Teresina) PI
Rio de Janeiro (Rio de Janeiro) RJ
Rio Grande do Norte (Natal) RN
Rio Grande do Sul
  (Pôrto Alegre) RS
Rondônia (Pôrto Velho) RO
Roraima (Boa Vista) RR
Santa Catarina (Florianópolis) SC
São Paulo (São Paulo) SP
Sergipe (Aracaju) SE
Tocantins (Miracema do
  Tocantins) TO

Canada

Canada has ten provinces and two territories, listed with capital cities and abbreviations. New Brunswick, Nova Scotia, and Prince Edward Is-

land are known as the Maritime Provinces.

PROVINCES
Alberta (Edmonton) AB
British Columbia (Victoria) BC
Manitoba (Winnipeg) MB
New Brunswick (Fredericton) NB
Newfoundland (St. John's) NF
Nova Scotia (Halifax) NS
Ontario (Toronto) ON
Prince Edward Island (Charlotte-
  town) PE
Quebec (Quebec) PQ
Saskatchewan (Regina) SK

TERRITORIES
Northwest Territory (Yellowknife) NT
Yukon Territory (Whitehorse) YT

METROPOLITAN AREAS
Edmonton: St. Albert
Halifax: Dartmouth
Hamilton: Burlington, Stoney Creek
Montreal: Anjou, Brossard,
Chateauguay, Dollard-des-Ormeaux,
Laval, Longueuil, Pierrefonds,
Repentigny, St. Huber, St. Laurent,
St. Leonard, Verdun
Ottawa-Hull: Gatineau, Gloucester,
Nepean
Quebec: Charlesbourg, Ste. Foy
St.Catharines-Niagara: Welland
Toronto: Brampton, Etobicoke,
Halton Hills, Markham,
Mississauga, Newmarket, North
York, Oakville, Pickering, Richmond
Hill, Scarborough, Woodbridge, York
Vancouver: Burnaby, Coquitlam,
Langley, New Westminster, North
Vancouver, Richmond, Surry

China

China has twenty-one provinces, five autonomous regions (not listed), and three municipalities.

Anhui (Hefei)
Fujian (Fuzhou)
Gansu (Lanzhou)
Guangdong (Guangzhou)

Guizhou (Guiyang)
Hebei (Shijiazhuang)
Heilongjiang (Harbin)
Henan (Chengchou)
Hubei (Wuhan)
Hunan (Haikou)
Jiangsu (Nanjing)
Jiangxi (Nanchang)
Jilin (Changchun)
Liaoning (Shenyang)
Qinghai (Xining)
Shaanxi (Xi'an)
Shandong (Jinan)
Shanxi (Taiyuan)
Sichuan (Chengdu)
Yunnan (Kunming)
Zhejiang (Hangzhou)

MUNICIPALITIES
Beijing; Shanghai; Tianjin

Costa Rica

Costa Rica's seven provinces are divided into cantons and districts. The provinces and their capitals are listed below.

Alajuela (Alajuela)
Cartago (Cartago)
Guanacaste (Liberia)
Heredia (Heredia)
Limón (Limón)
Puntarenas (Puntarenas)
San José (San José)

Hong Kong

Hong Kong is composed of three entities: Hong Kong Island including the port city of Hong Kong; Kowloon Peninsula (referred to as Kowloon); and the New Territories. Most business is conducted on Hong Kong Island and in Kowloon, but many factories operate in the New Territories.

India

India has twenty-three states and nine territories, listed with capitals.

Andhra Pradesh (Hyderabad)
Assam (Dispur)

Bihar (Patna)
Goa (Panaji)
Gujarat (Gandhinagar)
Haryana (Chandigarh)
Himachal Pradesh (Simla)
Jammu and Kashmir (Srinagar)
Karnataka (Bangalore)
Kerala (Trivandrum)
Madhya Pradesh (Bhopal)
Maharashtra (Bombay))
Manipur (Imphal)
Meghalaya (Shillong)
Nagaland (Kohima)
Orissa (Bhubaneshwar)
Punjab (Chandigarh)
Rajasthan (Jaipur)
Sikkim (Gangtok)
Tamil Nadu (Madras)
Tripura (Agartala)
Uttar Pradesh (Lucknow)
West Bengal (Calcutta)

TERRITORIES
Andaman and Nicobar Islands (Port Blair)
Arunachal Pradesh (Hangar)
Chandigarh (Chandigarh)
Dadra and Nagar Haveli (Silvassa)
Daman and Diu (Daman)
Delhi (Delhi)
Lakshadweep (Kavaratty)
Mizoram (Aizawl)
Pondicherry (Pondicherry)

Ireland

Ireland has twenty-six counties.

Carlow	Longford
Cavan	Louth
Clare	Mayo
Cork	Meath
Donegal	Monaghan
Dublin	Roscommon
Galway	Offaly
Kerry	Sligo
Kildare	Tipperary
Kilkenny	Waterford
Laoighis (Leix)	Westmeath
Leitrim	Wexford
Limerick	Wicklow

Italy

Italy has twenty regions subdivided into ninety-five provinces. Each province takes its name from its main city or town. This city or town is the capital of the province. Common English variations of names are shown in parentheses.

Agrigento	AG
Alessandria	AL
Ancona	AN
Aosta	AO
Arezzo	AR
Ascoli Piceno	AP
Asti	AT
Avellino	AV
Bari	BA
Belluno	BL
Benevento	BN
Bergamo	BG
Bologna	BO
Bolzano	BZ
Brescia	BS
Brindisi	BR
Cagliari	CA
Caltanissetta	CL
Campobasso	CB
Caserta	CE
Catania	CT
Catanzaro	CZ
Chieti	CH
Como	CO
Cosenza	CS
Cremona	CR
Cuneo	CN
Enna	EN
Ferrara	FE
Firenze (Florence)	FI
Foggia	FG
Forlì	FO
Frosinone	FR
Genova (Genoa)	GE
Gorizia	GO
Grosseto	GR
Imperia	IM
Isernia	IS
L'Aquila	AQ
La Spezia	SP
Latina	LT

Lecce	LE
Livorno (Leghorn)	LI
Lucca	LU
Macerata	MC
Mantova (Mantua)	MN
Massa Carrara	MS
Matera	MT
Messina	ME
Milano (Milan)	MI
Modena	MO
Napoli (Naples)	NA
Novara	NO
Nuoro	NU
Oristano	OR
Padova (Padua)	PD
Palermo	PA
Parma	PR
Pavia	PV
Perugia	PG
Pesaro	PS
Pescara	PE
Piacenza	PC
Pisa	PI
Pistoia	PT
Pordenone	PN
Potenza	PZ
Ragusa	RG
Ravenna	RA
Reggio Calabria	RC
Reggio Emilia	RE
Rieti	RI
Roma (Rome)	ROMA
Rovigo	RO
Salerno	SA
Sassari	SS
Savona	SV
Siena	SI
Siracusa	SR
Sondrio	SO
Taranto	TA
Teramo	TE
Terni	TR
Torino (Turin)	TO
Trapani	TP
Trento (Trent)	TN
Treviso	TV
Trieste	TS
Udine	UD
Varese	VA
Venezia (Venice)	VE

Vercelli	VC	Tottori (Tottori)
Verona	VR	Toyama (Toyama)
Vicenze	VI	Wakayama (Wakayama)
Viterbo	VT	Yamagata (Yamagata)
		Yamaguchi (Yamaguchi)
		Yamanashi (Kófu)

Japan

Japan has forty-seven prefectures, listed with their capitals.

Aichi (Nagoya)
Akita (Akita)
Aomori (Aomori)
Chiba (Chiba)
Ehime (Matsuyama)
Fukui (Fukui)
Fukuoka (Fukuoka)
Fukushima (Fukushima)
Gifu (Gifu)
Gunma (Maebashi)
Hiroshima (Hiroshima)
Hokkaido (Sapporo)
Hyogo (Kóbe)
Ibaraki (Mito)
Ishikawa (Kanazawa)
Iwate (Morioka)
Kagawa (Takamatsu)
Kagoshima (Kagoshima)
Kanagawa (Yokohama)
Kochi (Kochi)
Kumamoto (Kumamoto)
Kyoto (Kyoto)
Mie (Tsu)
Miyagi (Sendai)
Miyazaki (Miyazaki)
Nagano (Nagano)
Nagasaki (Nagasaki)
Nara (Nara)
Niigata (Niigata)
Oita (Oita)
Okayama (Okayama)
Okinawa (Naha)
Osaka (Osaka)
Saga (Saga)
Saitama (Urqwa)
Shiga (Otsu)
Shimane (Matsue)
Shizuoka (Shizuoka)
Tochigi (Utsunomiya)
Tokushima (Tokushima)
Tokyo (Tokyo)

Malaysia

Malaysia has fourteen states, listed with capitals and abbreviations.

Federal District (Kuala Lumpur)	
Johor (Johor Baharu)	JH
Kedah (Alor Setar)	KH
Kelantan (Kota Baharu)	KN
Malocca (Melaka)	MC
Negeri Sembilan (Seremban)	NS
Pahang (Kuantan)	PH
Penang (Penang)	PG
Perak (Ipoh)	PK
Perlis (Kangar)	PL
Sabah (Kota Kinabulu)	SH
Sarawak (Kuching)	SK
Selangor (Shuh Alam)	SL
Terengganu (Kuala Terengganu)	TG

Mexico

Mexico has thirty-one states and a federal district, listed with their capitals and abbreviations.

Aguascalientes (Aguascalientes)	AGS
Baja California Norte (Mexicali)	B.C.
Baja California Sur (La Paz)	B.C.S.
Campeche (Campeche)	CAMP
Chiapas (Tuxtla Gutierrez)	CHIS
or	CHIAP
Chihuahua (Chihuahua)	CHIH
Coahuila (Saltillo)	COAH
Colima (Colima)	COL
Distrito Federal* (Mexico City)	D.F.
Durango (Victoria de Durango)	DGO
Guanajuato (Guanajuato)	GTO
Guerrero (Chilpancingo de los Bravos)	GRO
Hidalgo (Pachuca de Soto)	HGO
Jalisco (Guadalajara)	JAL
México (Toluca de Lerdo)	MEX
Michoacán (Morelia)	MICH
Morelos (Cuernavaca)	MOR

Nayarit (Tepic)	NAY
Nuevo León (Monterrey)	N.L.
Oaxaca (Oaxaca de Juárez)	OAX
Puebla (Heroica Puebla de Zaragoza)	PUE
Querétaro (Querétaro)	QRO
Quintana Roo (Chetumal)	Q.R.
San Luis Potisí (San Luis Potisí)	S.L.P.
Sinaloa (Culiacàn)	SIN
Sonora (Hermosillo)	SON
Tabasco (Villahermosa)	TAB
Tamaulipas (Ciudad Victoria)	TAMPS
Tlaxcala (Tlaxcala de Xicohténcatl)	TLAX
Veracruz (Jalapa Enriquez)	VER
Yucatán (Mérida)	YUC
Zacatecas (Zacatecas)	ZAC

*The Federal District (Distrito Federal) includes Mexico City (Ciudad de México or Cd. de México) and is divided into districts (*delegaciones*) as follows. The first four *delgaciones* are part of Mexcio City.

Benito Juárez
Cuauhtémoc
Miguel Hidalgo
Venustiano Carranza

Alvaro Obregón
Azcapotzalco
Coyoacán
Cuajimalpa de Morelos
Gustavo A. Madero
Iztacalco
Iztapalapa
Magdalena Contreras
Milpa Alta
Tláhuac
Tlalpan
Xochimilco

Municipalities in the state of Mexico (Edomex) outside the Federal District:

Chimalhuacán
Coacalco
Cuautitlán de Romero Rubio
Cuautitlán Izcalli
Ecatepec

Huixquilucan
La Paz
Naucalpan
Nezahualcóyotl
Tlalnepantla
Tultitlán
Zaragoza

Nigeria

Nigeria has a federal territory and twenty-one states, listed with capitals.

Akwa Iborn (Uyo)
Anambra (Enugu)
Bauchi (Bauchi)
Bendel (Benin City)
Benue (Makurdi)
Borno (Maiduguri)
Cross River (Calabari)
Gongola (Yola)
Imo (Owerri)
Kaduna (Kaduna)
Kano (Kano)
Katsina (Katsina)
Kwara (Ilorin)
Lagos (Ikeja)
Niger (Minna)
Ogun (Abeokuta)
Ondo (Akure)
Oyo (Ibadan)
Plateau (Jos)
Rivers (Port-Harcourt)
Sokoto (Sokoto)

United Arab Emirates

The U.A.E. is composed of seven emirates; the head of government of each is an emir, or Muslim chief. Each emirate takes the same name as its capital: Abu Dhabi; Ajman; Dubai; Fujaira; Ras al-Khaimah; Sharjah; Umm-al-Qaiwain.

United Kingdom

Officially the United Kingdom of Great Britain and Northern Ireland, the country's major divisions are:
On the island of Great Britain: England; Wales; Scotland.

On the island of Ireland: Northern Ireland.

Crown dependencies: the Isle of Man and the Channel Islands (Jersey, Guernsey, and some smaller islands). Crown dependencies are not integral parts of the United Kingdom and have considerable self-government.

Counties in the U. K. are listed below. Most county names should not be abbreviated in mailing addresses. Abbreviations that British Royal Mail does allow are included below.

Aberdeenshire
Angus
Argyll
Avon
Ayrshire
Banffshire
Bedfordshire   Beds
Berkshire   Berks
Berwickshire
Buckinghamshire   Bucks
Caithness
Cambridgeshire   Cambs
Cheshire
Clackmannanshire
Cleveland
Clwyd
Cornwall
County Antrim   Co Antrim
County Armagh   Co Armagh
County Down   Co Down
County Durham   Co Durham
County Fermanagh   Co Fermanagh
County Londonderry
County Tyrone   Co Tyrone
Cumbria
Derbyshire
Devon
Dorset
Dumfriesshire
Dunbartonshire
Dyfed
East Lothian
East Sussex   E Sussex
Essex
Fife
Gloucestershire   Glos
Gwent

Gwynedd
Hampshire   Hants
Herefordshire
Hertfordshire   Herts
Inverness-shire
Isle of Arran
Isle of Barra
Isle of Benbecula
Isle of Bute
Isle of Canna
Isle of Coll
Isle of Colonsay
Isle of Cumbrae
Isle of Eigg
Isle of Gigha
Isle of Harris
Isle of Iona
Isle of Jura
Isle of Lewis
Isle of Mull
Isle of North Uist
Isle of Orkney
Isle of Rhum
Isle of Scalpay
Isle Of Shetland
Isle of Skye
Isle of South Uist
Isle of Tiree
Isle of Wight
Isles of Scilly
Kent
Kincardineshire
Kinross-shire
Kirkcudbrightshire
Lanarkshire
Lancashire   Lancs
Leicestershire   Leics
Lincolnshire   Lincs
London E
London EC
London N
London NW
London SE
London SW
London W
London WC
Merseyside
Middlesex   Middx
Mid Glamorgan   M Glam
Midlothian

Morayshire
Nairnshire
Norfolk
Northamptonshire   Northants
North Humberside   N Humberside
Northumberland   Northd
North Yorkshire   N Yorkshire
Nottinghamshire   Notts
Oxfordshire   Oxon
Peeblesshire
Perthshire
Powys
Renfrewshire
Ross-shire
Roxburghshire
Selkirkshire
Shropshire   Salop
Somerset
South Glamorgan   S Glam
South Humberside   S Humberside
South Yorkshire   S Yorkshire
Staffordshire   Staffs
Stirlingshire
Suffolk
Surrey
Sutherland
Tyne and Wear   Tyne & Wear
Warwickshire   Warks
West Glamorgan   W Glam
West Lothian
West Midlands   W Midlands
West Sussex   W Sussex
West Yorkshire   W Yorkshire
Wigtownshire
Wiltshire   Wilts
Worcestershire   Worcs

United States

The federal district and the fifty states, including their capitals and abbreviations, are listed. The traditional longer state abbreviation follows the capital. The two-letter abbreviation in the right column should be used in mailing addresses with ZIP codes.

Alabama (Montgomery) Ala.	AL
Alaska (Juneau) Alaska	AK
Arizona (Phoenix) Ariz.	AZ
Arkansas (Little Rock) Ark.	AR
California (Sacramento) Calif.	CA
Colorado (Denver) Colo.	CO
Connecticut (Hartford) Conn.	CT
Delaware (Dover) Del.	DE
District of Columbia (Washington) D.C.	DC
Florida (Tallahassee) Fla.	FL
Georgia (Atlanta) Ga.	GA
Hawaii (Honolulu) Hawaii	HI
Idaho (Boise) Idaho	ID
Illinois (Springfield) Ill.	IL
Indiana (Indianapolis) Ind.	IN
Iowa (Des Moines) Iowa	IA
Kansas (Topeka) Kans.	KS
Kentucky (Frankfort) Ky.	KY
Louisiana (Baton Rouge) La.	LA
Maine (Augusta) Maine	ME
Maryland (Annapolis) Md.	MD
Massachusetts (Boston) Mass.	MA
Michigan (Lansing) Mich.	MI
Minnesota (St. Paul) Minn.	MN
Mississippi (Jackson) Miss.	MS
Missouri (Jefferson City) Mo.	MO
Montana (Helena) Mont.	MT
Nebraska (Lincoln) Nebr.	NE
Nevada (Carson City) Nev.	NV
New Hampshire (Concord) N.H.	NH
New Jersey (Trenton) N.J.	NJ
New Mexico (Santa Fe) N.Mex.	NM
New York (Albany) N.Y.	NY
North Carolina (Raleigh) N.C.	NC
North Dakota (Bismarck) N.Dak.	ND
Ohio (Columbus) Ohio	OH
Oklahoma (Oklahoma) Okla.	OK
Oregon (Salem) Oreg.	OR
Pennsylvania (Harrisburg) Pa.	PA
Rhode Island (Providence) R.I.	RI
South Carolina (Columbia) S.C.	SC
South Dakota (Pierre) S.Dak.	SD
Tennessee (Nashville) Tenn.	TN
Texas (Austin) Tex.	TX
Utah (Salt Lake City) Utah	UT
Vermont (Montpelier) Vt.	VT
Virginia (Richmond) Va.	VA
Washington (Olympia) Wash.	WA
West Virginia (Charlestown) W.Va.	WV
Wisconsin (Madison) Wis.	WI
Wyoming (Cheyenne) Wyo.	WY

Variations on Place Names

Often places are known by names substantially different from the English name commonly used. For example, Germany is known as Allemagne in France and Deutschland in Germany. Differences in spellings occur for names that have been Romanized (that is, written in the alphabet used in this book). This includes Arabic, Chinese, Japanese, and Russian place names.

Until about twenty years ago, the predominant system for Romanizing Chinese ideograms was the Wade-Giles system; today it is the pinyin system. This switch accounts for many of the different spellings used for Chinese names, such as Peiping (Wade-Giles), Peking, and Beijing (pinyin) for the capital city of China.

Sometimes the names of places have completely changed. For example, after the demise of the USSR, the city of Leningrad reclaimed its pre-Soviet Union name of St. Petersburg.

The list below, while not comprehensive, serves to indicate possibilities for different spellings and to encourage you to look further if you cannot find a name listed where you expect it. For example, if you are looking for information on Japan in an Italian document, you should look under G for Giappone.

☞ See pages 211, 214, and 215 respectively for information on the Danish, Norwegian, and Swedish alphabets.

The left column shows a place name and in parentheses where that spelling is used. The right column gives the English language variation.

Place name (where used)	**Known in English as**
Afrique du Sud (France)	South Africa
Alemania (Spain, Mexico)	Germany
Allemagne (France)	Germany
Amerika Syarikat (Malaysia)	U.S.A
Angleterre (France)	England
Arabia Saudita (Italy)	Saudi Arabia
Autriche (France)	Austria
Bayern (Germany)	Bavaria
Belanda (Malaysia)	The Netherlands
Belgica (Spain)	Belgium
Belgio (Italy)	Belgium
Belgique (France)	Belgium
Brasile (Italy)	Brazil
Bruxelles (French-speaking Belgium)	Brussels
Bucuresti (Romania)	Bucharest
Cile (Italy)	Chile
Cipro (Italy)	Cyprus

Place name (where used)	Known in English as
Corea (Italy)	Korea
Corée (France)	Korea
Costarica (Italy)	Costa Rica
Danimarca (Italy)	Denmark
Dinamarca (Spain)	Denmark
Egitto (Italy)	Egypt
Eire (Ireland)	Ireland
El Djezair (Algeria)	Algiers
Estados Unidos (Spain)	United States
Es.Us. (Mexico)	United States
Etats-Unis (France)	United States
E.U.A. (Mexico)	United States
Filippine (Italy)	Philippines
Firenze (Italy)	Florence
Francia (Italy)	France
Frankreich (Germany)	France
Frankrijk (The Netherlands)	France
Genova (Italy)	Genoa
Giamaica (Italy)	Jamaica
Giappone (Italy)	Japan
Grecia (Italy)	Greece
Griechenland (Germany)	Greece
Großbritannien (Germany)	Great Britain
Guangzhou (preferred spelling)	Canton (used less today)
Holanda (Spain)	The Netherlands
Hongrie (France)	Hungary
Inde (France)	India
Inglaterra (Spain)	England
Islande (France)	Iceland
Japon (Mexico)	Japan
Jepun (Malaysia)	Japan
Kameroun (Italy)	Cameroon
København (Denmark)	Copenhagen
Köln (Germany)	Cologne
Kolumbien (Germany)	Colombia
Krung Thep (Thailand)	Bangkok
Livorno (Italy)	Leghorn
Lussemburgo (Italy)	Luxembourg
Makkah	Mecca (alternate spelling)
Malaisie (France)	Malaysia
Mantova (Italy)	Mantua
Maroc (France)	Morocco
Marocco (Italy)	Morocco
Mejico (Mexico)	Mexico
Messico (Italy)	Mexico
Milano (Italy)	Milan
Moskva	Moscow (alternate spelling)
Napoli (Italy)	Naples
Neuseeland (Germany)	New Zealand

Place name (where used)	Known in English as
Niederlande (Germany)	Netherlands
Noruega (Spain)	Norway
Norvège (France)	Norway
Norvegia (Italy)	Norway
Nuovo Zelanda (Italy)	New Zealand
Österreich (Germany)	Austria
Padova (Italy)	Padua
Paesi Bassi (Italy)	The Netherlands
Paises Bajos (Mexico)	The Netherlands
Pay-Bas (France)	The Netherlands
Peranchis (Malaysia)	France
Pologne (France)	Poland
Polonia (Italy)	Poland
Portogallo (Italy)	Portugal
Praha (Czech Republic)	Praque
Regno Unito di Gran Bretagna e Irlanda del Nord (Italy)	United Kingdom
Reino Unido (Mexico)	United Kingdom
Rep. Rakyat (Malaysia)	China
Repubblica del Sud Africa (Italy)	South Africa
Schweden (Germany)	Sweden
Schweiz (Germany)	Switzerland
Sepanyol (Malaysia)	Spain
's-Gravenhage (Netherlands)	The Hague
Siria (Italy)	Syria
Spagna (Italy)	Spain
Spanien (Germany)	Spain
Stati Uniti d'America (Italy)	U.S.A.
Südafrika (Germany)	South Africa
Südkorea (Germany)	South Korea
Suecia (Spain, Mexico)	Sweden
Suéde (France)	Sweden
Suisse (France)	Switzerland
Suiza (Spain, Mexico)	Switzerland
Sulawesi (Indonesia)	Celebes
Suomi (Finland)	Finland
Sverige (Sweden)	Sweden
Svezia (Italy)	Sweden
Svizzera (Italy)	Switzerland
Torino (Italy)	Turin
Tschechoslowakei (Germany)	Czechoslovakia
Turchia (Italy)	Turkey
Türkei (Germany)	Turkey
Turquia (Spain)	Turkey
Ungarn (Germany)	Hungary
Ungheria (Italy)	Hungary
Venezia (Italy)	Venice
Wien (Austria)	Vienna
Xianggang (China)	Hong Kong

Part 2

Business Words, Phrases, Abbreviations

The words, phrases, and abbreviations listed here frequently appear on letterhead stationery, on envelopes and mailing labels, on business cards, forms, in directories and other sources of information. Many describe the type of business organization, such as corporation and partnership. Some detail a person's title or position in the company.

☞ See pages 11–12, Words and Abbreviations in Addresses.

Fr = French, Gr = German, It = Italian, Pt = Portuguese, Sp = Spanish.

Aantal pagina's (Dutch) Total number of pages (as in a fax)

Abogado (Sp) Attorney.

Abschn (Gr) Abbreviation for *abschnitt*, section.

Abt (Gr) Abbreviation for *abteilung*, division.

ABW (Gr) Abbreviation for *abwicklung*, settlement, liquidation, transactions.

abwicklung See *ABW*.

A/C Account.

a.D. (Gr) Abbreviation for *ausser Dienst*, retired.

Advogado (Pt) Attorney.

Afdeling (Dutch) Department.

Afkomstig van (Dutch) From.

AG (Gr) Abbreviation for *aktiengesellschaft*, stock corporation.

Agare och chef (Swedish) Owner and principal.

Aksjeselskap See *A/S*.

Aktiengesellschaft See *AG*.

Aktieselskab See *A/S*.

An (Gr) To (as on a memo—To [someone])

Anwalt (Gr) Attorney.

Anwaltsbüro (Gr) Law firm.

Anwaltsfirma (Gr) Law firm.

Anwaltskanzlei (Gr) Law office.

Archt Abbreviation for architect.

A/S Abbreviation for *aksjeselskap* (Swedish) or *aktieselskab* (Norwegian), limited company.

ASBL abbreviation for *association sans but lucratif* (Fr), non-profit-making society.

Asocs Abbreviation for *asociados* (Sp), associates.

Association sans but lucratif See *ASBL*.

Asst Abbreviation for assistant.

Assurance (Fr) Insurance.

ausser Dienst See *a.D.*

Avdeiningskontor (Swedish) Branch office.

Avocat (Fr) Attorney.

Avvocato (It) Attorney.

Bank bankgiro (konto) (Gr) Bank transfer service.

Bankverbindung (Gr) Bank contact.

Banque (Fr) Bank.

Banque compte courant bancaire (Fr) Bank transfer service.

Barrister Lawyer (English term as opposed to American). Principally a trial lawyer. See solicitor.

Bedes anført ved besvarelse (Danish) "To which please refer." Used with a reference number.

Beratung (Gr) Consultant service.

Bericht (Dutch) Message (as on a memo or fax).

Besloten vennootschap See *BV*.

Bestemd voor (Dutch) To (as on a memo form).

Betriebsleiter (Gr) Works or plant manager.

Betrifft (Gr) Regarding, in reference to.

Bevollmächtige (Gr) Proxy, attorney, authorized agent.

Bilag (Danish) Enclosure(s).

BLZ (Gr) Abbreviation for *bankleitzahl*, bank number,

transit number, bank code number.

Bros Abbreviation for brothers.

Bürozeiten (Gr) Office hours.

BV or **bv** (Dutch) Abbreviation for *besloten vennootschap,* private limited company.

C (It) Abbreviation for *compagnía,* company.

CA (Sp) Abbreviation for *compañía anónima,* public limited company.

Cabinet d'avocat (Fr) Law firm.

Cabinet juridique (Fr) Law firm.

Caisse (Fr) Bank.

CC: stands for carbon copy or copy.

Chef (Fr., Swedish) Principal.

Chef d'atelier (Fr) Works or plant manager.

Cia (Pt) Abbreviation for *companhia,* company.

Cía (Sp) Abbreviation for *compañía,* company.

Cie (Fr) Abbreviation for *compagnie,* company.

Co Abbreviation for company or county.

Col Abbreviation for colonel.

Commanditaire vennootschap See *CV.*

Commerce en Gros (Fr) Wholesale.

Compagnía See *C.*

Compagnie See *Cie.*

Companhia See *Cia.*

Compañía See *Cía.*

Compañía anónima See *CA.*

Corporacion (Sp) Corporation.

Cta (Sp) Abbreviation for *cuenta,* account.

CV (Dutch) Abbreviation for *commanditaire vennootschap,* limited partnership.

Dato (Danish) Date.

Datum (Gr, Dutch) Date.

Dipl (Gr) Abbreviation for *diploma,* certificate. Combined with abbreviation for discipline, for example, *Dipl.-Ing.* (engineering), *Dipl.-*

Kauf. (business administration), *Dipl.-Wirt.* (economics).

Dir (Gr) Abbreviation for *direktor,* director.

Directeur des Achats (Fr) Purchasing manager.

Directeur des Services économiques (Fr) Financial manager.

Directeur des Ventes (Fr) Sales manager.

Directeur générale (Fr) Managing director.

d/o Abbreviation for daughter of.

Domaine d'exportation (Fr) Export area.

Domicilio (Sp) Address.

Dottorbolag (Swedish) Subsidiary.

Dr (Gr) abbreviation for *doktor,* doctor.

Eingetragner Verein See *eV.*

Einkaufsleiter (Gr) Purchasing manager.

Economichef (Swedish) Financial manager.

Empresa (Sp) Enterprise.

Enc Abbreviation for enclosure(s).

Engenheiro (Pt) Engineer.

Entreprise (Fr) Corporation.

Entwicklung (Gr) Development.

Esq Abbreviation for esquire, a title used by lawyers.

eV (Gr) Abbreviation for *eingetragner Verein,* registered society.

Exportchef (Swedish) Exports manager.

Exportgebiet (Gr) Export area.

Exportleiter (Gr) Exports manager.

Exportområde (Swedish) Export area.

Fáb (Sp) Abbreviation for *fábrica.*

Fábrica (Sp) Factory.

Fabrication et Exportation (Fr) Manufacture and export.

Fabrik (Gr, Swedish) Factory.

Fabril (Sp) manufacturing.

Fabrique (Fr) factory.

Fatura comercial (Pt) Commercial invoice.

Filiale (Gr, It, Fr) branch, affiliate.

Filialer (Swedish) Branches.

Finanzdirektor (Gr) Financial manager.

Firma (Gr) Corporation.

Försäljning (Swedish) Sale.

Försäljningschef (Swedish) Sales manager.

Frat (It) Abbreviation for *fratello*, brother.

Gabinete jurídico (Sp) Law firm.

Gebr (Gr) Abbreviation for *Gebrüder*, brothers.

Gebrüder See *Gebr*.

Gennemslag (Danish) Copy.

Gerente (Sp) manager, director.

Ges (Gr) Abbreviation for *Gesellschafter*, shareholder, stockholder, partner.

Geschäftsführender Direktor (Gr) Managing director.

Geschäftsführender Gesellschafter See *GeschfGes*.

Geschäftsführer See *Geschf*.

Geschäftsleitung See *Gesch.-Ltg*.

Geschäftsstunden (Gr) Office hours.

Geschf (Gr) Abbreviation for *Geschäftsführer*, general manager, managing director.

GeschfGes (Gr) Abbreviation for *Geschäftsführender Gesellschafter*, managing partner.

Gesch.-Ltg (Gr) Abbreviation for *Geschäftsleitung*, management.

Gesellschaft (Gr) Company, society. Often combined with other words, such as *beratungsgessellschaft*, a law firm; *treuhandgessellschaft*, a trust company; *aktiengessellschaft*, a joint stock company.

Gesellschafter See *Ges*.

Gesellschaft mit beschränkter Haftung See *GmbH*.

GmbH (Gr) Abbreviation for *Gesellschaft mit beschränkter Haftung*, a limited liability company or private limited company.

GM.K. (Japanese) Abbreviation for *gomei kaisha*, mercantile partnership.

Gomei kaisha See *GM.K.*

Goshi kaisha See *GS.K.*

Grosshandel (Gr, Swedish) Wholesale.

GS.K. (Japanese) Abbreviation for *goshi kaisha*, limited partnership.

(H) (Sp) Abbreviation for *hijo*, son.

Handelsmarke (Gr) Trademark.

Hermano (Sp) Brother.

Heures d'ouverture (Fr) Office hours.

Hijo (Sp) Son.

Hj Abbreviation for *haji*, a title used by someone of the Muslim faith who has made the pilgrimage to Mecca.

Hnos (Sp) Abbreviation for *hermanos*, brothers.

Hon Abbreviation for honorable, a title used with high-level government officials, such as judges.

Horario (Sp) Hours, as in business hours, or hours open.

Horas (Pt) Hours, as in business hours, or hours open.

Ihr Zeichen (Gr) Your reference. See *Unser Zeichen*.

Inc Abbreviation for incorporated.

Industrias (Sp) Industries.

Ing (Gr) Abbreviation for *ingenieur*.

Ingegnere (It) Engineer.

Ingeniero (Sp) Engineer.

Ingenieur (Gr) Engineer.

Ingénieur (Fr) Engineer.

Inh (Gr) Abbreviation for *inhaber*, proprietor, owner.

inhaber See *Inh*.

Inhaber und Geschäftsführer (Gr) Owner and principal

Inkopschef (Swedish) Purchasing manager.

J.nr. (Danish) Reference number.

Jr Abbreviation for junior.

Kabushiki kaisha See *KK*.

KG (Gr) Abbreviation for *Kommanditgesellschaft,* limited partnership.

KGaA (Gr) Abbreviation for *Kommanditgesellschaft auf Aktien,* limited partnership by shares.

KK (Japanese) Abbreviation for *kabushiki kaisha,* public limited company.

Kommanditgesellschaft See *KG.*

Kommanditgesellschaft auf Aktien See *KGaA.*

Konto Nr (Gr) Account number.

Kontorstid (Swedish) Office hours.

Kr (Gr) Abbreviation for *Kreis,* circle or in vicinity of. (A smaller town in the vicinity of a larger one.)

Kreis See *Kr.*

L, Lic, or **Lcdo** (Sp) Abbreviation for *licendado,* licensed.

L/CR (Fr) Abbreviation for *lettre de crédit,* letter of credit.

Lda (Pt) Abbreviation for *limitida,* limited.

Leiter (Gr) Principal.

Lief (Gr) Abbreviation for *lieferund,* number.

Limitada See *Lda, Ltda.*

Lizenznehmer (Gr) Licensee.

Ltd Abbreviation for limited.

Ltda (Sp) Abbreviation for *limitada,* limited.

Ltg (Gr) Abbreviation for *leitung,* management.

Man Dir Abbreviation for managing director.

Máquina (Sp) Machine.

Marchio (It) Trademark.

Marknadschef (Swedish) Marketing manager.

Marknadsföring (Swedish) Marketing.

Marque de fabrique (Fr) Trademark.

Maschinenfabrik (Gr) Machine factory.

Mdm Abbreviation for madam.

Me (Fr) Abbreviation for *maître,* lawyer.

Mgr Abbreviation for manager.

Mitglied (Gr) Member.

Naamloze vennootschap See *NV.*

Niederlassung (Gr) Branch.

No. Abbreviation for number.

Nr (Gr) Abbreviation for *nummer,* number.

N/Ref (Fr) Abbreviation for *notre référence,* our reference. Followed by a project, file or other number that is added to separate piece of correspondence. See *V/Ref.*

Numero verde (It) Toll-free number.

Numéro vert (Fr) Toll-free number.

Nummer (Dutch) Number.

NV (Dutch) Abbreviation for *naamloze vennootschap,* public limited company.

Of (Sp) Abbreviation for *oficina,* office.

Off. Abbreviation for office.

Offene Handelsgesellschaft See *OHG.*

Oficina See *of.*

OHG (Gr) Abbreviation for *Offene Handelsgesellschaft,* private trading company.

On (It) Abbreviation for *onorevole,* honorable.

Onderwerp (Dutch) Re, about, subject (as used on a memo form).

Osakeyhitiö See *Oy.*

Oy (Finnish, Russian) Abbreviation for *osakeyhitiö,* limited company.

Parkmöglichkeit (Gr) Possible parking available.

p/cta (Sp) Abbreviation for *por cuenta,* on account.

P.E. Abbreviation for professional engineer.

Personenvennootschap met beperkte aansprakelijkheid See *PVBA.*

PLC Abbreviation for public limited company.

Postanschrift (Gr) Mailing address.

Postfach (Gr) Post office box.

Präs (Gr) Abbreviation for *Präsident*, president.

Pres Abbreviation for president.

Produktionsbetrieb (Gr) production plant.

Produktion und Export (Gr) Manufacture and export.

Prof abbreviation for professor.

Prok (Gr) Abbreviation for *Prokurist*, officer with statutory authority.

Propriétaire-Directeur (Fr) Owner and principal.

Pty Abbreviation for proprietary.

Publicidad (Sp) Advertising.

Publicité (Fr) Advertising.

PVBA (Dutch) Abbreviation for *personenvennootschap met beperkte aansprakelijkheid*, private limited company.

Pvt Abbreviation for private.

RA (Gr) Abbreviation for *Rechtsanwalt*, counsel.

Rechtsanwalt See *RA*

Reklamchef (Swedish) Advertising manager.

Ret Abbreviation for retired.

Revisions (Gr) Accounting.

SA Abbreviation for *société anonyme* (Fr), *sociedade anônima* (Pt), *sociedad anónima* (Sp), public limited company.

Sàrl (It) Abbreviation for *société à responsabilité*, private limited company.

SAS (It) Abbreviation for *società in accomandita semplice*, limited partnership.

SCA (Sp) Abbreviation for *sociedad en comandita por acciónes*, limited partnership.

Schutzmarke (Gr) Trademark.

Schwestergesellschaft (Gr) Affiliate, associate, branch.

S de RL (Sp) Abbreviation for *sociedad de responsabilidad limitada*, private limited company.

Sdn Bhd (Malaysian) Abbreviation for *sendirian berhad*, private limited company.

Secy Abbreviation for secretary.

Sendirian berhad See *Sdn Bhd.*

Sequros (Sp) Insurance.

Service d'experts-conseil (Fr) Consulting service.

Servicios legales (Sp) Law firm.

Sez (It) Abbreviation for *sezione*, section.

SL (Sp) Abbreviation for *sociedad de responsabilidad limitada*, private limited company.

SNC (It) Abbreviation for *società in nome collettivo*, partnership.

s/o Abbreviation for son of.

Sociedad anónima See *SA.*

Sociedad de responsabilidad limitada See *S de RL* or *SRL.*

Sociedad en comandita por acciónes See *SCA.*

Società à responsabilità limita See *SRL.*

Società in accomandita semplice See *SAS.*

Società per Azioni See *SpA.*

Société anonyme See *SA.*

Société à responsabilité See *Sàrl.*

Société de personnes à responsabilité See *SPRL.*

Solicitor Lawyer (English term as opposed to American). Principally a lawyer who serves as a legal agent, represents clients in minor courts, and prepares cases for trial in superior courts. See barrister.

SpA (It) Abbreviation for *Società per Azioni*, a limited liability company.

SPRL (Fr) Abbreviation for *société de personnes à responsabilité*, private limited company.

Srio (It) Abbreviation for *secretario*, secretary.

SRL Abbreviation for *società à responsabilità limita* (It) or *sociedad de responsabilitad limitada* (Sp), private limited.

Stellv (Gr) Abbreviation for *Stellvertreter* or *Stellvertretender*, deputy.

Stellvertreter See *Stellv.*

Stellvertretender Vorsitzender See *Stellv Vors.*

Stellv Vors (Gr) Abbreviation for *stellvertretender Vorsitzender*, deputy chairman.

Studio legale (It) Law firm.

Styrelse (Swedish) Board.

Styrelseordförande (Swedish) Chairman of the board.

Suc (Sp) Abbreviation for *Sucursal*, subsidiary or branch.

Succ (Fr) Abbreviation for *succursal*, a branch office.

Sucursal See *Suc.*

Succursal See *Succ.*

Supt Abbreviation for superintendent.

Tillverkning och Export (Swedish) Manufacture and export.

Tochtergesellschaft (Gr) Subsidiary.

Treuhand (Gr) Trust.

Treuhandgesellschaft (Gr) Trust institution, trustee.

U (Gr) Abbreviation for *uhr*, hour.

Unser Zeichen (Gr) Our reference. See *Ihr Zeichen.*

Usine (Fr) Factory.

Utveckling (Swedish) Development.

VEB Abbreviation for *Volkseigener Betrieb* (Gr) People's enterprise.

Ventas (Sp) Sales

Verband (Gr) Association.

Vereniging zonder winstoogmerk See *VZW.*

Verkaufsbüro (Gr) Sales office.

Verkaufsleiter (Gr) Sales manager.

Verkst dir (Swedish) Managing director.

Verkstadschef (Swedish) Works or plant manager.

Versand (Gr) Shipping.

Versicherung (Gr) Insurance.

Vertreter (Gr) Representative.

Vertretung (Gr) Representation, agency.

Vertriebsgesellchaft (Gr) Distribution company.

Vertriebsleiter (Gr) Marketing manager.

Verumärkesnamn (Swedish) Trademark.

Volkseigener Betrieb See *VEB.*

Von (Gr) From (as on a memo— From [someone]).

Vors (Gr) Abbreviation for *Vorsitzender*, chairman.

Vorsitzender (Gr) Chairman.

Vorstand (Gr) Board of directors.

Vorstandsmitglied (Gr) Directors.

V/Ref (Fr) Abbreviation for *votre référence*, your reference. Followed by a number.

VZW Abbreviation for *vereniging zonder winstoogmerk* (Flemish), nonprofit-making society.

Werbeagentur (Gr) Advertising agency.

Werbeleiter (Gr) Advertising manager.

Werbung (Gr) Advertising.

Werke (Gr) Factory, works, as in *wasserwerke* (waterworks) and *stahlwerke* (steelworks).

Wirtsch (Gr) Abbreviation for *Wirtschaft*, industrial, economic, business, financial.

Wirtshaftsprüfer (Gr) certified public accountant.

ZIP code Term used in United States for postal code.

Zweigbetrieb (Gr) Branch works.

Zweigwerk (Gr) Branch works.

Part 3

Dates and Numbers

DATES

You will probably need to refer to forms, such as shipping papers, that have been prepared in another language. Therefore it is useful to be familiar with various ways of recording dates.

Formats of Dates

Dates are written in various ways throughout the world. On invoices, shipping papers, and other documents, brief forms consisting of all figures are often used. The month is referred to by number rather than name; for example, 3 for March, the third month of the year. Confusion arises when different sequences are used for the day, month, and year. In the United States, it is customary to put the month first:

> March 10, 1994, is written 3/10/94.

In other parts of the world, the day goes first:

> March 10, 1994, is written 10/3/94.

It is important to know the convention being used so you can tell whether 3/10/94 means March 10, 1994, or October 3, 1994.

Punctuation to separate the figures also varies—a clue as to the convention used. The slash (/) is common in the United States:

> 12/31/93

Periods are used elsewhere:

> 31.12.93

Dashes also may be used:

> 31-12-93

A range of days could be indicated like this:

> 16-24.3.1994

which refers to March 16 to 24, 1994. Other variations are not to abbreviate the year, and to place a 0 before single-digit figures, which gives all dates the same number of digits so they can be read and sorted by a computer. May 27, 1995, looks like this:

> 27.05.1995, or 1995-05-27.

Another variation uses a lowercase Roman numeral for the month. December 14, 1988 would be written:

> 14.xii.88

When spelling out the month's name, the day can precede or follow it:

5 September 1984 or September 5, 1984.

The best way to avoid misunderstanding is to spell out or abbreviate the name of the month, rather than use a number.

Days and Months

The names of days and months are given in seven languages in the tables below. It is customary to capitalize the names in English and German, but not in French, Italian, Portuguese, or Spanish.

There are various abbreviations for days and months. When an abbreviation spells another word, it can be confusing; for example, *ago*, an English word, is the Portuguese abbreviation for *agosto*. A traditional style of abbreviating is to raise the final letter or letters; for example, *dom^o* and *feb^o* for *domingo* and *febrero* in Spanish.

Days

English	French	German	Italian	Japanese	Portuguese	Spanish
Monday	lundi	Montag	lunedì	Getsuyoobi	segunda-feira	lunes
Tuesday	mardi	Dienstag	martedì	Kayoobi	terça-feira	martes
Wednesday	mercredi	Mittwoch	mercoledì	Suiyoobi	quarta-feira	miércoles
Thursday	jeudi	Donnerstag	giovedì	Mokuyoobi	quinta-feira	jueves
Friday	vendredi	Freitag	venerdì	Kinyoobi	sexta-feira	viernes
Saturday	samedi	Sonnabend or Samstag	sabato	Doyoobi	sábado	sábado
Sunday	dimanche	Sonntag	domenica	Niciyoobi	domingo	domingo

Months

English	French	German	Italian	Japanese	Portuguese	Spanish
January	janvier	Januar (or Jänner)	gennaio	Ichi-gatsu	janeiro	enero
February	février	Februar (or Feber)	febbraio	Ni-gatsu	fevereiro	febrero
March	mars	März	marzo	San-gatsu	março	marzo
April	avril	April	aprile	Shi-gatsu	abril	abril
May	mai	Mai	maggio	Go-gatsu	maio	mayo
June	juin	Juni	giugno	Roku-gatsu	junho	junio
July	juillet	Juli	luglio	Shichi-gatsu	julho	julio
August	août	August	agosto	Hachi-gatsu	agosto	agosto
September	septembre	September	settembre	Kyuu-gatsu	setembre	septiembre, setiembre
October	octobre	Oktober	ottobre	Juu-gatsu	outubro	octubre
November	novembre	November	novembre	Juuichi-gatsu	novembro	noviembre
December	décembre	Dezember	dicembre	Juuni-gatsu	dezembro	diciembre

Calendars

The Gregorian calendar is used throughout the international business world. It consists of the twelve months, January to December. The years are counted from the beginning of the Christian era. Other calendars are also in use although usually for religious observations and traditional festivals. A few are discussed on the following pages.

India

The national calendar of India is the Saka calendar. Chaitra is the first month, the other months have thirty or thirty-one days corresponding to the Gregorian calendar. Numerous other calendars are also used including the Muslim, Jewish, Buddhist, and Hindu calendars.

Islamic World

The months of the Hijri calendar are listed below. These are the twelve months of the Islamic lunar year. Several variations in spelling are given. The years are counted from the death of Mohammed, about 622 A.D.

Muharram (Moharram)	Rajab (Ragab)
Safar	Sha' ban (Shaban)
Rabi' Awal (Rabi I)	Ramadan
Rabi' Thani (Rabi II)	Shawal
Jumad Awal (Jumad I, Gumada I)	Dhul-Qu'dah (Thul-Kida)
Jumad Thani (Jumad II, Gumada II)	Dhul-Hijjah (Thul-Higga)

Japan

Japan counts years from the beginning of the imperial era. 1992 is the fourth year of the Heisei era, which began in 1989 when Emperor Akihito began his reign on the death of his father, Emperor Hirohito.

The Lunar Calendar

A 12-month lunar calendar is used in China along with the Gregorian calendar. On Taiwan, in Chinese communities elsewhere, and in Vietnam, the lunar calendar is observed mostly for traditional festivals.

Thailand

Observes the western twelve-month calendar in business. Religious and seasonal ceremonies follow lunar time.

☞ See pages 186–199 for holidays by country.

NUMBERS

Although numbers are usually precise and easily understood, ambiguities can occur. Europeans often handwrite the number 7 with a slash through it to distinguish it from the 1. The slash is not used in a printed 7. Americans usually write the 7 without the slash.

Ordinal Numbers

Ordinal numbers are *first, second, third, fourth,* etc. as distinguished from *one, two, three,* etc. In English, they may be written in abbreviated form: *1st, 2nd, 3rd, 4th,* etc. Abbreviations are also used in other languages. In French, 1st is written *1ier* or *1ière* (*premier* or *première*). The second floor would be the *2ième étage,* short for *deuxième étage,* the third floor the *3ième étage.* Traditional style uses superscript for the final letters in abbreviated forms but these are not always typeset.

Thousands and Fractions

Commas and periods are used to separate parts of a number. In some countries commas are used to separate amounts of a thousand and periods to separate fractions, that is, amounts less than one. In the United States you would use the commas and periods as follows:

> $1,000.50 (one thousand dollars and fifty cents)

In the Netherlands, Germany, Italy, and other countries of western Europe, a comparable number would be written this way:

> Dfl 1.000,50 (one thousand guilders and 50 cents)

Or you might see this:

> 6,5 mio, meaning 6.5 million (*Mio* is an abbreviation used in Germany)

The following phrases say the same thing. The first two phrases might be written in Costa Rica, the second two in the United States.

> 5 Costa Rican centimos equal 0,05 Costa Rican colon.
> In Costa Rica there is a bill worth 20,00 colons.

> 5 Costa Rican centimos equal 0.05 Costa Rican colon.
> In Costa Rica there is a bill worth 20.00 colons.

Very Large Numbers

The terms for very large numbers may be different in the United States from those used in the United Kingdom. For example, the number 1,000,000,000,000 is 1 trillion in the United States but may be called 1 billion or a million millions in the United Kingdom.

In countries where very large amounts of currency are used, phrases like "a thousand million" (for one billion) may be used.

Part 4

Personal Names

How to Use Personal Names

When addressing someone it is important to use the person's name correctly. Many countries have a rich variety of cultures and their citizens follow different customs. Be aware of these customs so that you use the name the way the person prefers. The information below is a guide, and it may or may not apply in any given situation.

Surname and Given Name

In most cultures, a person's full name consists of two kinds of names: a given name (given to one member of the family) and a family name or surname (shared with other members of the family).

The order of the parts of the name and the number of names of each kind vary from culture to culture. Sometimes the given name goes first and sometimes it goes last. For this reason, the commonly used American terms "first name" and "last name" may be confusing. A "first" name could appear last in the name, and a "last" name first.

Formal Names

Some cultures distinguish between surname and formal name. The formal name is used with titles and may include several family names, such as both the mother's and the father's (as with Spanish and Arabic names). In other places the formal name may not be the family name.

Prefixes and Particles in Names

Names sometimes contain small words—particles, prefixes, articles, or prepositions—with meanings such as "of," "on," "from," "and," "son of," "the." Here are some examples:

Andrea del Sarto   *del* is Italian meaning "from" or "of the."
Konrad von Gesner   *von* is German meaning "from."
Charles de Gaulle   *de* is French meaning "from."
Ibn Saud   *Ibn* is Arabic meaning "son of."

Rules vary about whether to capitalize or lowercase these words and whether to include them when the surname stands alone or goes first. Would you address Marie Van Renssalaer as Ms. Renssalaer or Ms. Van Renssalaer? When trying to reach Mr. Tawfiq al-Hakim at his hotel would you ask the operator for Mr. al-Hakim or Mr. Hakim? Try to determine when you first meet people how they prefer to be called to avoid embarrassment later.

Inverting the Order in the Name

Sometimes people simplify or alter the appearance of their name in business communication to conform to western form. For example, in Japan and Hungary the family name goes before the given name. However, before you invert a Hungarian or Japanese name, be sure it has not already been inverted. It might have been inverted on stationery and business cards to be given to business contacts from the West.

Women's Titles

In Europe and many other parts of the world, it is traditional to use the same title (such as Madame or Signora) for all women over twenty-one years of age whether married or not. In the United States, the title Miss has traditionally been used for unmarried women of any age. Today the title Ms. is preferred by many American women.

Pronunciation

Unfamiliar names may be difficult to pronounce. However it is easy to learn the correct pronunciation with a little effort.

The first time you have to pronounce someone's name make a point of asking if you are doing it correctly. Repeat after the other person says it to be sure you have it right. Don't worry if your accent is not perfect; you mainly want your pronunciation to be recognizable.

Spell the name whatever way helps you remember the correct pronunciation. Imagine answering a phone call from a businessperson to whom you have written but never spoken with before. His name is Antonio Pacheco. You write down "pe' jhio" to remind you not to say "Pah cheek' o" when you to need to pronounce his name.

Arabic

In Arabic names, the surname follows the given name. Often people use several names, making it difficult to know where the surname begins. You must ask Youseff Abou-el Ezz if he should be addressed as Mr. Abou-el Ezz or Mr. Ezz or Mr. el Ezz.

Some common particles and prefixes are: *Abu-* (father of), *Abd, Abdel, Abd-el, Abdoul, Abou, Aboul, Abu, Ahu-* (brother), *bin-, ad-, al-* (the), *ar-, as-, at-, az-, el-* (the), *ibn-* (son of), *umm-* (mother).

In the Arabic alphabet there are no capital and lowercase letters. When transliterated into the Roman alphabet (the one used in this book), the articles *al-* and *el-* are not capitalized. But words like *Abu* are often capitalized.

Chinese

The Chinese custom is to place the family name before the given name. Usually the family name is one syllable and the given name two, although it is not always easy to distinguish between the two.

> Zheng Liangyu, or Mayor Zheng
> Liu Hongru, or Vice Minister Liu

Dutch

Common particles and prefixes include *de, ten, van,* and *van der.* The particles are generally not capitalized. However, Americans of Dutch descent often capitalize the particles in their names.

English

A person with a hyphenated surname is generally known by the combined name: Howard Jones-Atley or Mr. Jones-Atley.

French

French names may contain the articles *le, la, les, de, du, des* (often not capitalized). The articles *le, la, les, du, des* are not dropped when using the last name alone. The article *de* or *d'* often is dropped:

> M. Henri du Plessy or M. du Plessy
> Mme Annette de Latour or Mme Latour

German

In German common particles in personal names include *im, von, zu, zum, zur.* German practice is to drop the particle when using just the last name. Therefore it would be acceptable to refer to Heinrich von Steuben as Mr. Steuben. The particles in German names are not customarily capitalized. Americans of German descent often capitalize the particles in their names.

Hungarian

The family name precedes the given name. However, the name may have already been inverted to conform to western style.

Indian

The given name is first, the surname last. *Sen* and *Das* should be considered part of the last name. Each part of the name is capitalized.

Indonesian

Javan Indonesian names have only one part. It is a personal name, not a family name. An additional name may be added to conform to western style. An Arabic name may be added by a person of Muslim faith.

Italian

In Italian common particles in personal names include *da, dalla, della, delle, di.* Follow individual preference for capitalizing or not and for including as part of the surname.

Japanese

The surname or family name precedes the given name. However when people write their names in western alphabets, they often invert their name to conform to western style and print it this way on stationery and business card. If you are not sure if the name has already been inverted the better procedure would be to ask, not assume. In Japanese there are no capital and lowercase letters. Capitalize the initial letter of each part of a Japanese name when writing it in the Roman alphabet.

Korean

The surname or family name precedes the given name in Korean custom. People in frequent contact with the West may choose to invert their name to conform to western style. They will show it in this inverted way of given name first, family name last on stationery and business card. If you are not sure if the name has already been inverted to conform to western style, the best thing is to ask.

There are relatively few (some 200) family names. If you recognize these, you will know whether a name has been inverted or not. When you see one of the following you can be fairly certain it is the family name regardless of its placement: Kim, Lee, Pak, An, Chae, Cho, Choi, Chong, Chung, Han, Ku, Ko, Im, Oh, No, Park, Shin, Yu, Yun.

Portuguese

The given name is first, surname or surnames last. The full name often includes the family names of both mother and father. The father's family name goes first. People are referred to by either the father's family name or by both names. Silvio dos Santos Gutiérrez might be called Mr. dos Santos or Mr. dos Santos Gutiérrez. You would use whatever he uses. Common particles and prefixes include *de, do, da, dos, das.* Particles are not capitalized.

Russian

The given name is first, surname is last. A middle name (patronymic) is customary. The patronymic is the name of someone in the father's family, perhaps an important ancestor. When Russians refer to someone by their given name they often use the patronymic as well. Mikhail Gorbachev is often called Mikhail Sergeyevich. Men's and women's names have different endings. Rostov would be the masculine ending and Rostova the feminine. Use the feminine ending if the woman uses it; not all do.

Spanish

The given name is first, surname or surnames last. The full name often includes the family names of both mother and father. The father's family name goes first. People are referred to by either the father's family name or by both names. Luis Portillo Sanchez might be called Mr. Portillo or Mr. Portillo Sanchez. You would use whatever he uses. Sometimes *y*, meaning "and," is used to separate the two family names: Luis Portillo y Sanchez. The particles *de*, *de la* and *y* are not capitalized.

The word *hijo* or *h.* means "son" and is similar to junior in English. You would not use it in a salutation in a letter. However, if you were calling a company you might be asked if you want the father or son.

In Spain and South America, women do not change their name when they marry.

Thai

The given or personal name is first, the surname last. A person is usually known by the personal name, not the family name. In other words, the formal name is the given or personal name, not the family or surname.

United States

In the United States, people speak of having a first, middle, and last name. The last name, or surname, is traditionally the father's family name. Usually, only the initial letter of the middle name is used: Mary L. Jones. A person might spell out the middle name to avoid confusion with another person with the same first and last name, or to honor the mother as well as the father (when the middle name is the mother's family name).

The hyphenated surname is becoming more common in the United States, especially among married women. A married woman may retain her own family name and add her husband's family name: Mary Jones-Smith. The first part of the hyphenated last name (Jones) is the woman's family name before she married. The second part is her husband's family name (Smith). Married women sometimes use their maiden name (name before marrying) in business and their married name (their husband's family name) in private life.

> Ms. Mary Jones in business, professional life
> Mrs. Robert Smith in private life

ACCENTS

Many languages use accents and diacritical marks, which pose a problem for someone not familiar with them. Their purpose is to indicate emphasis in a word or to change the sound of a letter.

The names of some accents and diacritical marks are listed below.

acute accent (á, é)	tilde (ñ)
grave accent (à)	cedilla (ç)
dieresis or umlaut (ö)	circumflex (ê)

If you need to type accents, you have several options. If you plan to use them a lot, you can adapt your typewriter or computer keyboard by replacing characters that you do not use with accented letters.

If you use a typewriter you can create some accents and symbols by striking two characters over each other. To make a £ symbol, type a hyphen over the letter *t* or the letter *f* over *L* to see which looks best.

With a computer, you can put in many accents by typing the ASCII code. Your printer must be able to print the accents you have encoded.

☞ See page 71 for ASCII codes.

Another option is to handwrite the accents, which may not look neat. A better choice is to ignore the accents. Most people do not mind if their name is typed without accents and understand that others do not have the equipment to handle them.

Do not think that because you cannot type the exact accent required that a similar one will do. Accents and diacritical marks indicate a specific emphasis or sound and are an integral part of the language. Using them incorrectly is worse than not using them at all.

If your word processor uses ASCII, you can type in many accents and marks using the codes in the following list. Hold down the Alt key and type the code number on the numeric key pad. Do not type the letter first or you will get the letter twice, with and without the accent. You will not get the accent or mark you want if your printer is unable to print them, even though they show on your screen. Before typing a lot of ASCII codes, do a test run to see what your printer can do.

â 131	é 130	ñ 164	ù 151
ä 132	É 144	Ñ 165	ú 163
à 133	ê 136	ô 147	Ü 154
å 134	ë 137	ö 148	ÿ 152
á 160	è 138	ò 149	æ 145
Ä 142	ï 139	Ö 153	Æ 146
Å 143	î 140	ó 162	
ç 135	ì 141	ü 129	
Ç 128	í 161	û 150	

With some software, you can create the following characters as well.

Á 199	Ë 203	Ó 209	Ù 213
Â 200	Ì 204	Ô 210	Ú 214
À 182	Í 205	õ 177	Ÿ 216
Ã 183	Î 206	Ø 178	ß 217
ã 176	Ï 207	ø 179	Ž 218
È 201	Õ 184	Š 211	œ 180
Ê 202	Ò 208	š 212	Œ 181

FORMS OF ADDRESS

It is worthwhile spending a few minutes before calling or writing someone to determine the appropriate form of address. Although a business deal might not be lost, things go more smoothly if you are sensitive to the comfort of the other person. Be alert to cues they give.

Formal or Informal

Some people (including many Americans) are informal from the start whereas others are formal. As a general rule, it is better to be formal until you know the other person is comfortable with an informal style. When speaking, use the appropriate title: Mr., Mrs., Ms., or Miss.

Some people like you to use their professional title, such as engineer or doctor, in the salutation or in the address. However, unless you are quite sure of the title, you may be better off simply using Mr. or Mrs. Avoid first names and nicknames until you know what is preferred. Even though you may have established a rapport, you each represent different companies and different countries. Others in the company will read your correspondence and may expect formality. It is possible to be both cordial and formal.

Salutations

Depending on the style of your correspondence you may open with a salutation, such as *Dear Mr.——* or *Ladies and Gentlemen.*

In Europe it is customary to address a woman over the age of twenty-one as Mrs. (or *Madame* in French, *Signora* in Italian, *Mevrouw* or *Mw* in Dutch) regardless of her marital status. This custom is not usually followed in the United States; however, the title Ms. is often used by businesswomen regardless of marital status.

See the following table for abbreviated forms of titles. The titles Mr., Messrs. (plural of Mr.), and Mrs. are never spelled out. Ms. is not an abbreviation and has no other form. Miss (plural Misses) does not have an abbreviated form. Periods are used with Mr. and Mrs. in American practice but not in British practice.

English	French	German	Italian	Spanish
Mr.	Monsieur (M)	Herr	Signor (Sig.)	Señor (Sr.)
Messrs.	Messieurs (MM.)	Herren	Signori (Sigg.)	Señores (Sres.)
Mrs.	Madame (Mme)	Frau (Fr.)	Signora (Sig.ra)	Señora (Sra.)
Mesdames	Mesdames (Mmes)		Signore (Sig.re)	Señoras (Sras.)
Miss	Mademoiselle (Mlle)	Fräulein (Frl.)	Signorina (Sig.na)	Señorita (Srta.)
Misses	Mesdemoiselles (Mlles)	Fräulein (Frl.)	Signorine (Sig.ne)	Señoritas (Srtas.)

People use many other titles with their name to indicate professional experience, academic status, company position, and so on. In the United States, titles are not widely used in the salutation of business correspondence but are used with the person's name in the address and following their signature. In other countries, they may be used frequently. Try to determine the individual's preference and follow it.

Formal Occasions

Many rules that apply to the use of names and titles can be overlooked in everyday communication but should be observed on formal occasions. If you need a source for this kind of information, refer to a style manual or consult with someone at a cultural organization, consulate, or embassy.

For example, if the abbreviation Esq. for esquire is used following the name of a lawyer, a title should not also be used before the name:

> Judith L. Test, Esq.

not

> Ms. Judith L. Test, Esq.

☞ See pages 78–81 for more on letter styles.
☞ See pages 51–56 for more on titles.

Part 5

Letter Writing

LANGUAGE USAGE

This book assumes that most readers will be writing in English whether or not it is their first language and that they will be receiving letters in English. English is spoken around the world and is the most commonly used language for business.

In international correspondence it is important to write clearly and simply because although most people will probably have some command of English, that command may be weak and, even more to the point, the version of English with which they are familiar may differ from the version of English that you are using.

Slang and Colloquialisms

Slang and colloquial expressions do not travel well. They may be misunderstood and may embarrass or annoy others. Therefore, it is a good idea to avoid them. In business correspondence, the best style is one that is clear and straightforward.

Although you may, if you are American, tell your manager that you plan to "put on a real dog and pony show," not everyone will know what you are talking about. A better way to say this to your international contact would be that you plan to give a presentation that will be complete, impressive, elaborate, flamboyant, or whatever best describes your intent.

Using slang is often an excuse to avoid saying precisely what you mean—another reason not to use it.

Jargon and Acronyms

Your company may use jargon and acronyms that to you are so familiar you do not realize others outside the company as well as outside the country will not understand them. If you are in the habit of referring to products, forms, and procedures by code names, be sure to clarify what you mean for others. You will find it difficult to do business with someone who does not know what you are talking about.

Your warehouse staff may know what to send if you ask them to ship an M642 Iro, but your customer should be told that you are sending the Ink Roller to fit in the Model 642 Electronic Check Writer.

Business jargon may not be understood by everyone. Rather than saying you are going to run a P & L, it would be better to say that you are going to do a profit-and-loss study.

British vs. American English

In international business correspondence, one soon realizes that, contrary to what was taught in school, there is often more than one acceptable way to punctuate, spell certain words, and capitalize. In Great Britain periods are not used with abbreviations ending with the last letter of the word. For example, the British do not put periods at the end of Mr and Mrs but Americans do. Shortened forms of British county names do not end with a period—for example, Bucks for Buckinghamshire (leading an unwary American to think there is a Bucks County in England the same as in Pennsylvania).

Capitalization and punctuation vary from language to language. For example, in French, Italian, Spanish, and Portuguese, the names of the days of the week and the months are not capitalized as they are in English. Some people use a colon at the end of the salutation of a business letter; others do not observe this style.

Many minor differences exist between British and American spellings. Here are just a few:

British (American)

acknowledgement (acknowledgment)
aeroplane (airplane)
analyse (analyze)
catalogue* (catalog)
centre* (center)
cheque* (check)
colour* (color)
councillor* (councilor)
counselled* (counseled)
defence (defense)
enrol (enroll)
favour* (favor)
fibre (fiber)
flavour* (flavor)
fulfil (fulfill)
grey (gray)
harbour* (harbor)
honour* (honor)
instalment* (installment)
judgement* (judgment)
kerb (curb)
labour* (labor)
litre* (liter)
manoeuvre* (maneuver)
metre* (meter)
mould (mold)
neighbour* (neighbor)
organisation (organization)
plough (plow)
theatre* (theater)
travelled (traveled)
travelling (traveling)
tyre (tire)
woollen (woolen)

* also used in Canada

The many differences in how Americans and British speak English are a source of humor as well as confusion. This book, written by an American, contains a short list of British-English words followed by their American equivalents to illustrate these differences.

British	American Equivalent
bank account	savings account
bank holiday	legal holiday

car park	parking lot
chemist	pharmacist, drug store
commercial traveller	traveling salesperson
current account	checking account
deposit account	savings account
fortnight	two weeks, fourteen days
hire	rent (as in hire a car from Hertz)
hire purchase	installment plan
lift	elevator
limited company	incorporated company
jumper	sweater
managing director	general manager or chief executive officer (CEO)
never-never	installment plan
phone through	call on telephone
roundabout	rotary or traffic circle
stockist	supplier
trade cycle	business cycle
trades union	labor union
tradesman	storekeeper
trading estate	industrial park
visiting card	business card
unit trust	mutual fund

Here are examples of different meanings for the same word or phrase.

Word/Phrase	British	American
to bomb	to succeed	to fail
to fill someone in	to hit over the head	to inform
intercourse	conversation	sex

Examples of British idiomatic expressions.

bank holiday week	a week in which Monday was a bank holiday
the Bank	the Bank of England, whose chief customer is the government
Monday week	a week from Monday or Monday a week ago
today fortnight	two weeks from today

Writing Guides

There are many excellent style manuals and guides on how to write well and prepare copy, including these:

- *Chicago Manual of Style*
- *Webster's Secretarial Handbook*
- *Words into Type*
- *Write to the Point: Letters, Memos, and Reports That Get Results*

☞ See Part 14, pages 233–236, Sources of Information, for details on the above titles as well as other useful publications.

FORMAT OF THE LETTER

An international business letter should contain most of the following features.

Return address Include country name.

Telephone/fax/telex numbers Include country code as well as city or area code.

Interior address (address of the recipient of the letter). Be sure to spell everything correctly, include all necessary elements—such as floor or suite number—and the person's correct title.

Date See page 59 on dates.

Attention Line You may use the attention line to give the appearance of addressing your letter to the company rather than the individual. The word *attention* might be followed by a department name rather than a person's name. This option may be preferred because it looks more businesslike.

Salutation Your greeting to the letter's recipient. This reads "Dear ———" in standard U.S. business usage. Another acceptable and widely used option is to skip the salutation. In some European countries, the practice is to write to the department of the company not the individual, except at senior level. This may be preferred since it appears more businesslike. It also solves several problems:

1. What to do when you do not know if the person should be addressed as Mr., Mrs. or Ms.
2. When you only have the person's name in a handwritten signature that is not legible.

Since both formats are correct you can use either without difficulty. You may follow the style of the letter sent to you first, if there is one.

☞ See pages 71–72 on forms of address.

Subject Line This is optional but is more important if you have not included an individual's name in either the address or salutation. By indicating the subject of the letter you help guide it to the right person or department.

Reference Number Some businesses assign reference numbers to all correspondence for easier filing and retrieval. If you are responding to a letter in which there is a request to use a reference number in any reply, you should do it. This is especially important when your letter is not addressed to an individual. When your letter arrives at its destination anyone can quickly locate previous correspondence by the reference number and give it to the correct person.

You may assign a reference number to your letter with the understanding that it will appear on any response you receive.

Body of Letter The text of the letter.

Complimentary Close This may be a simple "Yours truly," something more wordy, more formal, more personal, or nothing at all. The best is something brief, pleasant sounding, not too casual. If the person writing to you has used a closing that seems too formal or flowery, remember that it is a convention. You can use a closing with which you feel more comfortable. You probably would not use a complimentary close if you have not used a salutation.

Name/Signature/Title/Company Name Any and all of these may be used in conjunction with the closing.

Reference Initials The initials in capital letters of the writer of the letter followed by a colon and lowercase initials of the person who typed the letter.

Enclosure If additional papers are to be enclosed with the letter you can indicate this. Either the word Enclosure or Encl. is typed below the signature and possibly a brief description of what is enclosed.

Copy Notation This starts with cc: (carbon copy), pc: (photocopy) or c: followed by the name of the person or people who will receive copies of the letter.

Four sample letters follow.

#1

```
              Foldham Publishing
               11 Maple Avenue
             New London, CT 06320
                    U.S.A.
         Telephone: +1 203 444-0000
             Fax: +1 203 443-1111

3 August 1993
ABC Cie
65, rue Mazarines
F-75006 Paris
FRANCE

Dear M——:


(body of letter)



Sincerely yours,
(signature)
Mary Arekalian (Mrs.)
Manager, Reference Department

MA/ma
Encl: Annual Report
```

Letter #1 (preceding page) has a salutation and complimentary close. The sender's telephone and fax number include the international country code for the United States (+1). Mary Arekalian typed the letter herself and wants to be referred to as Mrs. Arekalian.

#2

> **Wolf Electronics**
> **59483 Keefer Court**
> **Hamilton, ON L8E 4V4**
> **CANADA**
>
> ```
> August 4, 1993
> A & T Technology
> Research Department
> PO Box XXX
> Dublin 20
> IRELAND
>
>
> (body of letter)
>
>
> FRITZ OTTERMEYER
> ENGINEERING MANAGER
> ```

Letter #2 has no salutation or complimentary closing and is sent to a department. The writer's name and title are typed in capital letters.

#3

> **(letterhead)**
>
> ```
> By facsimile: 1 203 443 0000
>
> Nels Foldham
> Foldham Publishing
> 11 Maple Avenue
> New London, CT 06320
> U.S.A.
>
> Dear Mr. Foldham:
> TRADE INQUIRY
>
>
> (body of letter)
>
>
> Yours truly,
> TRADE DEVELOPMENT BOARD
>
> Phillip Laydon
> ```

Letter #3 (preceding page) was sent by fax; the fax number includes the international country code. The subject line indicates that the letter is a response to a trade inquiry. It was written by Phillip Laydon on behalf of the Trade Development Board.

#4

```
                        (letterhead)
        Your Ref. 88.04/885-A/93
        Our Ref. TBG 94/02/789-93

        21.09.1993
        A & T Technology
        Attn: M. D. Edberg
        PO Box XXX
        Dublin 20
        IRELAND

        Gentlemen:


        (body of letter)


        Very truly yours,
        Tam Electronics Company

        Ralph Wing
        Public Relations Director

        kl
        pc: Soon-Yi Delgado
```

Letter #4 includes the reference number (Your Ref.) taken from the letter to which it is responding. The date of the letter is September 21, 1993 (21.09.1993). The salutation "Gentlemen" may be used if referring only to men. If women are included then "Ladies and Gentlemen" would be appropriate.

STATIONERY

If you expect to conduct business internationally on a regular basis, you may want to reprint your stationery, business cards, and forms to include information needed by your contacts in other countries.

User-Friendly Stationery

As an aid to your international business contacts, the international telephone country code should appear with your telephone and fax numbers on your business stationery. If you have a telex or cable number include it as well. Your country name should be included in the address.

The Paper Stock

It is not necessary to use ultra lightweight airmail stationery for international mail. In the United States, the minimum rate for an international letter at the time of this writing applies up to .5 ounce, which is the weight of about five sheets of standard bond paper. If you purchase new stationery however it would be worthwhile considering weight. The minimum rate for U.S. domestic mail applies to weight up to 1 full ounce.

Business stationery and cards are printed in varying sizes. If the size is important, for example, if you plan to insert a page in a folder, be sure it will fit. In the United States the most common size of business stationery is 8.5 inches x 11 inches and of business cards is 3.5 inches x 2 inches. Another common stationery size is 21 centimeters x 29.5 centimeters.

Business Cards

Business cards are important in international trade. Some countries emphasize the exchange of cards on first meeting. They provide evidence that you are who you say you are. They also make it easier for someone to pronounce an unfamiliar name.

By giving people your card you make it easier for them to contact you at a later time. A card with the telephone number is helpful when the telephone system is difficult to use, telephone directories are not available, or the person does not speak your language well and would have difficulty going through an operator or switchboard.

Business cards provide the correct spelling of your name and your title, saving others the embarassment of having to ask for this information later.

In some situations you may want to have your business card printed in two languages. For example, it is not uncommon for Japanese businesspeople to have cards printed in Japanese on one side and English on the other. A bilingual business card indicates you are serious about being in international business.

Part 6
===

Section	Page

Mailing Letters and Packages

PUBLIC POSTAL SERVICE VS. PRIVATE COMPANIES

When sending letters and packages to international addresses you may use the public postal service or a private shipping company such as Federal Express, UPS (United Parcel Service), DHL Worldwide Express Ltd., Airborne Express, Emery, and TNT Express Worldwide. The government-run postal service offers less expensive, but not always as speedy, delivery. The postal service only handles letters and small packages whereas many private companies handle large industrial shipments as well. The following pages discuss the mailing of small packages and letters—the kind that would be sent from an office.

Before you settle on one organization to handle your international mail, find out which ones best serve your area and what each can offer. Some serve certain parts of the world better than others. Prices, speed of delivery, and specific services will vary. Ask for a complete package of international mailing information including a description of each service offered, instructions for filling out the waybill, rates, schedules, and countries served. Some organizations also provide detailed country by country information, such as the following:

- The correct forms to use with each kind of shipment
- Services offered and to which areas within the country
- Billing options, which vary from country to country
- Information on specific commodities
- Addresses and phone numbers of their service centers

The service center information can be helpful if you plan to travel to that country and want to send packages back home. You may be able to use the same waybill as you use in your own country or you may have to use a different one but can still use your account number.

The commodities information may tell you what documents are required by that country (e.g. when shipping electronic parts you must provide an international waybill and a commercial invoice), which commodities are prohibited from entering the country, and so on.

Business documents—such as correspondence and reports—do not usually require extensive customs documentation. Nevertheless, different forms may be required if your package is over a certain weight. The following list provides examples of what may qualify as business documents. This list will not apply to all countries. Also note that in any given country any one of the items could be prohibited from entering. Contact your shipper for specific information.

Examples of Business Documents

Airline tickets	Catalogs	Newsletters
Annual reports	Charts	Passports
Bids	Computer printouts	Price lists
Blueprints	Magazines	Proposals
Brochures	Manuals	Specification sheets
Business cards	Manuscript	Traveler's checks
Calendars	Negatives	Visa applications

If you use the postal service or one shipping company a lot, you should open an account. Listed below are some possible advantages and disadvantages of public and private services. We say *possible* because every mailing situation is different; find out which organization best meets your own needs.

Advantages of the Postal Service

- Only the U.S. Postal Service can deliver to post office boxes, APO (Army/Air Force Post Office) and FPO (Fleet Post Office) boxes. (There are exceptions to this so check with the private company you want to use.)
- The postal service's first-class airmail is far less expensive than the least expensive service of the private companies.
- The postal service offers bulk mailing—M-bag (for mail going to one addressee), combined air and surface mail, and surface mail, all at lower rates than first class.
- Express mail of the postal service may be less expensive and just as quick as comparable service of a private company.
- The post office may deliver on Saturday at no additional charge whereas private companies may charge more for weekend delivery.
- If no one is at the address to receive your package it will be returned to the post office where the addressee can pick it up. Usually with private companies you have to wait for them to redeliver, which could be a problem for a small company or an individual.
- The postal service picks up from drop boxes on weekends and holidays so packages mailed at these times may be delivered faster than through a private company.

Advantages of Private Shipping Companies

- The private companies are generally considered to be more reliable. They may guarantee faster delivery than the postal service to any given area.
- They provide express delivery to more places in the world than the postal service.

- They have efficient tracking systems, so they know where your package is at all times, when it will be delivered, and what to do in case of a problem.
- They provide excellent telephone assistance on how to fill out a waybill, on delivery time and prices, on customs documentation, and so on.
- They handle large shipments as well as letters and packages.
- If customs duty and taxes are owed on your package, you may have the option with a private company of being billed for these amounts. In this case the company advances you the amounts, probably charging a fee for the service. You might choose this option when you do not want the recipient to have to pay duty and taxes (for example, when you are sending a gift or a package to a potential customer). However, you must check with the shipper to see if this option is available for the country where you are shipping. For packages mailed through the postal service, the recipient must pay duty and taxes.
- If you are traveling outside your own country and want to send a package home, you can use your private company account number and possibly the same international waybill that you use at home. This may be more convenient than making a trip to the post office and paying postage.
- The private company shipping and billing documentation may be more detailed or better suited to your record keeping needs.

What Both the Postal Service and Private Companies Offer

- Both provide packaging free of charge (letter envelopes, small package envelopes, mailing tubes and boxes) and mailing labels or waybills. You can order these supplies by phone. Be sure to specify that you want ones for international not domestic mail.
- Both have drop boxes in various locations. One service may be located more conveniently than others.
- Both pick up packages from your office on request for a fee.
- Both allow you to set up an account with them for billing and provide mailing labels imprinted with your name and address, account number, and, if you want, with a receiver address, which is helpful if you mail a lot to the same address.

SPECIFIC POSTAL SERVICE REQUIREMENTS

Different postal systems have different preferences on how envelopes and labels should be addressed. Although your letter or package probably will get to its destination if you do not follow their directions exactly, try to conform especially when mailing to other countries and preparing bulk mailings. Optical character scanners and other automated devices used to speed up delivery work most efficiently when scanning a standard format. You might want to obtain instructions from the national postal system of a country to which you plan to mail in quantity.

You will have to deal with conflicts between preferred practices of different countries. For example, the U.S. Postal Service requests that only the country name be in all capital letters. Other systems put the city as well as the country in all capital letters. Always type or clearly print the address.

☞ See pages 18–38, for information on placement of postal codes, inclusion of regional names, and so on, by country.

☞ See pages 38–45, for province and state names, by country.

☞ See pages 12–17, for words and abbreviations used in addresses.

Canada

The Postal Code Directory of Canada requests the following use of the postal code:

1. Always show the postal code as the last item of the address. (On international mail to Canada put the code before Canada.)
2. Always print the postal code in block capitals.
3. Do not use periods or other punctuation marks anywhere in the postal code.
4. Leave a clear space of one character between the two parts of the postal code.
5. Never underline the postal code.
6. Place the postal code on a line by itself at the end of the address:

   Mr. F. Khan
   46 Pine Trail
   NEPEAN, Ontario
   K2G 5A5
   CANADA

7. If it is impossible to use a separate line, the postal code can appear on the same line as city and province providing it is separated from the province name by a space *at least* two characters wide as in the following example:

   Mr. B. Cloutier
   150 Nepean Street
   OTTOWA, Ontario   K2P 0B6
   CANADA

8. If you use any subscription or account numbers on the envelope, they should be written above the address and not placed where they could be confused with the code.
9. No part of the address should appear below the code on the envelope. "For attention of . . ." and similar messages should be shown above the address.
10. Write the entire address, including the street and number, and the apartment or suite number if applicable, on all mail.
11. All previous zone numbers are withdrawn. The zone numbers are not incorporated into the code.

Canadian postal codes all begin with a letter that indicates a specific part of Canada. In the address above for Mr. Cloutier, the letter K tells you the address is in eastern Ontario. Here are the regions (in both English and French) and their letters.

A	Newfoundland/Terre-Neuve
B	Nova Scotia/Nouvelle-Écosse
C	Prince Edward Island/Île-du-Prince-Édouard
E	New Brunswick/Nouveau-Brunswick
G	Quebec East/Est du Québec
H	Montreal Metropolitan/Montréal Métro
J	Quebec West/Ouest du Québec
K	Eastern Ontario/Est de l'Ontario
L	Central Ontario/Centre de l'Ontario
M	Toronto Metropolitan/Toronto Métro
N	Southwestern Ontario/Sud-Ouest de l'Ontario
P	Northern Ontario/Nord de l'Ontario
R	Manitoba
S	Saskatchewan
T	Alberta
V	British Columbia/Colombie-Britannique
X	Northwest Territories/Territoires du Nord-Ouest
Y	Yukon

For Canadian postal information, contact Canadian Post Office, Postal Headquarters, Ottawa, ON, K1A OB1 Canada.

Germany

Following the reunification of East and West Germany in 1990, the German post office recommended using the letter O (for *Ost*, or East) or W (for West) before the postal code to distinguish between cities in the eastern and western parts of the country. This would be particularly helpful when two cities have similar names, such as Frankfurt/Main in the western part of the country and Frankfurt/Oder in the eastern.

Ministerium für Tourismus
Stellingstrasse 2102
O-2755 Schwerin, Germany

☞ See page 20 for European postal codes.

Spanish-Speaking Countries

It is worth remembering Spanish names often include the family names of both mother and father. The father's family name goes first, then the mother's. When a letter to John Smith Andrews at a Spanish address arrives at the post office a postal worker might think that Smith is the name the person goes by rather than Andrews. This could be important when using General Delivery or Poste Restante. When Mr. Andrews goes to pick up his package he may be told it is not there, because it has been filed under Smith not Andrews. If Mr. Andrews is aware of this he can ask the post office to look under Smith as well.

☞ See page 98 for more on poste restante.

United Kingdom

The often lengthy British address is confusing to the uninitiated. The following information is extracted from the *Complete Guide to Postcode Products* published by Royal Mail. This guide and other information may be obtained from the National Postcode Centre, 4 St. Georges Business Centre, St. Georges Square, Portsmouth PO1 3AX, United Kingdom.

A correct postal address consists of the following:

(1) name of addressee (person or company)
(2) number (or name) of house and street name
(3) locality name (if required)
(4) post town (in block capitals)
(5) county name (if required)
(6) postcode

Other elements may also appear in the address or some may not appear. Here are several examples. Refer to the preceding numbered key.

(1) Capscan Ltd
(2) Tranley House
(2) Tranley Mews
(2) 144 Fleet Road
(4) LONDON
(6) NW3 2QW

The above address has a house name and two street names—Tranley Mews and Fleet Road. The more recognizable name would probably be

Fleet Road. A mews is a small street behind a main street. Below are more examples.

(1) The WSA Consultancy Ltd
(2) 257 High Road
(4) BROXBOURNE
(5) Hertfordshire
(6) EN10 6PZ

(1) Centre File Ltd
(2) 75 Leman Street
(4) LONDON
(6) E1 8EX

(1) Future Office Systems Ltd
(2) Firs House
(2) High Street
(3) Whitchurch
(4) AYLESBURY
(5) Bucks
(6) HP22 4JU

Most British county names should be spelled out in mailing addresses.

☞ See pages 44–45 for a list of county abbreviations that Royal Mail does allow.

The name of the county must be included in the address except for those cities and towns in the following list:

Aberdeen	Carlisle	Hounslow	Northampton	Shrewsbury
Antrim	Chelmsford	Huddersfield	Norwich	Slough
Armagh	Chester	Hull	Nottingham	Southampton
Ayr	Clackmannan	Inverness	Oldham	South Wirral
Banff	Colchester	Ipswich	Orkney	Southend On
Bath	Coventry	Kinross	Oxford	Sea
Bedford	Crewe	Kirkcudbright	Peebles	Stafford
Belfast	Croydon	Lanark	Perth	Stirling
Berwick Upon	Dartford	Lancaster	Peterborough	Stoke On
Tweed	Derby	Leeds	Plymouth	Trent
Birmingham	Dumbarton	Leicester	Portsmouth	Sunderland
Blackburn	Dumfries	Lincoln	Preston	Swansea
Blackpool	Dundee	Liverpool	Reading	Torquay
Bolton	Durham	London	Redhill	Twickenham
Bournemouth	Edinburgh	Londonderry	Renfrew	Walsall
Brighton	Exeter	Luton	Romford	Warrington
Bristol	Falkirk	Manchester	Salford	Warwick
Bromley	Glasgow	Milton Keynes	Salisbury	Watford
Buckingham	Gloucester	Nairn	Selkirk	Wolverhampton
Cambridge	Hereford	Newcastle	Sheffield	Worcester
Cardiff	Hertford	Upon Tyne	Shetland	York

Postcodes have been allocated to every address in the United Kingdom (but note the Channel Islands do not use postal codes). The postal code uses a combination of letters and numbers, grouped in a variety of ways. Although many postcodes follow a uniform set of rules, there are also many exceptions.

British postcodes are made up of combinations of five to seven numbers and letters. The postcode begins with one or two letters, which are based on letters from a city, town, or district in the area. A letter with the post code MK42 8LA is going to an address in the area of Milton Keynes. Exceptions include London codes, which begin with E, EC, N, NW, SE, SW, W, and WC.

The number following the letters on the left, either one or two digits, refers to a district within the larger area. Referring again to the postcode MK42 8LA, "42" refers to a district within Milton Keynes. Next there is a space followed by another number and two letters representing yet smaller areas.

The possible formats of the postcode, with A representing an alphabetic character and N representing a numeric character, are as follows. As you can see, the second half of the code is always a number followed by two letters.

Format	Example
AN NAA	M2 5BQ
ANN NAA	M34 3AB
AAN NAA	DN5 7XY
AANN NAA	DN16 9AA
ANA NAA	W1A 4WW
AANA NAA	EC1A 1HQ
AAA NAA	GIR 0AA

Following is a complete list of postcode areas the initial letters represent.

AB	Aberdeen	CM	Chelmsford	DH	Durham
BA	Bath	CH	Chester	EH	Edinburgh
BT	Belfast	TS	Cleveland	EN	Enfield
B	Birmingham	CO	Colchester	EX	Exeter
BB	Blackburn	CV	Coventry	FK	Falkirk
FY	Blackpool	CW	Crewe	TD	Galashiels,
BL	Bolton	CR	Croydon		Selkirkshire
BH	Bournemouth	DL	Darlington	G	Glasgow
BD	Bradford, West	DA	Dartford	GL	Gloucester
	Yorkshire	DE	Derby	GU	Guildford
BN	Brighton	DN	Doncaster, South	HX	Halifax
BS	Bristol		Yorkshire	HG	Harrogate
BR	Bromley	DT	Dorchester, Dorset	HA	Harrow
CB	Cambridge	DY	Dudley, West Mid-	HP	Hemel Hempstead,
CT	Canterbury		lands		Hertfordshire
CF	Cardiff	DG	Dumfries	HR	Hereford
CA	Carlisle	DD	Dundee	HD	Huddersfield

HU	Hull	LU	Luton	UB	Southall, Middlesex
IG	Ilford, Essex	M	Manchester	SO	Southampton
IV	Inverness	ME	Medway	SS	Southend On Sea
IP	Ipswich	MK	Milton Keynes	AL	St Albans,
KW	Kikwall, Orkney	ML	Motherwell,		Hertfordshire
KA	Kilmarnock,		Lanarkshire	SG	Stevenage,
	Ayrshire	NE	Newcastle Upon		Hertfordshirie
KT	Kingston Upon		Tyne	SK	Stockport, Cheshire
	Thames, Surrey	NP	Newport, Gwent	ST	Stoke On Trent
KY	Kirkcaldy, Fife	NN	Northampton	SR	Sunderland
LA	Lancaster	NR	Norwich	SM	Sutton, Surrey
LS	Leeds	NG	Nottingham	SA	Swansea
LE	Leicester	OL	Oldham	SN	Swindon
ZE	Lerwick, Shetland	OX	Oxford	TA	Taunton, Somerset
LN	Lincoln	PA	Paisley,	TF	Telford, Shropshire
L	Liverpool		Renfrewshire	TN	Tonbridge, Kent
LD	Llandrindod Wells,	PH	Perth	TQ	Torquay
	Powys	PE	Peterborough	TR	Truro, Cornwall
LL	Llandudno,	PL	Plymouth	TW	Twickenham
	Gwynedd	PO	Portsmouth	WF	Wakefield, West
E	London E	PR	Preston		Yorkshire
EC	London EC	RG	Reading	WS	Walsall
N	London N	RH	Redhill	WA	Warrington
NW	London NW	RM	Romford	WD	Watford
SE	London SE	SP	Salisbury	WN	Wigan, Lancashire
SW	London SW	S	Sheffield	WV	Wolverhampton
W	London W	SY	Shrewsbury	WR	Worcester
WC	London WC	SL	Slough	YO	York

United States

If there is an attention line, put it first, above the company or person's name. On the line below the name put the street or post office box number and suite or room number, if necessary. The city, state, and ZIP code go on the same line, below the street.

The postal code in the United States is called the ZIP code. It is either a five-digit number (no spaces) or a nine-digit number with a hyphen before the last four digits. The first few digits of the ZIP code can give you an idea of the location. The ZIP code directory can give you a complete list of U.S. codes. The post office requests that the two-letter abbreviations for state names be used rather than longer abbreviations.

> Attn: Susan J. Crane
> ABC International
> 123 Anytown Ave. Rm. 31
> Markstown, NY 10010-5104
> U.S.A.

☞ See page 45 for state abbreviations.

An address in a foreign language is permissible provided the names of the city, province, and country are also in English. The last line of the address must show only the country name, written in full (no abbreviations) and in capital letters. Foreign postal codes (numeric or alpha), if used, should be placed on the line above the country of destination.

Jacques Moliere
Rue de Champaign
06570 St. Paul
FRANCE

Ms. J. Meggs
Apartado 3068
46807 Puerto Vallarta, Jalisco
MEXICO

If you plan to do a lot of mailing from the United States to other parts of the world on a regular basis you should consider subscribing to the *International Mail Manual.* The Manual gives current rates of the U.S. Postal Service for all kinds of international mail and details on various services, eligibility of contents, dangerous substances, preparation requirements, and more. The price is about $14 per year. You can order it from Superintendent of Documents, U.S. Government Printing Office, 941 N Capitol Street NE, Washington DC 20402-9371 U.S.A.

CLASSES OF U.S. POSTAL SERVICE INTERNATIONAL MAIL

The following, based on *International Postal Rates and Fees*, a United States Postal Service publication, applies to mail sent from the United States. International rates are higher than domestic rates. At the time of this writing, the minimum international rate applies to letters and letter packages weighing up to .5 ounce in contrast to the minimum domestic rate, which applies up to 1 ounce. Details on current rates, weight limits, and time of delivery can be obtained from any local post office. Similar information can be obtained from the postal services of other countries.

Airmail is available to all countries from the United States for all classes of mail up to a certain weight limit, generally 44 pounds per piece.

Surface mail is available to all countries. It is less expensive and delivery time is longer, usually four to six weeks.

Letters and Letter Packages

Items of mail containing personal handwritten or typewritten communications having the character of current correspondence must be sent as letters or letter packages. Unless prohibited by the country of destination, merchandise or other articles within the applicable weight and size limits also may be mailed at the letter rate of postage. Weight limit to all countries: 4 pounds.

Postcards

Postal cards and postcards consist of single cards sent without a wrapper or envelope. Folded (double) cards must be mailed in envelopes at the letter rate of postage.

Aerogrammes

Aerogrammes are air letter sheets that can be folded into the form of an envelope and sealed. Tape or stickers must not be used to seal aerogrammes. Enclosures are not permitted. The rate for sending an aerogramme is less than for a letter.

Printed Matter

Printed matter means paper on which words, letters, characters, figures, or images, or any combination of them not having the character of a bill or statement of account or of correspondence, have been reproduced by any process other than handwriting or typewriting. This classification includes regular printed matter, books and sheet music, and publishers' periodicals (second class). Not acceptable as printed matter are articles of stationery; stamps of various kinds, whether used or not; framed photographs and certificates; photographic negatives and slides; films; microfilm and microfiche; sound or video recordings; punched paper tapes or ADP cards, and playing cards.

M Bag

Customers mailing printed matter in quantities of 15 pounds or more to a single addressee may, under certain conditions, enclose such matter in mail sacks addressed directly to the addressee. The weight of the contents cannot be less than 15 pounds. The combined weight of the sack and its contents cannot be more than 66 pounds.

Small Packets

Small packets provide a class of mail for sending small items of merchandise, commercial samples, or documents that do not have the character of current and personal correspondence. The postage rates are lower than those for letter packages or parcel post. The weight limit for most countries is 4 pounds.

Parcel Post

Resembles domestic (U.S) zone-rated fourth-class mail. Packages of merchandise or any other articles that are not required to be mailed at letter postage rates can be sent as parcel post. Written communications having the nature of current and personal correspondence are not permitted. Parcel post is the only class of mail that can be insured. Maximum weight limits for parcel post items vary by country, but are usually 22 or 44 pounds. See *International Postal Rates and Fees* for rates and service availability.

Express Mail International Service (EMS)

EMS offers reliable high-speed mail service to many countries. The Custom Designed Service provides delivery on a fixed schedule—tailored to the need of the customer—from any location in the United States. The On-Demand Service provides delivery when shipments cannot be made on a regular basis. Express Mail International Service includes merchandise and document reconstruction insurance at no additional charge and provides an Express Mail Corporate Account option. Unlike domestic Express Mail, there is no service guarantee for International Express Mail. Weight limit is generally 44 pounds.

International Priority Airmail Service (IPA)

This service is intended to meet an increasing demand by business mailers for an international service that is faster than regular mail. Mailers must meet specific minimum volume and sortation requirements. This service is available for all LC and AO classes.

☞ See page 106 for explanation of AO and page 107 for explanation of LC.

Service is available from the United States to all foreign countries except Canada.

International Surface Air Lift (ISAL)

ISAL is a shipping method that provides expedited dispatch and transportation for all types of printed matter, including advertising material, catalogs and directories, publications, and books. The cost of the mailing is designed to be lower than airmail, while the service is much faster than that provided by ordinary surface mail. ISAL shipments are brought by the customer to designated U.S. acceptance cities where they are flown to a foreign destination. Upon arrival in the destination country, the shipments are entered into the surface mail system for delivery to the addressee. Rates vary by country of destination.

INTELPOST Service

INTELPOST, or International Electronic Post service, offers same or next-day delivery of facsimile documents from post offices in major U.S. cities to addresses in Canada, Europe, South America, and the Near and Far East. Letters, documents, bills of lading, blueprints—any item that can be photocopied—can be sent in minutes. INTELPOST mail is transmitted through state-of-the-art equipment that produces high-quality black and white photocopies that can be picked up by your addressee overseas within an hour, delivered by regular mail the next day, or by special delivery the same day, depending upon the time differences around the world. Rates are $10 for the first page, and $6 for each additional page. The special handling and delivery fee is $5.

International Business Reply Mail

Available for certain countries, this service allows businesses to mail prepaid airmail reply postcards and envelopes.

Types of Services

When time is not a factor, consider the U.S. Postal Service, which delivers letters and small packages at a lower cost than private services.

Whomever you use, remember that international delivery of letters and packages probably will take longer than domestic delivery, depending on the distance. If a letter or package has to cross the international date line, this may add a day to the delivery time. Service between adjacent countries, for example between Canada and the United States, may be the same or similar to domestic service.

The Postal Service

For some of the following services there is a small fee. Check with your local post office for details.

Registered Mail. Registered, or insured, mail provides secure handling for letter-class mail, small packets, and all printed matter to practically all destinations in the world. It is often used for valuable papers, such as contracts, checks, warehouse receipts, and stock certificates. Valuable papers that have no intrinsic value can be insured for the cost of their preparation.

Registered service is not available for items paid at the parcel post rate. The base fee (about $4.50) is less than for private express mail services for a letter but it will take longer.

Insurance. Insurance offers indemnity for loss of or damage to items paid at the parcel post rate. It is available to many countries. Indemnity limits vary by country and can be found in *International Postal Rates and Fees*. Insurance is not available for letter-class mail, small packets, or printed matter.

Return Receipt. Provides evidence of delivery of registered or insured mail for a small fee. Return receipts must be purchased at the time of mailing. Return Receipt service is available at no charge for Express Mail International Service items to some countries.

Restricted Delivery. A service that generally limits who may receive an item. Details of the service, however, are governed by the internal legislation of the destination country. Available to many countries for registered mail.

Recorded Delivery. A service that provides the mailer with a mailing receipt and the post office of destination retains a record of delivery. No record is kept at the post office of mailing. Recorded Delivery service is available for letter-class mail, small packets, matter for the blind, and all printed matter with little or no value. No insurance coverage is provided.

Special Delivery. Provides more expeditious delivery of letter-class mail, small packets, and printed matter at the office of addressee, according to the special delivery regulations of the country of destination. Available to most countries. Special delivery is not available for items paid at the parcel post rate.

Special Handling. Provides for preferential handling to the extent practical in dispatch and transportation from the office of mailing to the U.S. Office of Dispatch. Does not offer preferential dispatch from the United States or special treatment in the country of destination. The purchase of special handling service is at the sender's option. Available only for parcel post, printed matter, matter for the blind, and small packets sent at surface rates.

International Postal Money Orders. Available to transfer funds to individuals or firms in countries that have entered into agreements with the U.S. Postal Service for the exchange of postal money orders. The maximum for a single order is $700.

International Reply Coupons. The sender of a letter may prepay a reply by purchasing reply coupons that are sold and exchangeable for postage stamps at post offices in member countries of the Universal Postal Union. One coupon is exchangeable in any other member country for a stamp or stamps representing the minimum postage on an unregistered air letter.

Poste Restante or General Delivery. On occasion you might want to send mail to someone who is traveling and does not have a permanent address. Use *Poste Restante* to indicate that the mail should be held at the post office in the city where the person will pick it up. The number of days that *poste restante* mail will be held varies among countries. The French term *poste restante* is universally accepted and means the same as general delivery. Write the address as follows:

> name of person
> Poste Restante
> name of city or town
> country

Private Shipping Companies

Private companies do not offer identical services. If several are required to meet your needs, then open accounts with more than one. You may save your company money and get the job done better. Some of the services offered by private shipping companies are listed here:

- A choice of speed of delivery at a top rate and somewhat slower service at an economical rate
- Insurance
- Service centers where you can drop off packages, pick up supplies, get information
- Self-service units where you can pick up supplies
- Drop boxes
- Hold-for-pickup service
- Descriptive billing

Many more kinds of service are available for shipping freight.

☞ See page 86 for more on private companies.

PREPARING THE INTERNATIONAL LETTER OR PACKAGE

International letter mail can be sent in a normal, sturdy envelope. The full address should be typed or clearly handwritten (handwriting styles differ so make every effort to make yours clear). For nonexpress mail add the correct amount of postage, which is higher than domestic mail but lower than express mail. For express mail be sure to use the correct waybill and packaging for international mail. They are different from the ones used for domestic mail.

If your package contains dutiable items, you will have to provide customs declarations and may have to pay duty and tax.

☞ See pages 103–106 for a discussion of customs.
☞ See pages 100–103 for filling out a waybill.

Sender's Return Address

The sender's name and address, including postal or ZIP code and country of origin, should appear on all mail. In the event a letter or parcel cannot be delivered, this will ensure that it is returned.

It is also recommended that the name and address of the sender and addressee be included inside packages. This way if a package is damaged in transit and the outside label becomes unreadable the package can still be delivered to the addressee or returned to the sender.

Packaging

When sending a package to an international destination take extra care to make it secure. The package will be handled more often and perhaps more roughly than a domestic shipment. The wrapping and labeling will have to be sturdy enough to withstand possibly being opened in a customs check and resealed.

Use plastic tape, not water-activated tape or string, to fasten packages. Remove old mailing labels if you are reusing shipping packages or cartons. Use filling to keep loose items from sliding.

Your package may sit in very cold, hot, or damp conditions while waiting to clear customs. Take extra precautions if your goods can be damaged by these conditions.

If you are sending computer disks, use extra packing, not just a cardboard mailer, and write on the outside "Do not X-ray."

If important, use internationally recognized cautionary symbols to indicate which end should be kept up and whether fragile items are within. Special labels can be purchased with pictures to indicate various instructions, such as "Do Not Roll," "Keep Dry," "Keep Frozen," "Use No Hooks," and "Lift Here."

The Express Mail Waybill or Air Waybill

To send a letter by international express, either through the postal system or a private shipping company, fill out an international waybill and attach it to the envelope. To send a package by international express mail, add customs information to the waybill. You must include postage or indicate another choice of payment, such as billing your account.

The air waybill is provided by the airline or shipping company to indicate that it has received goods to transport by air to a specific destination. It is a receipt for the goods and a contract to carry them to a destination. A bill of lading is the document used for similar purposes when the transportation is by land or sea.

The information you will be asked to provide on a shipper's international waybill is described below.

Sender's name, address, phone number, account number with the shipper. You are the sender.

Recipient or consignee's name, address, phone or telex number, account number with the shipper. The recipient or consignee is the person to whom you are sending the package.

Always include your phone number and the recipient's phone number so that the shipper can contact either one if there is a problem in making the delivery. Always include the postal, or ZIP, code even when using a private company. The private company may use the ZIP code to identify the location and for sending invoices, announcements and other mail through the postal system to you.

The recipient's account number is not necessary if you are agreeing to pay all the charges.

Level of service. Indicate which you want—priority, standard, economy, or whatever the choices. There also may be a place to indicate delivery instructions, such as hold for pickup or deliver on weekday. You may have to call the shipper to be sure the service you want is available at the destination of your package.

Sender or customer's reference number. This is optional. The sender may add one to identify the package and to appear on the invoice.

Payment options. You must indicate whether you want transportation costs charged to your account, your credit card, to the consignee, or to a third party. Some companies offer still other payment options. If you choose a third party you must provide that party's account number. If the third party fails to pay then you will be held liable, so be sure the third party agrees to pay and that you have the correct account number.

When using a private company you also may choose among several options for payment of customs duties and taxes. When using the postal service, any customs duties and taxes will be collected from the consignee at the time of delivery.

Declared Value of the Contents for Customs. This information is required for your package to clear customs at the border of the country where you are sending it. Be sure to specify the currency in which you have stated the value (U.S. dollars or Canadian dollars, for example). This amount will help determine any duty or taxes you have to pay. This amount should be the selling price, even if you do not plan to sell the item, or the cost of its replacement.

Description of the contents. Also necessary for customs. If the contents are business correspondence, contracts, reports, and similar papers you can describe the contents as "business documents."

Business documents generally are considered to have **no commercial value**, which may be abbreviated **ncv** on the customs form. However some shipping companies and some countries do not allow the designation ncv. In this case, you must list a nominal value—just a few dollars. Of course if the contents have commercial value—if they could be sold—you must list the value. When the contents are something other than business documents be as specific as possible in describing them to decrease the chances of your package being opened and delayed in customs.

☞ See page 86 for a list of items that can be included in the description of business documents.

You may be asked to list the weight (in pounds or kilograms), the dimensions, and the country of origin. If the contents are a .5 inch thick business report typed on 8.5 by 11 inch paper in your office, then use these dimensions and list the country where the office is located as the country of origin.

What makes an item have commercial value? Items with commercial value include anything for which you have paid money or that can be sold. This would include gifts you bought with money.

If your package contains business documents you do not list a **harmonized code** or **commodity code.** If the contents have commercial value you must provide the correct **harmonized code**. The harmonized code refers to the worldwide system for classifying industrial goods and services. In the United States, the SIC codes were used in the past instead. You can obtain the correct harmonized code from your shipper.

☞ See page 114 for information on SIC codes.

If you are sending something as a gift or as a sample of your merchandise you may not have to pay customs duty or tax, depending on where you are sending it. Some shipping companies will not handle items traveling under an ATA carnet.

☞ See page 106 for a description of carnets.

The waybills of private companies usually include space where you fill in all this customs information. The U.S. Post Office Express Mail waybill does not. This means you must use its international mailing envelope, which has a green customs form printed on it, or obtain a customs form from the post office.

Declared Value for Carriage or Shipment. You may also see a place on the waybill to provide this information. Carriage refers to the act of carrying your package from one place to another. This is not used for customs but is used in case of damage or loss of your package. If you do not fill in an amount, then the payment to you by the shipper will be minimal. If you fill in an amount you will be charged accordingly and if the package is lost or damaged the payment due you will be based on the declared value for carriage. In other words, by listing a declared value for carriage you are buying insurance to cover your package while in transit.

There may be space on the waybill for additional information and documentation, which are required for large and high-value shipments. These include a shipper's export declaration (SED), required on U.S. exports; a consignee's identification number; and an Internal Revenue Service Employer Identification Number (IRS EIN) or Social Security number (SSN). You do not have to fill in this information when shipping business documents or small packages of little value.

CUSTOMS

Customs is the authority of a country to collect duties on imports and exports. The term *customs* also applies to the procedures for collecting duty. Customs regulations allow certain articles to enter, and restrict or prohibit others. Each country has its own customs service and its own procedures for clearing articles through customs.

The purpose of customs regulations is to raise revenue, to protect the country's industries from unfavorable competition, and to protect its citizens from exposure to unacceptable or dangerous articles.

When company A in country A sells (or exports) merchandise to company B in country B the merchandise must clear customs of country B, not country A. When a U.S. company ships its products to a company in Germany it must comply with German customs. If the same U.S. company also makes a shipment of its products to Brazil, that shipment must comply with Brazilian customs.

If you want to export goods from the United States and need advice, do **not** call the U.S. Customs Service. Call the U.S. Department of Commerce, a trade representative of the country to which you are shipping, a freight forwarder, or a delivery service like Federal Express. They can help you with customs regulations of the country to which you are shipping. Call the U.S. Customs Service (part of the Department of the Treasury) for help with goods you want to bring into the United States.

Prohibited or Restricted Items

Customs regulations determine which classes of goods will be allowed into the country and which are restricted or prohibited. Countries sometimes restrict imports of goods that will compete with goods made within the country. Agricultural products, leather goods, artwork may fall in this category. Often firearms, hazardous materials (including chemicals and explosives), and pornographic materials are restricted. Medicine, living plants and animals are other examples. Some goods are prohibited for religious reasons; for example, liquor cannot be taken into Muslim countries. Also unused traveler's checks, personal and payroll checks, credit cards, blank and undated airline tickets, securities payable to the bearer, currency, and other valuables may be prohibited.

Large Shipments

When making a large or highly valuable shipment you have to complete the usual customs documents as well as additional documents. This book will not go into detail on the subject of large shipments of goods for sale in other countries. This a complex process and needs to be handled by experts. Exporters use the services of specialists, such as freight forwarders, whose business is to handle international transportation and customs clearance, and customs brokers, whose business is to help companies through customs clearance.

☞ See Part 7, pages 111–114, for information on shipping documents.

Numerous publications explain the details of international shipping, ranging from *A Basic Guide to Exporting*, published by the U.S. Department of Commerce for about $15, to Dun's *Exporter's Encyclopedia*, published annually by Dun & Bradstreet with monthly updates, for more than $500.

Letters and Small Packages

Letters sent to other countries do not have to pass through customs and only need the correct address and postage for delivery.

Small packages as well as large shipments do require completed customs papers. A typical business package might include a computer printout of sales activity, a mailing list, a business plan or report, a manuscript, a training or user manual, a collection of letters and memos, or contracts. You might have occasion to send any of these items to a partner or manager who is traveling in another country or to a potential client. In this case you would describe the contents of the package as "business documents" and list the declared valued as "no commercial value" (ncv).

☞ See page 86 for examples of what qualifies as a document.

Neither you nor the recipient will have to pay duty on a package with no commercial value; in other words, it is nondutiable. (Exceptions:

New Zealand, Japan, Canada, Philippines do not allow the description "no commercial value" and so in order to clear customs in those countries you must include a nominal amount such as $1.)

Whether the package is dutiable or nondutiable you must fill out a customs form because countries want to know what is entering them. Even if you fill out the forms accurately your package may be opened by customs officials if they want to verify the description or value of the contents.

U.S. Postal Service

If you use a post office in the United States for packages, you must obtain the necessary customs forms from that post office or use its international express mail package with a customs form printed on it.

Small Packets, Dutiable Printed Matter. Use customs green label on which you must provide the following information:

> description of contents
> status (indicate gift or sample of merchandise)
> value
> weight

If you do not want the description of the contents to appear on the outside of the package or if the value exceeds a certain amount, then attach only part of the green form on the outside and indicate that the customs declaration is enclosed within the package. In this case the package will be opened by customs for inspection.

Parcel Post. You use a different form for parcel post. It is either a single form or a three-part form, depending on the country to which it is going. You provide the same information as on the green label. It must be itemized if more than one item is enclosed.

To insure the package, you must tell the amount to the post office employee, who will complete the insurance section of the form.

Express Mail International Service (EMS). You use either the green label for small packets or the single form for parcel post as described above.

Private Delivery Services

If you send your package through a private delivery service, such as UPS or Federal Express, you use an international waybill. This is similar to the domestic waybill except that it includes space to fill out customs information. The waybill also is the mailing label, since it contains the address of the recipient and the sender.

Because we are mostly concerned in this book with packages that are nondutiable, that is, no customs duty will be owed, we will only mention some of the information asked for on the waybill.

☞ See pages 100–103 for a discussion of filling out the waybill.

CARNETS

Often people want to take items into another country for a short period of time to use for display and demonstration purposes. Such items might include commercial samples, tools of the trade, advertising materials, cinematographic, audiovisual, scientific, or other professional equipment. They may do this without having to pay customs duty by obtaining an ATA Carnet in advance. ATA stands for *admission temporaire*—temporary admision.

The ATA Carnet is a customs document to obtain temporary duty-free admission of certain items. It may be used in countries that are signatories to the ATA Convention, which include: Australia, Austria, Belgium, Bulgaria, Canada, Cyprus, Czechoslovakia, Denmark, Finland, France, Germany, Gibraltar, Greece, Hong Kong, Hungary, Iceland, India, Iran, Ireland, Israel, Italy, Ivory Coast, Japan, Luxembourg, Mauritius, Netherlands, New Zealand, Norway, Poland, Portugal, Romania, Senegal, Singapore, Sri Lanka, South Africa, South Korea, Spain, Sweden, Switzerland, Turkey, United Kingdom, United States.

You need to apply for a carnet and pay a fee. In the United States, to find out more about carnets and participating countries, contact the U.S. Council for International Business, 1212 Avenue of the Americas, New York, NY 10036 U.S.A. Or contact a freight forwarder.

MULTILINGUAL GLOSSARY OF MAILING TERMS

Abandonné (Fr) Abandon, do not return to sender or try to forward.

Addressee Person to whom a package or letter is addressed. The recipient or consignee.

AO See *Autres Objets.*

APO Abbreviation for Army or Air Force Post Office.

A.R. See *Avis de reception.*

A remettre en main propre (Fr) Deliver to addressee in person. Restricted or personal delivery. In other words, the letter or package must be delivered only to the person to whom it is addressed. Sometimes addressee must sign a receipt on delivery. In some countries, the letter or package may be delivered to an agent of the addressee, or the country requires only a postal official's signature on the return receipt.

Autres Objets (Fr) Other articles, one of three main categories of international mail, which includes regular printed matter, books and sheet music, matter for the blind, small packets, and publishers' periodicals (second class). See also *LC* and *CP*.

Avis de reception (Fr) Return receipt.

Cadeau (Fr) Gift.

Colis de poste, or **colis postaux** or **CP** (Fr) Parcel post, one of the three main categories of international mail. See also *AO* and *LC*.

consignee The person to whom a shipment is sent.

correo aereo (Sp) Airmail.

CP See *Colis de poste*.

Désignation détaillée du contenu (Fr) Detailed description of contents.

Destinaire (Fr) Receiver.

Dispositions de l'expediteur (Fr) Instructions of sender.

Douane (Fr) Customs.

EIN Abbreviation for Employer Identification Number.

En cas de non-livraison (Fr) If parcel is undeliverable.

Énchantillon de marchandises (Fr) Sample of merchandise.

Endorsement The marking that shows the classification under which something is mailed, for example, "Printed Matter" or "Small Packet."

Expéditeur (Fr) Sender.

Expres (Fr) Special delivery.

FPO Abbreviation for Fleet Post Office.

General delivery See Poste restante.

Kyoku dome yubin (Japanese) Poste restante.

LC See *Lettres et Cartes*.

Lettres et Cartes or **LC** (Fr) Letters and cards, one of the three main categories of international mail, which consists of letters, letter packages, aerogrammes and post cards. See also *AO* and *CP*.

Numéro d'assurance (Fr) Insurance number.

Packchen (Gr) Small packet.

Par Avion (Fr) Airmail.

Pequeño Paquet (Sp) Small packet.

Petit Paquet (Fr) Small packet.

Poids (Fr) Weight.

Poste restante (Fr) Mail addressed to poste restante is held at a central post office for addressee to pick up.

Recipient Person receiving a letter or package.

Réexpédié à (Fr) Forward to.

Restricted delivery See *A remettre en main propre*.

Special delivery *Expres*.

SSN Abbreviation for Social Security number.

Valeur (Fr) Value.

Part 7

Shipping Terms and Documents

Any business exporting its products needs to prepare a variety of shipping documents dealing with terms and conditions of the sale, finances, transportation, and government control. For detailed information on shipping documents consult with a freight forwarder, the Department of Commerce, the Small Business Administration, or other organizations serving the export business.

A set of shipping terms published by the International Chamber of Commerce provides the recognized international standard used in exporting. Known as *Incoterms* these terms help to eliminate difficulties that arise because of language and cultural differences.

Incoterms clarify the responsibilities and obligations assumed by the seller and buyer in the sale of goods. The seller may quote a price as CFR or whatever to indicate that the price does or does not include transportation, insurance, customs, or other costs and responsibilities. For more information on Incoterms contact the International Chamber of Commerce Publishing Company (156 Fifth Ave., Suite 820, New York, NY 10010 USA). Following is a brief description of some of the shipping documents and terms commonly used in international export.

Ad valorem See duty.

Bill of lading A document prepared by the seller on a form supplied by the company transporting the goods. It defines the terms of transportation, billing and paying, sender and recipient addresses, etc. Various kinds of bills of lading are the air waybill, inland bill of lading, and ocean bill of lading.

Bonded warehouse A warehouse authorized by customs where goods may be stored until customs duty has been paid.

Certificate of origin (CO) A declaration made by the seller stating in which country the goods being shipped were produced. The CO is required by some countries and may need to be notarized.

CFR or Cost and Freight to a named port of import overseas The seller agrees to pay cost of transporting goods to a named port. Cost does not include insurance. Term is applied mainly to ocean shipments. (Incoterm)

CIF or Cost, Insurance, and Freight to a named port of import overseas The seller agrees to pay the cost of transporting the goods, including insurance, to a named port. This term is applied mainly to ocean shipments. (Incoterm)

CIP or Carriage and Insurance Paid to a named destination Like CIF only applied to shipments by some mode other than water. (Incoterm)

Commercial invoice A bill for the goods from the seller to the buyer, including delivery and payment terms. Some governments use it to determine customs duty.

Consular invoice A government document required by some countries on goods entering the country. It describes the contents and value of the shipment and provides information on the buyer and seller. It may have to be prepared in the language of the importing country and be authorized by its consul in the exporter's country.

CPT or **Carriage Paid to a named destination** Like CFR only applied to shipments by some mode other than water. (Incoterm)

Customs union A group of countries that have agreed to eliminate all customs duties among members of the group and have agreed on a common tariff on all imports from outside the group.

DAF or **Delivered At Frontier of a named place** The seller's obligations are fulfilled when the goods reach the frontier, before customs, of the buyer's country. (Incoterm)

DDP or **Delivered Duty Paid to a named place of destination** The seller assumes responsibility to deliver the goods to the buyer's premises including paying customs. (Incoterm)

DDU or **Delivered Duty Unpaid to named place of destination** (Incoterm)

DEQ or **Delivered Ex Quay at named port of destination** The seller assumes the cost and risks only to get the goods to the quay (wharf) in the buyer's country. (Incoterm)

DES or **Delivered Ex Ship at named port of destination** The seller agrees to make the goods available to the buyer on the ship in the port of destination named in the contract and assumes all costs up to this point. (Incoterm)

Destination control statement This appears on the commercial invoice, bill of lading or air waybill, and shipper's export declaration. It notifies the carrier and all foreign parties that the item may only be exported to certain destinations.

Distributor A foreign agent who sells for a supplier directly and maintains an inventory of the supplier's products.

Dock receipt This document transfers accountability for the goods between the domestic and international ocean carrier.

Duty A tax imposed on imports by the customs authority of the country. The amount of duty may be based on the value of the goods (ad valorem duty); on weight, quantity, or some other factor (specific duty); or a combination of value and other factors (compound duty).

EIN Employer's Identification Number. An EIN is assigned to all U.S. corporations. Also called an IRS number, Employer's Federal Identification Number, or payroll tax number. An individual doing business alone may use his or her Social Security number for an EIN.

Export licenses The General Export License is a broad grant of authority by the U.S. government to all U.S. exporters for certain categories of products not requiring special application. The Individually Validated License (IVL), granted for a limited time, is required for goods affecting national security, foreign policy, or in short supply.

Export management company A company that serves as the export department for another company. Its services include market research, overseas representation, and distribution. In return it may receive a commission, a salary, or commission plus retainer.

Export packing list This is a detailed itemization of the material in each individual package being shipped. It indicates the type of package—box, crate, drum, carton, etc. It may show the individual net, legal, tare and gross weights and measurements for each package in both Imperial and metric systems. Package markings should be shown along with the shipper's and buyer's references. The packing list should be in or attached to the outside of the package in a waterproof envelope marked "packing list enclosed." The list is used by the shipper or forwarding agent to ascertain the total shipment weight and volume, in addition to determining whether the correct cargo is being shipped. Customs officials may use the list to check the cargo.

Export trading company Similar to an export management company.

EXW or Ex Works at a named point of origin (ex factory, ex mill, ex warehouse) The seller only agrees to make the goods available at a certain time at the point of origin. The buyer is responsible for transportation from there and all other costs. (Incoterm)

FAS or Free Alongside Ship at a named port of shipment The seller pays the cost to deliver the goods alongside the ship in the country of export. The buyer assumes responsibility thereafter including the cost of loading, ocean transportation, and insurance. (Incoterm)

FCA or Free Carrier to a named place The seller is responsible for the cost of delivering the goods to the carrier at the named point. The carrier is responsible for transporting by road, rail, air, sea, or a combination of modes. This term is used for multimodal transport such as containers and roll on, roll off. (Incoterm)

FOB or Free on Board at a named port of export The seller assumes costs up to and including delivery aboard a ship for overseas transportation. (Incoterm)

Foreign sales agent A person or company that serves as foreign representative for a person or company that seeks to sells its product abroad.

Foreign Trade Zone See free port.

Free port A port (airport or seaport) designated by the government as an area where goods may enter the country duty free. While warehoused there, they can be worked on, processed, relabelled, displayed and shipped out of the country. If they enter the country, duty must be paid. Hong Kong is a free port. Another term for free port is free trade zone. There are more than 100 free trade zones in the United States.

Free trade The term *free trade* refers to international trade that is free of protective quotas and duties; it may be subject to tariffs imposed to raise revenue. Free trade exists among various countries, for example, between the United States, Canada, and Mexico, and among European countries. The general trend throughout the world is to increase free trade, easing the flow of goods internationally.

Free Trade Area Duties are eliminated between the member countries of a free trade area group. Each member country can negotiate its own tariffs with other countries outside the group. See also customs union.

Free Trade Zone See free port.

Freight forwarder A service company that arranges export shipments for other companies. A freight forwarder is an excellent source of information on domestic and foreign regulations and documentation and shipping methods.

HS or Harmonized System The Harmonized System (HS) is the international method of classifying goods used by more than fifty countries, including the United States, since 1989. Schedule B lists the code number for each class of goods; this code number is used to identify goods on shipping documents. To find out the correct code for a product, service, or technology in the United States, it may be necessary to refer to SIC and SITC codes as well. See SIC and SITC. Contact a local or state office of the U.S. Department of Commerce or a freight forwarder for assistance.

Inspection certificate Some purchasers and countries require this certificate which attests to the specifications of the goods shipped and which is usually performed by a third party, such as an independent testing organization.

Insurance certificate This document assures the buyer that the goods are covered by insurance while in transit.

Intellectual property Trademarks, copyrights, service marks, patents, and trade secrets are considered intellectual property.

L/C or **Letter of credit** A document issued by a bank at the request of the buyer guaranteeing payment to the seller upon receipt at the bank of certain documents that indicate terms and conditions of the transaction have been fulfilled. In addition to a description of the goods, it contains a shipping date and expiration date. Letters of credit are widely used in international trade. There are many kinds of letters of credit, including advised letter of credit, back-to-back letter of credit, clean letter of credit, commercial letter of credit, confirmed letter of credit, export and import letters of credit, irrevocable and revocable letters of credit, transferable letter of credit, unconfirmed letter of credit.

License A license or permit to export, issued by the country of the exporter. Or a license to import issued by the country of the importer.

Proforma invoice An invoice provided by the seller prior to shipment to notify the buyer of the kinds and quantities of goods to be shipped, their value, weight, size, etc.

Purchasing agent An agent who purchases goods in his or her own country on behalf of foreign importers.

Quota A limitation on the quantity of goods of a specific kind that a country allows to be imported. Amounts that exceed the quota may be restricted or subject to additional duty. Quotas may vary by country and by year.

Quotation An offer to sell goods at a stated price and perhaps under specific conditions. The quotation may be good only for a specific amount of time.

Schedule B See HS.

Shipper's Export Declaration (SED) Required for U.S. exports and used by the U.S. government to gather export statistics and administer international trade.

SIC Standard Industrial Code. A numerical system used in the United States to classify goods and products. See HS, used in international shipping by the United States and more than fifty other countries.

SITC Standard Industrial Trade Classification. A numerical code system developed by the United Nations to classify goods used in international trade. Used by international organizations.

SSN Social Security number. A number assigned to U.S. citizens for purposes of taxation and government benefits.

Standard Industrial Classification See SIC.

Standard Industrial Trade Classification See SITC.

Tariff 1. Charges or rate. 2. Duties imposed on imports or exports. 3. A freight or service rate.

Warehouse receipt See dock receipt.

Part 8

Measures

METRIC AND OTHER SYSTEMS

The metric system was planned and adopted in France in 1799. Later several systems of measure based on the metric system were developed and became widely used. In 1960 the 11th General Conference on Weights and Measures adopted the International System of Units, or Le Système International d'Unités. This system is used in virtually all countries of the world today.

Metric units of measure are also referred to as SI units (from Système International), whereas units in the inch–pound measurement system of the United States are referred to as U.S Customary units. The U.S. Customary System was inherited from the British Imperial System, or English System, but now differs in certain units.

☞ See page 119 for comparison of Imperial, metric, and U.S. Customary measures.

The fundamental units of measure in the British and U.S. systems are the yard and the pound (avoirdupois). Seven units serve as the base of the metric system and other units are derived from them. They are as follows:

> length — meter (or metre)
> mass — kilogram
> time — second
> electric current — ampere
> thermodynamic temperature — kelvin
> amount of substance — mole
> luminous intensity — candela

Virtually all countries today officially are on the metric system, notable exceptions being the United States and the United Kingdom, although both these countries are moving toward that standard. Other countries have only recently become metric officially and still refer to previously used systems, whether British Imperial, U.S. Customary, or other traditional measures. These are discussed below. Countries like Canada and India that had strong ties to the United Kingdom in the past may use Imperial measures, as well as traditional local measures and the metric system.

Australia

On metric system, but Imperial measures still referred to informally.

Canada

On metric system but in many areas of commerce, such as tools, measures are given in metric equivalents not true metrics. Reference also may be made to British Imperial measures.

China

On metric system. Traditional weights and measures also used:

> 1 mu = 0.0667 hectares (ha)
> 1 jin = 0.5 kilograms (kg)

Egypt

On metric system. Some traditional Egyptian measures also used.

Hong Kong

On metric system. Imperial and Chinese measures in limited use.

India

On metric system but the Imperial System is still in use, as are traditional Indian measures.

> 1 tola = 11.66 grams
> 1 seer = 933.1 grams
> 1 maund = 37.32 kg

Ireland

Import/export commerce is metric. Imperial System still in use locally.

Israel

On metric system. 1 dunum = 1,000 square meters

Malaysia

On metric system. Imperial measures and traditional weights still used.

> Weights:
> 1 tahil = 1 1/3 oz (37.8 grams)
> 16 tahil = 1 kati = 1 1/3 lb (604.8 grams)
> 100 katis = 1 picul = 133 1/3 lb (60.48 kg)
> 40 piculs = 1 koyan = 5,333 1/3 lb (2419 kg)
> Capacity:
> 1 chupak = 1 Imperial quart (1.136 liters)
> 1 gantang = 1 Imperial gallon (4.546 liters)

Pakistan

On metric system but Imperial and local measures also used.

> 1 maund = 82.28 lb (37.32 kg)
> 1 seer = 2.057 lb (933 grams)
> 1 tola = 180 grains (11.66 grams)

Singapore

On metric system but local units are also used.

> Weights:
> 1 tahil = 1 1/3 oz (37.8 grams)
> 16 tahil = 1 kati = 1 1/3 lb (604.8 grams)
> 100 katis = 1 picul = 133 1/3 lb (60.48 kg)
> 40 piculs = 1 koyan = 5,333 1/3 lb (2419 kg)
> Capacity:
> 1 chupak = 1 Imperial quart (1.136 liters)
> 1 gantang =1 Imperial gallon (4.546)

South Africa

On metric system but a number of traditional measures still used.

Taiwan

On metric system but some traditional Chinese measures also used.

Thailand

On metric system but some traditional measures also used.

United Kingdom

The Imperial System of weights and measures is in force; however, conversion to metric is in progress. Business is increasingly on the metric system, including construction, farming, and much of manufacturing. Pharmaceutical products, petroleum products, wholesaling, and freight tariffs use metric units. Clothing and many other goods are marked in both metric and Imperial units of measure.

Contact the International Trade Administration of the U.S. Department of Commerce (at the nearest DOC office), a distributor or freight forwarder for information on which to use for a given product.

The Imperial fluid ounce, pint, quart, and gallon differ from U.S. Customary ounces, pints, quarts, and gallons. In the Imperial System, units of dry measure (capacity) are the same as liquid measures, whereas in the U.S. system liquid and dry measures are different.

☞ See page 121 for liquid and dry measures.

Below are Imperial, metric, and U.S. Customary equivalents:

Imperial	Metric	U.S. Customary
1 fluid ounce	28.4 milliliters	.961 fl. ounce
1 pint	0.6 liter	1.032 dry pint
		1.2 liq. pints
1 quart	1.136 liters	1.032 dry quart
		1.2 liq. quart
1 gallon	4.5 liters	1.2 gallons

Metric	Imperial	U.S. Customary
1 milliliter	.035 fluid ounce	.034 fluid ounce
1 liter	1.66 pints	1.72 dry pints
		2 liquid pints
1 liter	.88 quart	.91 dry quart
		1.06 liquid quarts
1 liter	.22 gallon	.267 gallon

In the British system a hundredweight (cwt), also called a quintal, equals 112 pounds; in the U.S. system a hundredweight equals 100 pounds.

United States

The United States still predominantly uses its U.S. Customary System of measures. However it is gradually converting to the metric system. The automotive industry, pharmaceutical industry, and science all use the metric system, as do other technical fields.

When using certain weights (ounces and pounds) it may be necessary to indicate whether they are avoirdupois, troy, or apothecaries' weights. It may also be necessary to indicate whether liquid or dry measures are used. See the preceding discussion for differences with the British Imperial System.

CONVERSIONS

From U.S. to Metric

Follow these directions to convert U.S. Customary units to metric equivalents. For example, to convert inches to an equivalent amount in centimeters or feet to an equivalent amount in meters, use the following:

1 inch ×	2.54	=	2.54 centimeters
2.5 feet ×	0.3048	=	0.762 meters

☞ See pages 125–126 for more terms and abbreviations used in connection with weights and measures.

Linear

Multiply		by	To get:
inches	×	25.4	= millimeters (mm)
inches	×	2.54	= centimeters (cm)
feet	×	0.3048	= meters (m)
yards	×	0.9144	= meters (m)
miles	×	1.6093	= kilometers (km)

Area

Multiply		by		To get:
square inches (inches^2)	×	645.16	=	millimeters^2 (mm^2)
square inches (inches^2)	×	6.4516	=	centimeters^2 (cm^2)
square feet (feet^2)	×	0.0929	=	meters^2 (m^2)
square yards (yards^2)	×	0.8361	=	meters^2 (m^2)
acres	×	0.4047	=	hectares
square miles (miles^2)	×	2.590	=	kilometers^2 (km^2)

Volume or Capacity

Multiply		by		To get:
cubic inches (inches^3)	×	16387	=	millimeters^3 (mm^3)
cubic inches (inches^3)	×	16.387	=	centimeters^3 (cm^3)
cubic inches (inches^3)	×	0.016387	=	liters (L)
cubic feet (feet^3)	×	28.317	=	liters (L)
cubic feet (feet^3)	×	0.02832	=	meters^3 (m^3)
cubic yards (yards^3)	×	0.7646	=	meters^3 (m^3)
fluid ounces	×	29.573	=	milliliters (mL)
liquid quarts	×	0.94635	=	liters (L)
dry quarts	×	1.101	=	liters (L)
gallons	×	3.7854	=	liters (L)

Mass or Weight

Multiply		by		To get:
ounces (av)	×	28.35	=	grams (g)
ounces (troy)	×	31.10	=	grams (g)
pounds (av)	×	0.4536	=	kilograms (kg)
tons (2000 lb. or short ton)	×	907.18	=	kilograms (kg)
tons (2000 lb. or short ton)	×	0.90718	=	metric ton (t) or megagram (Mg)
tons (2240 lb. or long ton)	×	1.016	=	metric ton

From Metric to U.S.

Perform the following operations to convert metric units to U.S. Customary equivalents. For example, to convert 1 centimeter to an equivalent amount in inches or hectares to an equivalent amount in acres, follow this format:

1 centimeter	×	0.3937	=	0.3937 inch
14.75 hectares	×	2.471	=	36.44725 acres

Linear

Multiply		by		To get:
millimeters (mm)	×	0.03937	=	inches
centimeters (cm)	×	0.3937	=	inches
meters (m)	×	3.281	=	feet
meters (m)	×	1.0936	=	yards
kilometers (km)	×	0.6214	=	miles

Area

Multiply		by		To get:
millimeters^2 (mm^2)	×	0.00155	=	square inches (inches^2)
centimeters^2 (cm^2)	×	0.155	=	square inches (inches^2)
meters^2 (m^2)	×	10.764	=	square feet (feet^2)
meters^2 (m^2)	×	1.196	=	square yards (yards^2)
hectares	×	2.471	=	acres
kilometers^2 (km^2)	×	0.3861	=	square miles (miles^2)

Volume or Capacity

Multiply		by		To get:
millimeters^3 (mm^3)	×	0.000061	=	cubic inches (inches^3)
centimeters^3 (cm^3)	×	0.06102	=	cubic inches (inches^3)
milliliters (mL^3)	×	0.03381	=	fluid ounces
liters (L)	×	1.0567	=	liquid quarts
liters (L)	×	0.2642	=	gallons
liters (L)	×	0.03531	=	cubic feet (feet^3)
liters (L)	×	61.024	=	cubic inches (inches^3)
meters^3 (m^3)	×	35.315	=	cubic feet (feet^3)
meters^3 (m^3)	×	1.3080	=	cubic yards (yards^3)

Mass or Weight

Multiply		by		To get:
grams (g)	×	0.03527	=	ounces (av)
grams (g)	×	0.03215	=	ounces (troy)
kilograms (kg)	×	2.2046	=	pounds (av)
kilograms (kg)	×	0.001102	=	tons (2000 lb. or short ton)
metric ton (t) or megagram (Mg)	×	1.1023	=	tons (2000 lb. or short ton)

U.S. Customary Units and U.S. Equivalents

☞ See page 119 for comparison to British Imperial System.

Linear

1 inch	= 0.083 foot
1 foot	= 12 inches; 1/3 yard
1 yard	= 36 inches; 3 feet
1 mile (land)	= 1,760 yards; 5,280 feet

Area

1 square inch	= 0.0007 square foot
1 square foot	= 144 square inches
1 square yard	= 1,296 square inches; 9 square feet
1 acre	= 43,560 square feet; 4,840 square yards
1 square mile	= 640 acres

Volume or Capacity

1 cubic inch	= 0.00058 cubic foot
1 cubic foot	= 1,728 cubic inches
1 cubic yard	= 27 cubic feet

Liquid Measures

1 fluid ounce	= 8 fluid drams; 1.804 cubic inches
1 pint	= 16 fluid ounces; 28.875 cubic inches
1 quart	= 2 pints; 57.75 cubic inches
1 gallon	= 4 quarts; 231 cubic inches

Dry Measures

1 pint	= 1/2 quart; 33.6 cubic inches
1 quart	= 2 pints; 67.2 cubic inches
1 peck	= 8 quarts; 537.605 cubic inches
1 bushel	= 4 pecks; 2,150.42 cubic inches

Weight (Avoirdupois)

1 grain	= 0.036 dram; 0.002285 ounce
1 dram	= 27.344 grains; 0.0625 ounce
1 ounce	= 16 drams; 437.5 grains
1 pound	= 16 ounces; 7,000 grains
ton (short)	= 2,000 pounds
ton (long)	= 1.12 short tons; 2,240 pounds
1 hundredweight	= 100 pounds

Metric Units and Metric Equivalents

Linear

10 millimeters (mm)	= 1 centimeter (cm)
10 centimeters	= 1 decimeter (dm)
10 decimeters	= 1 meter (m)
10 meters	= 1 dekameter (dam)
10 dekameters	= 1 hectometer (hm) or 100 meters
10 hectometers	= 1 kilometer (km) or 1,000 meters

Area

100 square millimeters (mm^2)	= 1 square centimeter (cm^2)
10,000 square centimeters	= 1 square meter (m^2)
100 square meters	= 1 are (a)
100 ares	= 1 hectare (ha)
100 hectares	= 1 square kilometer (km^2)

Volume

10 milliliters (mL)	=	1 centiliter (cL)
10 centiliters	=	1 deciliter (dL)
10 deciliters	=	1 liter (L)
10 liters	=	1 dekaliter (daL)
10 dekaliters	=	1 hectoliter (hL)
10 hectoliters	=	1 kiloliter (kL)

Cubic Measure

1,000 cubic millimeters (mm^3)	=	1 cubic centimeter (cm^3)
1,000 cubic centimeters	=	1 cubic decimeter (dm^3)
1,000 cubic decimeters	=	1 cubic meter (m^3)

Weight

10 milligrams (mg)	=	1 centigram (cg)
10 centigrams	=	1 decigram (dg) or 100 milligrams
10 decigrams	=	1 gram (g) or 1,000 milligrams
10 grams	=	1 dekagram (dag)
10 dekagrams	=	1 hectogram (hg)
10 hectograms	=	1 kilogram (kg)
1,000 kilograms	=	1 metric ton (t)

Temperature

The metric temperature system uses the Celsius scale. Freezing occurs at 0°C and water boils at 100°C. The Fahrenheit scale, used in the United States, registers freezing at 32°F and water boils at 212°F.

To convert degrees Celsius to degrees Fahrenheit use the formula below.

degrees Celsius × 9/5 + 32 = degrees Fahrenheit

25° × 9/5 + 32 = 77°

To convert degrees Fahrenheit to degrees Celsius use the formula below.

degrees Fahrenheit - 32 × 9/5 = degrees Celsius

37° - 32 × 9/5 = 9°

The term *centigrade* is sometimes used to mean *Celsius*, although not officially correct.

TERMS AND ABBREVIATIONS

The following terms are useful when working with various systems of measure. An understanding of them can make it easier to describe a product, understand a product description, or fill out shipping forms. For example, the different types of weight—gross weight, legal weight, net weight, tare—are important when customs duty is determined by weight.

☞ See the Conversions section on pages 120–124 for abbreviations of units of measure in both the U.S. Customary system and the SI system as well as the following under SI system and U.S. Customary system.

apothecaries' weight A system of weights used primarily for drugs.

av., avdp., avoir All are abbreviations for avoirdupois.

avoirdupois weight The system of weights based on a pound containing 16 ounces. Used in the United States and Great Britain, for goods other than gems, precious metals, and drugs. See apothecaries' weight and troy weight.

cu Abbreviation for cubic.

cwt Abbreviation for hundredweight.

dutiable weight The difference between the gross weight and the net weight. Also known as *tare*.

gallon 1. A U.S. Customary unit of volume or capacity, used to measure liquid, equal to 231 cubic inches or 4 quarts. 2. A slightly larger British Imperial System unit of volume, used in dry and liquid measure, equal to 277.420 cubic inches.

gross weight Total weight of the goods and all interior and exterior packing.

legal weight Weight of goods and the interior containers.

net weight Weight of goods only, with no packing material.

ounce 1. A U.S. Customary avoirdupois unit of weight equal to 437.5 grains or 16 drams. There are 16 ounces in a pound. 2. A U.S. Customary unit of volume or capacity used in liquid measure, equal to 8 fluid drams or 1.805 cubic inches. There are 16 ounces in a pint. 3. A British Imperial unit of volume or capacity used in dry and liquid measure equal to 1.734 cubic inches. 4. A unit of apothecaries' weight equal to 480 grains or 1.097 avoirdupois ounces.

The ounce as a liquid measure is also called the fluid ounce in both British and U.S. systems.

pint A unit of measure used for volume or capacity in both U.S. Customary and British Imperial Systems for dry and liquid measures. The amounts vary slightly.

quart A unit of measure used for volume or capacity in both U.S. Customary and British Imperial Systems for dry and liquid measures. The amounts vary slightly.

SI unit abbreviations Not followed by a period.

a are	dl, dL deciliter	km kilometer
cc cubic centimeter	dm decimeter	l, L, or lit liter
cg centigram	g, gm gram	m meter
cl, cL centiliter	ha hectare	mg milligram
cm centimeter	hg hectogram	ml, mL milliliter
dag dekagram	hl, hL hectoliter	mm millimeter
dal, daL dekaliter	hm hectometer	MT, t metric ton
dam dekameter	kg kilogram	
dg decigram	kl, kL kiloliter	

sq Abbreviation for square.

stone One of various units of weight. In the United Kingdom, a stone is equivalent to 14 pounds or 6.4 kg.

tare The difference between the gross weight and the net weight. Also known as *dutiable weight*.

ton Various meanings are given to the word *ton*. Since shipping rates are determined by the ton it is important to know exactly what is meant—the short ton, long ton, or metric ton. See below.

You will also hear the terms "one ton weight" and "one ton measure." One ton weight could mean 2,000 pounds (a short ton) or 2,204 pounds (a metric ton). One ton measure equals 40 cubic feet of space or one cubic meter. A small but heavy shipment would be charged by weight and a large but light shipment would be charged by measure.

    1. Long ton. A unit of weight equal to 2,240 pounds avoirdupois. Used in Great Britain.

    2. Short ton. A unit of weight equal to 2,000 pounds avoirdupois. Used in the United States.

    3. Metric ton. A unit of measure in the SI system equal to 1,000 kg.

troy weight A system of weights used primarily for gems and precious metals.

U.S. Customary unit abbreviations May or may not be followed by period:

A. a. acre	gal. gallon	pt, p. pint
bar., bl. barrel	in., " inch	qt, q. quart
bu, bsh, bushel	lb. pound	rd. rod
cwt, c., C. hundred-	mi. mile	T., t., tn. ton
weight	oz. ounce	yd. yard
ft., ' foot	pk. peck	

Part 9

Currency

CURRENCIES OF THE WORLD

Currency is another word for money. When involved in international business you have to know about other currencies besides your own. Buying and selling between countries usually involves several currencies. Having an understanding of exchange rates is important.

A number of countries use the same name for their unit of currency. For example, the currency of Australia, Canada, Hong Kong, New Zealand, the United States, and a number of other countries is the dollar. Other commonly used names of currencies are franc, pound, peso, and dinar. The British pound is also referred to as the pound sterling. The currency of both Italy and Turkey is the lira. It is important to indicate the country's currency to which you are referring. Here are a few examples of how amounts of currency might be written.

> This item has a value of C$900.
> This item has a value of Can$900.
> This item has a value of CAD$900.
> *(This item has a value of 900 Canadian dollars.)*
>
> They are willing to pay $1000 U.S.
> *(They are willing to pay 1,000 U.S. dollars.)*
>
> The price is 50 USD.
> *(The price is 50 U.S. dollars.)*
>
> Please quote the terms in US$ or DM.
> *(Please quote the terms in U.S. dollars or deutsche (German) marks.)*
>
> The loans amount to NKr2bn, or US$346m.
> *(The loans amount to 2 billion Norway krone, or 346 million U.S. dollars.)*
>
> The stock rose L520 to L13,200.
> *(The stock rose 520 Italian lire to 13,200 lire)*
>
> The shoes sell for Lit 83,000.
> *(The shoes sell for 83,000 Italian lire.)*

Some very small countries use the currency of a larger neighbor. For example, Liechtenstein uses the Swiss franc and Monaco uses the French franc. The currency used in most of the Commonwealth of Independent States, as of 1992, is the Russian ruble. Several, however, are moving to establish their own separate currencies.

☞ See pages 133–138 for information on the convertibility of currency, exchange rates, and other currency topics.

Symbols and Abbreviations

Symbols, used to write currency amounts in shortened form, often are a letter with a slash or bar through it. If your typewriter or computer cannot handle this, you can abbreviate, for example C for Costa Rican colon or PP for Philippine peso. The Society for Worldwide Interbank Financial Telecommunications (SWIFT), headquartered in Belgium, is used for automated international transfer of funds. SWIFT uses the following symbols for the principal trading currencies.

ATS	Austrian schilling	BEF	Luxembourg (see Belgian franc)
BEF	Common Belgian franc	BEC	Luxembourg (see Belgian franc)
BEC	Convertible Belgian franc	BEL	Luxembourg (see Belgian franc)
BEL	Financial Belgian franc	NLG	Netherlands guilder
CAD	Canadian dollar	NOK	Norwegian krone
DKK	Danish krone	SGD	Singapore dollar
FIM	Finnish markka	ESP	Spanish peseta
DEM	German mark	ESA	Spanish peseta (Acc. A)
GRD	Greek drachma	ESB	Spanish peseta (Acc. B)
HKD	Hong Kong dollar	SEK	Swedish krona
IRP	Irish pound	CHF	Swiss franc
JPY	Japanese yen	GBP	U.K. pound sterling
CHF	Liechtenstein (see Swiss franc)	USD	U.S. dollar

Basic Units

Following is a list of basic units (such as the dollar), abbreviations or symbols (such as $), and subunits (such as the cent). Refer to a dictionary for information on currencies not listed.

Algeria

Abbrev./symbol: DA
1 dinar = 100 centimes

Angola

Abbrev./symbol: Kz
1 new kwanza = 100 lwei

Argentina

Abbrev./symbol: AP
1 peso = 100 centavos

Armenia

The monetary unit is the ruble; see Russia.

Australia

Abbrev./symbol: $A
1 Australian dollar = 100 cents

Austria

Abbrev./symbol: S
1 schilling = 100 groschen

Azerbaijan

The monetary unit is the ruble; see Russia.

Belarus

The monetary unit is the Belarusian ruble.

Belgium

Abbrev./symbol: BF
1 Belgian franc = 100 centimes
The Belgian franc has parity with the Luxembourg franc.

Brazil

Abbrev./symbol: Cz$
1 cruziero = 100 centavos

Bulgaria

Abbrev./symbol: Lv
1 leva = 100 stotinki

Canada

Abbrev./symbol: Can$
1 dollar = 100 cents

Chile

Abbrev./symbol: Ch$
1 peso = 100 centavos

China

Abbrev./symbol: Y
1 yuan = 10 jiao = 100
fen
Chinese currency is
called renminbi (RMB),
"people's money."
Foreigners exhanging
currency are supplied
with Foreign Exchange
Certificates (FEC).

Colombia

Abbrev./symbol: Col$
1 peso = 100 centavos

Commonwealth of Independent States

See each country. Most
use Russian ruble.

Costa Rica

Abbrev./symbol: C
1 colon = 100 centimos

Czechoslovakia

Abbrev./symbol: Kcs
1 koruna = 100 haleru
New Czech and Slova-
kian currency to replace
Koruna.

Denmark

Abbrev./symbol: Dkr
1 krone = 100 oere

Dominican Republic

Abbrev./symbol: RD$
1 peso = 100 centavos

Ecuador

Abbrev./symbol: S/
1 sucre = 100 centavos

Egypt

Abbrev./symbol: LE, £E
1 pound = 100 piastres;
1 piastre = 10 milliemes

Estonia

The monetary unit is
the ruble (see Russia),
to be replaced with the
kroon.

Finland

Abbrev./symbol: Fmk
1 Markka (FIM) =
100 penni
(markka = finmark)

France

Abbrev./symbol: F
1 franc = 100 centimes

Georgia

The monetary unit is
the ruble (see Russia),
to be replaced with the
maneti.

Germany

Abbrev./symbol: DM
1 mark = 100 pfenning

Guatemala

Abbrev./symbol: Q
1 quetzal = 100 centavos

Hong Kong

Abbrev./symbol: HK$
1 dollar = 100 cents

Hungary

Abbrev./symbol: Ft
1 forint = 100 filler

India

Abbrev./symbol: Re
(plural Rs)
1 rupee = 100 paise

Indonesia

Abbrev./symbol: Rp
1 rupiah = 100 sen

Ireland

Abbrev./symbol: £Ir
1 Irish pound (or punt)
= 100 pence

Israel

Abbrev./symbol: IS
1 new shekel =
100 agorot

Italy

Abbrev./symbol: Lit
1 lira = 100 centisimi

Japan

Abbrev./symbol: ¥
1 yen = 100 sen

Kazakhstan

The monetary unit is
the tanga.

Korea, Rep. of

Abbrev./symbol: W
1 won = 100 cheun

Kyrgyzstan

The monetary unit is
the ruble; see Russia.

Latvia

The monetary unit is the
ruble (see Russia), to be
replaced with the lat.

Lithuania

The monetary unit is
the ruble (see Russia),
to be replaced with litas.

Luxembourg

Abbrev./symbol: LuxF
1 franc = 100 centimes
The Luxembourg franc
has parity with the Belgian franc.

Malaysia

Abbrev./symbol: M$
1 ringgit (dollar) =
100 sen

Mexico

Abbrev./symbol: Mex$
1 peso = 100 centimes

Moldova

The monetary unit is
the ruble; see Russia.

Netherlands

Abbrev./symbol: f
1 guilder = 100 cents
The guilder is also
known as a florin and
by the abbreviations
gld, Dfl, or Fl.

New Zealand

Abbrev./symbol: $NZ
1 dollar = 100 cents

Nigeria

Abbrev./symbol: N
1 naira = 100 kobo

Norway

Abbrev./symbol: NKr
1 krone = 100 oere

Pakistan

Abbrev./symbol: PRe
1 rupee = 100 paisa

Peru

Abbrev./symbol: NS
1 new sol = 100
centimos

Philippines

Abbrev./symbol: PP
1 peso = 100 centavos

Poland

Abbrev./symbol: Zl
1 zloty = 100 groszy

Portugal

Abbrev./symbol: Esc
1 escudo = 100 centavos

Romania

Abbrev./symbol: L
1 lev = 100 bani

Russia

Abbrev./symbol: R
1 ruble = 100 kopecks

Saudi Arabia

Abbrev./symbol: SR
1 Saudi riyal = 20
qursh = 100 halalahs

Singapore

Abbrev./symbol: S$
1 dollar = 100 cents

Slovakia

See Czechoslovakia.

South Africa

Abbrev./symbol: R
1 rand = 100 cents

Spain

Abbrev./symbol: pta
1 peseta = 100 centimos

Sweden

Abbrev./symbol: SKR
1 krona = 100 oere

Switzerland

Abbrev./symbol: SwF
1 Swiss franc =
100 centimes

Taiwan

Abbrev./symbol: T$
1 new Taiwan dollar =
100 cents

Tajikistan

The monetary unit is
the ruble; see Russia.

Thailand

Abbrev./symbol: B
1 baht = 100 stangs

Turkey

Abbrev./symbol: LT
1 lira = 100 kurus

Turkmenistan

The monetary unit is
the ruble. See Russia.

Ukraine

The monetary unit is
the ruble (see Russia),
to be replaced with the
hrynnia.

United Arab Emirates

Abbrev./symbol: Dh
1 dirham = 100 fils

United Kingdom

Abbrev./symbol: £
1 pound sterling = 100
pence (singular: penny)

United States

Abbrev./symbol: US $
1 dollar = 100 cents.

Uzbekistan

The monetary unit is
the ruble. See Russia.

Venezuela

Abbrev./symbol: B
(plural Bs)
1 bolivar = 100 centimos

CURRENCY EXCHANGE

Money, or currency, of one country may be sold, or exchanged, for an equivalent amount of another country's currency. Rates of exchange fluctuate, or change, constantly. One U.S. dollar today may be worth 92 percent of one unit of currency of Country X, whereas six months ago the dollar might have been worth only 87 percent of the same unit of currency.

Suppose your company is located in the United States and has to purchase a certain part to use in equipment it manufactures. The part can be purchased from two companies—one in the United States and the other in South Korea. You need to buy 10,000 parts. The U.S. company sells its part for $24.00 each. The South Korean company sells its for 17,000 won. If the won is worth .0013985 dollars, the part will cost you about $23.77 each. This is a savings of 23 cents over the U.S. part, or $2,300 for 10,000 parts. On price of the part alone, your company would be better off buying from the South Korean company.

Three months later the company has not yet bought the part. The South Korean price of 17,000 won still holds. But the value of the won has gone up and is now worth .00141 U.S. dollars. This means your company will pay $23.97, only 3 cents less than the U.S. price. The savings is now $300 per 10,000 units. If you agree to purchase the part from the South Korean company now, you will not save as much.

This example illustrates why international trade prices often are quoted as good for only a specific and short time. This allows companies to adjust prices when exchange rates change. Of course there are many other considerations, such as transportation costs and delivery time.

Because of the uncertainty of future exchange rates, exporters and importers use various methods to avoid losing money. One method, to insist that payment be made in a single currency to avoid fluctuations in exchange rates, will be unfair to one party in the deal. Therefore other methods are preferable. Explanations of these, in greater or lesser detail, can be found in many books on exporting.

Here are definitions of frequently used terms. **Appreciation** is the rise in the value of one currency in relationship to another. **Depreciation** is a drop in the value of a currency in relationship to another. **Devaluation** occurs when the currency of one country is officially lowered in value in terms of one or more other currencies. **Eurodollars** are U.S. dollars deposited in banks outside the United States, usually in Europe. **Asian dollars** may be used for U.S. dollars deposited in Asia and the Pacific Rim. When a currency is **strong** it can be exchanged for a larger amount of foreign currency than when the same currency is **weak**.

Where to Find Exchange Rates

To determine the rate of exchange on any given day, you can call a bank (ask for the department that handles foreign exchange); look in a major newspaper, such as *The New York Times* or *The Wall Street Journal*; call an exchange (a company that buys and sells foreign currency), or call a travel agency.

Look in the business section of the paper for a table labeled Exchange Rates, Foreign Exchange, or something similar. A larger table will list forty to fifty countries and give two kinds of information: in a U.S. paper, for example, the amount in U.S. dollars that equals one unit of each foreign currency and the amount in each foreign currency that equals one U.S. dollar.

☞ See page 135 for sample exchange rates table.

Here is how to read the sample exchange rates table, which is adapted from *The Wall Street Journal*. The numbers under the heading "U.S. $ equiv." are the amount of U.S. dollars that 1 unit of the currency to the left is worth (US$0.12927 is equivalent to 1 Hong Kong dollar). The numbers under the heading "currency per U.S. $" are the amounts of the currency to the left that you will get in exchange for 1 U.S. dollar (1 U.S. dollar can be exchanged for 7.7355 Hong Kong dollars).

Daily exchange rates vary slightly depending on who is making the exchange and the amount of money involved. The bank may quote you a slightly different rate from what is printed in the newspaper.

The Number of Decimal Places

Exchange rates usually will be given with more than two decimal places. They are shown this way because they may be applied to large amounts of money: $1 million and more. If the rates are rounded up to fewer digits or they change a little, the amount of money involved in the transaction may change substantially. Look at the three calculations below for exchanging $1 million into another currency at three different rates. As you can see there is a difference of as much as 9,800 units of the other currency depending on which rate you use.

$1,000,000 × .8098 = 809,800
$1,000,000 × .8001 = 801,000
$1,000,000 × .80 = 800,000

Rates may be shown with as many as eight decimal points. For example, the exchange rate of the Polish zloty to U.S. dollars was around .00006789 in late 1992.

EXCHANGE RATES (Tuesday, February 2, 1993)

COUNTRY	U.S. $ equiv.		Currency per U.S. $	
	Tues.	Mon.	Tues.	Mon.
Argentina (Peso)	1.01	1.01	.99	.99
Australia (Dollar)	.6795	.6750	1.4717	1.4815
Austria (Schilling)	.08662	.08686	11.55	11.51
Belgium (Franc)	.02953	.02967	33.86	33.70
Brazil (Cruzeiro)	.0000573	.0000577	17460.02	17325.02
Britain (Pound)	1.4440	1.4595	.6925	.6852
Canada (Dollar)	.7910	.7915	1.2643	1.2635
Czechoslovakia (Koruna) ...	.0352113	.0355366	28.4000	28.1400
Chile (Peso)	.002682	.002679	372.84	373.28
China (Renminbi)	.171233	.171233	5.8400	5.8400
Colombia (Peso)	.001583	.001583	631.55	631.55
Denmark (Krone)	.1576	.1587	6.3454	6.3024
Ecuador (Sucre)	.000557	.000557	1796.01	1796.01
Finland (Markka)	.17740	.17649	5.6368	5.6662
France (Franc)	.18010	.18067	5.5525	5.5350
Germany (Mark)	.6094	.6114	1.6410	1.6355
Hong Kong (Dollar)	.12927	.12928	7.7355	7.7350
Hungary (Forint)	.0120744	.0122055	82.8200	81.9300
India (Rupee)	.03453	.03453	28.96	28.96
Indonesia (Rupiah)	.0004850	.0004850	2062.03	2062.03
Ireland (Punt)	1.4823	1.4934	.6746	.6696
Israel (Shekel)	.3654	.3615	2.7367	2.7660
Italy (Lira)	.0006567	.0006601	1522.86	1514.90
Japan (Yen)	.008026	.007994	124.60	125.10
Malaysia (Ringgit)	.3810	.3811	2.6250	2.6240
Mexico (Peso)	.3221649	.3221649	3.10	3.10
Netherlands (Guilder)	.5415	.5434	1.8466	1.8404
New Zealand (Dollar)	.5160	.5148	1.9380	1.9425
Norway (Krone)	.1435	.1437	6.9693	6.9591
Pakistan (Rupee)	.0387	.0387	25.85	25.85
Peru (New Sol)	.6105	.6105	1.64	1.64
Philippines (Peso)	.04040	.04040	24.75	24.75
Poland (Zloty)	.00006465	.00006534	15468.02	15304.02
Portugal (Escudo)	.006745	.006749	148.26	148.18
Saudi Arabia (Riyal)	.26702	.26702	3.7450	3.7450
Singapore (Dollar)	.6066	.6065	1.6485	1.6487
South Africa (Rand)	.3231	.3237	3.0948	3.0893
South Korea (Won)	.0012594	.0012594	794.00	794.00
Spain (Peseta)	.008593	.008606	116.38	116.20
Sweden (Krona)	.1346	.1339	7.4288	7.4693
Switzerland (Franc)	.6572	.6589	1.5215	1.5177
Taiwan (Dollar)	.039620	.039246	25.24	25.48
Thailand (Baht)	.03915	.03915	25.54	25.54
Turkey (Lira)	.0001127	.0001131	8875.00	8841.03
U.A.E. (Dirham)	.2723	.2723	3.6725	3.6725
Venezuela (Bolivar)	.01246	.01248	80.23	80.13

Parity

Occasionally two currencies achieve parity, meaning that one unit in one currency can be exchanged for one unit of the other currency. If one Swiss franc can be exchanged for $.66, parity is much closer between U.S. and Swiss currency than in the case of U.S. and Thai currency where one baht can be exchanged for about $.04.

Calculating Currency Exchange

The following text illustrates how to calculate currency exchange, using U.S. dollars and British pounds as examples. Be sure to use the latest figures for your calculations.

Exchanging Foreign Currency to U.S. Dollars. Here is how to calculate the value of a certain amount of currency in U.S. dollars. Suppose you want to know how much 20 British pounds are worth in U.S. dollars. Refer to the table above of exchange rates for February 2, 1993, which shows one pound as equivalent to $1.4440 U.S. dollars. You multiply the number of pounds by the U.S. dollar equivalent.

$$20 \text{ pounds} \times \$1.4440 = \$28.88$$

On that day you could have converted 20 pounds to $28.88, which is what you would have paid for an item costing 20 pounds. Remember that the exchange rates change daily so you have to check each time you do a calculation. Although the difference is likely to be only a few cents, it makes a big difference when large amounts of money are involved.

Exchanging U.S. Dollars to Foreign Currency Now suppose you have an item you want to sell in Great Britain for an amount of pounds that is equal to about $15. To determine the amount of pounds equivalent to $15, you divide $15 by the dollar amount that one pound equals.

$$\$15/1.444 \text{ pounds} = 10.387811 \text{ pounds}$$

On that day you could sell the item for 10.39 pounds to make about $15 on it. Here are examples of what $15 was worth in other currencies, again using the table of sample exchange rates.

$$\$15/.001583 \text{ Colombian pesos} = 9{,}476 \text{ Colombian pesos}$$
$$\$15/.12927 \text{ Hong Kong dollars} = 116.04 \text{ Hong Kong dollars}$$

There is another way to do this calculation if you prefer to multiply rather than divide. On the exchange rates table, refer to the right column, which shows the amount of foreign currency that one U.S. dollar purchased on February 2, 1993. One U.S. dollar purchased .6925 British pounds.

Therefore:

> $15 \times .6925 = 10.39$ British pounds
> $15 \times 631.55 = 9,473.25$ Colombian pesos
> $15 \times 7.7355 = 116.03$ Hong Kong dollars

Although fluctuations in rates of exchanges are usually minor from day to day, they can change a lot from year to year. Check a newspaper or bank for daily exchange rates.

If you work regularly with foreign currencies you should have a calculator to figure exchanges. Sometimes there are major differences between two currencies—for example, one unit of one may be worth 2,000 units of another, making it difficult to keep track of how many zeros to use. A salary of 20,000 units of one could be equivalent to 40,000,000 in the other.

Where to Buy Foreign Currency

Suppose you or someone in your office will be making a trip and wants to obtain some money used in the country to be visited. You want to buy foreign currency, or in other words, convert your currency to another currency.

Places where you can buy foreign currency include the following.

- **Commercial Banks** Savings banks usually do not exchange currency.
- **Exchanges or Money Brokers** These are companies that specialize in buying and selling currencies. A major company in this business is Thomas Cook Foreign Exchange, which has branches around the world. A large exchange is the best place to try if you want to buy a currency in less frequent demand. Exchanges are located in larger cities and at international airports. They are listed under Foreign Money Brokers in the Yellow Pages.
- **Travel Agents** Large ones in major cities can usually convert currency.
- **Hotels** Those that regularly have a lot of international visitors may be able to convert currency. They will probably not have a wide variety of currencies and may charge more for the service than the previously mentioned places.

Some countries do not allow their currency to be sold outside their own borders. In those cases, you have to take cash or traveler's checks and when you arrive at your destination make your exchange. See the next section on convertibility of currency.

Before leaving on a trip, you might consider buying foreign currency traveler's checks, which eliminates the need to wait in airport lines or to search for a bank when you arrive. You may also reduce conversion fees. Contact an exchange to find out what foreign currency traveler's checks are available. Checks may be ordered by mail.

Currency Convertibility

Convertibility refers to the ability to freely exchange a currency to another. Many of the major international trading nations have free currencies or put only limited restrictions on currency conversion. A free currency can be freely exchanged for another currency without concern for restrictions preventing this.

A common form of moderate currency control is to require that import transactions be done on a letter of credit. Stronger currency controls not only record the flow of currency but make it much harder for the currency to leave the country. Strict controls are likely to be used in a country where there is extensive black market activity. One result may be that it is not possible to buy the currency outside of the country. If you plan to travel to that country you will not be able to buy its currency before arriving or take any of it out when leaving. In countries that impose strict currency controls violators are subject to severe penalties.

Hard currencies are currencies that can be easily traded, such as the U.S. dollar, the German mark, and currencies of other major industrial countries. Soft currencies are those that are not freely convertible into other currencies.

Part 10

Time
Considerations

12-Hour and 24-Hour Time Systems

In the United States, a 12-hour a.m. and p.m system is used in business. Many other countries use the 24-hour system. In the 24-hour system, the first twelve hours are 1 a.m. to noon, as in the a.m./p.m. system. From noon on, the hours are numbered 13 to 24. In the United States, the armed forces, international shipping, airlines, most computers, and the scientific community use the 24-hour system.

There are various styles of writing time in the 24-hour system. See the examples below.

> 1000 to 1500 hours *means* 10 a.m. to 3 p.m.
> 0930 to 1130 hours *means* 9:30 a.m. to 11:30 a.m.
> 0830 to 1630 hours *means* 8:30 a.m. to 4:30 p.m.

or

> 10 00 to 15 00 *means* 10 a.m. to 3 p.m.
> 23 30 *means* 11:30 p.m.

or

> 8.30 to 16.30 *means* 8:30 a.m. to 4:30 p.m.

Time Zones

There are twenty-four time zones around the world. A few countries observe time that is a half hour different from zone time. The time in India for example is half an hour ahead of time in neighboring Pakistan. The time in central Australia is half an hour behind eastern Australia and an hour and a half ahead of western Australia.

The International Date Line goes through the Pacific Ocean. When you cross the line going east (towards the United States), you set the date back one day. When you cross the line going west (towards Japan), you advance the date one day.

Greenwich Mean Time (GMT) is the standard used to illustrate time differences for much of the world. For example, you might see that the time in the Philippines is GMT + 8 (Greenwich Mean Time plus 8 hours). At 1 p.m. Greenwich Mean Time, it is 9 p.m. in the Philippines.

Greenwich refers to Greenwich, England, and Greenwich Mean Time is the time in effect in Great Britain. Portugal observes the same time and the rest of western Europe is Greenwich Time +1, that is, the time is one hour ahead. The twenty-four time zones are numbered starting with 0 for the zone that includes Greenwich, England.

Time in the United States

The United States crosses six zones and observes six times: Eastern, Central, Mountain, Pacific, Alaskan, and Hawaiian. The states observing each time are listed below. States marked with an asterisk observe different times in different areas.

Eastern Time Connecticut, Delaware, Florida,* Georgia, Indiana,* Kentucky,* Maine, Maryland, Massachusetts, Michigan,* New Hampshire, New Jersey, New York, North Carolina, Ohio, Pennsylvania, Rhode Island, South Carolina, Tennessee,* Vermont, Virginia, Washington, D.C., West Virginia

Central Time Alabama, Arkansas, Illinois, Iowa, Kansas,* Louisiana, Minnesota, Mississippi, Missouri, Nebraska,* North Dakota,* Oklahoma, South Dakota,* Texas,* Wisconsin

Mountain Time Arizona, Colorado, Idaho,* Montana, New Mexico, Utah, Wyoming

Pacific Time California, Nevada, Oregon,* Washington

Alaskan Time Alaska

Hawaiian Time Hawaii

The following are major cities in states where two times are observed.

FLORIDA **Eastern**—Most major cities. **Central**—Tallahassee.

IDAHO **Mountain**—Boise, Idaho Falls, Twin Falls. **Pacific**—Lewiston.

INDIANA **Eastern**—Elkhart, Fort Wayne, South Bend. **Central**—Evansville, Gary.

KANSAS **Central**—Lawrence, Topeka, Wichita. **Mountain**—Goodland.

KENTUCKY **Eastern**—Ashland, Florence, Frankfort, Lexington. **Central**—Owensboro.

MICHIGAN **Eastern**—Most major cities. **Central**—Iron Mountain.

NEBRASKA **Central**—Lincoln, North Platte, Omaha. **Mountain**—Scottsbluff.

NORTH DAKOTA **Central**—Bismarck, Fargo, Grand Forks. **Mountain**—Dickinson

OREGON **Mountain**—Rome. **Pacific**—Bend, Eugene, Klamath Falls, Portland, Salem.

SOUTH DAKOTA **Central**—Pierre, Sioux Falls. **Mountain**—Hot Springs, Rapid City.

TENNESSEE **Eastern**—Knoxville . **Central**—Chattanooga, Memphis, Nashville.

TEXAS **Central**—Most major cities. **Mountain**—El Paso.

Time in Canada

Canada observes six times. The boundaries of Eastern, Central, Mountain, and Pacific times are closely aligned with the U.S. ones of the same names. The others are Atlantic time and Newfoundland time, which lie to the east of Eastern time. Newfoundland is 30 minutes earlier than Atlantic time. The times observed in the Canadian provinces are as follows.

Alberta (Mountain)	Ontario (Eastern and Central)
British Columbia (Pacific)	Prince Edward Island (Atlantic)
Manitoba (Central)	Quebec (Atlantic and Eastern)
New Brunswick (Atlantic)	Saskatchewan (Mountain and Central)
Newfoundland (Newfoundland)	Northwest Territory (Atlantic, Eastern,
(excluding Labrador, which is Atlantic)	Central, Mountain)
Nova Scotia (Atlantic)	Yukon Territory (Pacific)

The times of major Canadian cities (with provinces) are as follows.

Newfoundland—Gander, NF; St. John's, NF.
Atlantic—Charlottetown, PE; Fredericton, NB; Yarmouth, NS.
Eastern—London, ON; Ottawa-Hull, ON; Québec City, PQ; Toronto, ON.
Central—Kenora, ON; Regina, SK; Winnipeg, MB.
Mountain—Calgary, AB; Edmonton, AB; Yellowknife, NT.
Pacific—Vancouver, BC; Victoria, BC; Whitehorse, YT.

Time in Mexico

Mexico has three times: Central, Mountain, and Pacific. Times of major Mexican cities (with states) are as follows.

Central—Acapulco, GRO; Aguascalientes, AGS; Campeche, CAMP; Cancun, Q.R.; Chetumal, Q.R.; Chihuahua, CHIH; Chilpancingo de los Bravos, GRO; Ciudad Victoria, TAMPS; Colima, COL; Cuernavaca, MOR; Durango, or Victoria de Durango, DGO; Guadalajara, JAL; Guanajuato, GTO; La Paz, B.C.S.; Manzanillo, COL; Matamoros, TAMPS; Mérida, YUC; Mexico City, or Ciudad de Mexico, D.F.; Oaxaca, OAX; Pachuca, HGO; Puebla, or Heróica Puebla de Zaragosa, PUE; Queretaro, QRO; Saltillo, COAH; San Luis Potosí, S.L.P.; Toluca, or Toluca de Lerdo, MÉX; Tuxtla Gutierrez, CHIS; Veracruz, or Veracruz Llave, VER; Villahermosa, TAB.
Mountain—Culiacán, SIN; Hermosillo, SON; Tepic, NAY.
Pacific—Ensenada, B.C.N.; Mexicali, B.C.N.; Navohoa, SON; Tijuana, B.C.N.

DAYLIGHT SAVING TIME

Some countries modify standard time for part of the year to prolong daylight hours in the evening. This is called daylight saving time (DST), summertime, or fast time. The clocks are set ahead, usually one hour, at the beginning of local summer and set back at the end. (Remember, "Spring forward, fall back.") The exact dates for doing this vary by country and from one year to the next.

Most parts of the United States, Canada, and Europe observe daylight saving time. Western Europe goes on daylight saving time earlier than the United States. The United Kingdom stays on it a little longer than Continental Europe. Many Asian countries do not observe daylight saving time. Mexico, as of 1992, does not observe daylight saving time except in some cities bordering the United States.

In the southern hemisphere, daylight saving time starts when it is fall in the northern hemisphere and ends with the northern spring. Countries near the equator tend not to observe daylight saving time.

When a country is on daylight saving time then the time difference changes by one hour.

The monthly publications of the Official Airline Guides provide exact dates for starting and ending daylight saving time in most countries of the world, including details regarding regional variations and times of outlying territories, such as the Canary Islands of Spain.

Time Tables

The seven tables that follow show standard time in many countries of the world when it is 9 a.m., noon, and 5 p.m. Greenwich Mean Time, and U.S. Eastern, Central, Mountain, Pacific, Alaskan, Hawaiian times.

If you are in a place that is on Mountain Standard Time (MST) use that table to find the time elsewhere in the world. You will see that at 9 a.m. in Denver it is 12 midnight (or 00 00 hours) in Malaysia. In the far right column for Malaysia the number +15 indicates that the time in Malaysia is 15 hours ahead of Denver. (If you are in Malaysia you can use the same chart to find the time in Denver.)

The time is shown on the tables two ways, according to the 12-hour a.m./p.m. system and the 24-hour system. For example, the Eastern Standard Time table tells you that at 9 in the morning in Philadelphia, it is 3 p.m, or 15 00, in Amsterdam. This would be a good time to place a call to Amsterdam. If you waited until 2 p.m. in Philadelphia it would be 20 00, or 8 p.m., in Amsterdam. This would be all right if you were calling someone at home, but not if you were calling the office.

You may also need to take into consideration daylight saving time, or summer time, which is observed in opposite months in the southern hemisphere from the northern hemisphere. The tables below refer to standard time.

When your time and the time in another location are 11 to 15 hours different it may be difficult to find a good time to call someone there. It may be necessary to stay late or arrive early at your office to make the call.

Most countries do not observe more than one time. In those cases only the name of the country has been shown in the tables below. For example, in France the time in all locations is the same. China, although geographically very large, also observes only one time. When it is 9 a.m. in Beijing, it is 9 a.m. everywhere else in China as well. For countries that observe more than one time, one major city for each time is shown on the table.

☞ See page 143 for more on daylight time.
☞ See page 141 for more on 12-hour and 24-hour time.

Greenwich Mean Time

(Cities shown only when country observes more than one time.)	9:00 AM (09 00)	12:00 M (12 00)	5:00 PM (17 00)	GMT +/- Hrs
ALGERIA	10.00 AM (10 00)	1:00 PM (13 00)	6:00 PM (18 00)	+1
ANGOLA	10:00 AM (10 00)	1:00 PM (13 00)	6:00 PM (18 00)	+1
ARGENTINA	6:00 AM (06 00)	9:00 AM (09 00)	2:00 PM (14 00)	-3
ARMENIA	12:00 M (12 00)	3:00 PM (15 00)	8:00 PM (20 00)	+3
AUSTRALIA				
Adelaide, SA	6:30 PM (18 30)	9:30 PM (21 30)	2:30 AM* (02 30*)	+9.5
Perth, WA	5:00 PM (17 00)	8:00 PM (20 00)	1:00 AM* (01 00*)	+8
Sydney, NSW	7:00 PM (19 00)	10:00 PM (22 00)	3:00 AM (03 00*)	+10
AUSTRIA	10:00 AM (10 00)	1:00 PM (13 00)	6:00 PM (18 00)	+1
AZERBAIJAN	12:00 M (12 00)	3:00 PM (15 00)	8:00 PM (20 00)	+3
BELARUS	11:00 AM (11 00)	2:00 PM (14 00)	7:00 PM (19 00)	+2
BELGIUM	10:00 AM (10 00)	1:00 PM (13 00)	6:00 PM (18 00)	+1
BRAZIL	6:00 AM (06 00)	9:00 AM (09 00)	2:00 PM (14 00)	-3
BULGARIA	11:00 AM (11 00)	2:00 PM (14 00)	7:00 PM (19 00)	+2
CANADA (See page 143 for additional Canadian cities.)				
Edmonton, AB	2:00 AM (02 00)	5:00 AM (05 00)	10:00 AM (10 00)	-7
Halifax, NS	5:00 AM (05 00)	8:00 AM (08 00)	1:00 PM (13 00)	-4

12:00 M (12 00) = Noon; 12:00 PM (00 00) = Midnight; * = Next day

(continues)

Greenwich Mean Time —*continued*

(Cities shown only when country observes more than one time.)	9:00 AM (09 00)	12:00 M (12 00)	5:00 PM (17 00)	GMT +/- Hrs
Regina, SK	3:00 AM (03 00)	6:00 AM (06 00)	11:00 AM (11 00)	-6
St. John's, NF	5:30 AM (05 30)	8:30 AM (08 30)	1:30 PM (13 30)	-3.5
Toronto, ON	4:00 AM (04 00)	7:00 AM (07 00)	12:00 M (12 00)	-5
Vancouver, BC	1:00 AM (01 00)	4:00 AM (04 00)	9:00 AM (09 00)	-8
CHILE	5:00 AM (05 00)	8:00 AM (08 00)	1:00 PM (13 00)	-4
CHINA	5:00 PM (17 00)	8:00 PM (20 00)	1:00 AM* (01 00*)	+8
COLOMBIA	4:00 AM (04 00)	7:00 AM (07 00)	12:00 M (12 00)	-5
COSTA RICA	3:00 AM (03 00)	6:00 AM (06 00)	11:00 AM (11 00)	-6
CZECHOSLOVAKIA	10:00 AM (10 00)	1:00 PM (13 00)	6:00 PM (18 00)	+1
DENMARK	10:00 AM (10 00)	1:00 PM (13 00)	6:00 PM (18 00)	+1
DOMINICAN REPUBLIC	5:00 AM (05 00)	8:00 AM (08 00)	1:00 PM (13 00)	-4
ECUADOR	4:00 AM (04 00)	7:00 AM (07 00)	12:00 M (12 00)	-5
EGYPT	11:00 AM (11 00)	2:00 PM (14 00)	7:00 PM (19 00)	+2
ESTONIA	11:00 AM (11 00)	2:00 PM (14 00)	7:00 PM (19 00)	+2
FINLAND	11:00 AM (11 00)	2:00 PM (14 00)	7:00 PM (19 00)	+2
FRANCE	10:00 AM (10 00)	1:00 PM (13 00)	6:00 PM (18 00)	+1
GEORGIA	12:00 M (12 00)	3:00 PM (15 00)	8:00 PM (20 00)	+3
GERMANY	10:00 AM (10 00)	1:00 PM (13 00)	6:00 PM (18 00)	+1
GUATEMALA	3:00 AM (03 00)	6:00 AM (06 00)	11:00 AM (11 00)	-6
HONG KONG	5:00 PM (17 00)	8:00 PM (20 00)	1:00 AM* (01 00*)	+8
HUNGARY	10:00 AM (10 00)	1:00 PM (13 00)	6:00 PM (18 00)	+1
INDIA	2:30 PM (14 30)	5:30 PM (17 30)	10:30 PM (22 30)	+5.5

12:00 M (12 00) = Noon; 12:00 PM (00 00) = Midnight; * = Next day

Greenwich Mean Time

(Cities shown only when country observes more than one time.)	9:00 AM (09 00)	12:00 M (12 00)	5:00 PM (17 00)	GMT +/- Hrs
INDONESIA				
Jakarta, Java	4:00 PM (16 00)	7:00 PM (19 00)	12:00 PM (00 00)	+7
Pontianak, Borneo	5:00 PM (17 00)	8:00 PM (20 00)	1:00 AM* (01 00*)	+8
IRELAND	9:00 AM (09 00)	12:00 M (12 00)	5:00 PM (17 00)	
ISRAEL	11:00 AM (11 00)	2:00 PM (14 00)	7:00 PM (19 00)	+2
ITALY	10:00 AM (10 00)	1:00 PM (13 00)	6:00 PM (18 00)	+1
JAPAN	6:00 PM (18 00)	9:00 PM (21 00)	2:00 AM* (02 00*)	+9
KAZAKHSTAN				
Alma Ata	3:00 PM (15 00)	6:00 PM (18 00)	11:00 PM (23 00)	+6
Atyubinsk	2:00 PM (14 00)	5:00 PM (17 00)	10:00 PM (22 00)	+5
KOREA, REPUBLIC OF	6:00 PM (18 00)	9:00 PM (21 00)	2:00 AM* (02 00*)	+9
KYRGYZSTAN	2:00 PM (14 00)	5:00 PM (17 00)	10:00 PM (22 00)	+5
LATVIA	11:00 AM (11 00)	2:00 PM (14 00)	7:00 PM (19 00)	+2
LITHUANIA	11:00 AM (11 00)	2:00 PM (14 00)	7:00 PM (19 00)	+2
LUXEMBOURG	10:00 AM (10 00)	1:00 PM (13 00)	6:00 PM (18 00)	+1
MALAYSIA	5:00 PM (17 00)	8:00 PM (20 00)	1:00 AM* (01 00*)	+8
MEXICO (See page 143 for additional Mexican cities.)				
Hermosillo, SON	2:00 AM (02 00)	5:00 AM (05 00)	10:00 AM (10 00)	-7
Mexico City, D.F.	3:00 AM (03 00)	6:00 AM (06 00)	11:00 AM (11 00)	-6
Tijuana, B.C.N.	1:00 AM (01 00)	4:00 AM (04 00)	9:00 AM (09 00)	-8
MOLDOVA	11:00 AM (11 00)	2:00 PM (14 00)	7:00 PM (19 00)	+2
NETHERLANDS	10:00 AM (10 00)	1:00 PM (13 00)	6:00 PM (18 00)	+1
NEW ZEALAND	9:00 PM (21 00)	12:00 PM (00 00)	5:00 AM* (05 00*)	+12

(continues)

Greenwich Mean Time —*continued*

(Cities shown only when country observes more than one time.)	9:00 AM (09 00)	12:00 M (12 00)	5:00 PM (17 00)	GMT +/- Hrs
NIGERIA	10:00 AM (10 00)	1:00 PM (13 00)	6:00 PM (18 00)	+1
NORWAY	10:00 AM (10 00)	1:00 PM (13 00)	6:00 PM (18 00)	+1
PAKISTAN	2:00 PM (14 00)	5:00 PM (17 00)	10:00 PM (22 00)	+5
PERU	4:00 AM (04 00)	7:00 AM (07 00)	12:00 M (12 00)	-5
PHILIPPINES	5:00 PM (17 00)	8:00 PM (20 00)	1:00 AM* (01 00*)	+8
POLAND	10:00 AM (10 00)	1:00 PM (13 00)	6:00 PM (18 00)	+1
PORTUGAL	9:00 AM (09 00)	12:00 M (12 00)	5:00 PM (17 00)	
ROMANIA	11:00 AM (11 00)	2:00 PM (14 00)	7:00 PM (19 00)	+2
RUSSIA				
Arkhangelsk	12:00 M (12 00)	3:00 PM (15 00)	8:00 PM (20 00)	+3
Irkutsk	4:00 PM (16 00)	7:00 PM (19 00)	12:00 PM (00 00)	+7
Kaliningrad	10:00 AM (10 00)	1:00 PM (13 00)	6:00 PM (18 00)	+1
Kazan	12:00 M (12 00)	3:00 PM (15 00)	8:00 PM (20 00)	+3
Khabarovsk	7:00 PM (19 00)	10:00 PM (22 00)	3:00 AM* (03 00*)	+10
Magadan	8:00 PM (20 00)	11:00 PM (23 00)	4:00 AM* (04 00*)	+11
Moscow	12:00 M (12 00)	3:00 PM (15 00)	8:00 PM (20 00)	+3
Murmansk	12:00 M (12 00)	3:00 PM (15 00)	8:00 PM (20 00)	+3
Nakhodka	7:00 PM (19 00)	10:00 PM (22 00)	3:00 AM* (03 00*)	+10
Nizhny Novgorod .... (formerly Gorky)	1:00 PM (13 00)	4:00 PM (16 00)	9:00 PM (21 00)	+4
Novorosslisk	12:00 M (12 00)	3:00 PM (15 00)	8:00 PM (20 00)	+3
Novosibirsk	4:00 PM (16 00)	7:00 PM (19 00)	12:00 PM (00 00)	+7
Omsk	3:00 PM (15 00)	6:00 PM (18 00)	11:00 PM (23 00)	+6

12:00 M (12 00) = Noon; 12:00 PM (00 00) = Midnight; * = Next day

Greenwich Mean Time

(Cities shown only when country observes more than one time.)	9:00 AM (09 00)	12:00 M (12 00)	5:00 PM (17 00)	GMT +/- Hrs
St. Petersburg .... (formerly Leningrad)	12:00 M (12 00)	3:00 PM (15 00)	8:00 PM (20 00)	+3
Samara	1:00 PM (13 00)	4:00 PM (16 00)	9:00 PM (21 00)	+4
Sverdlovsk	2:00 PM (14 00)	5:00 PM (17 00)	10:00 PM (22 00)	+5
Tomsk	4:00 PM (16 00)	7:00 PM (19 00)	12:00 PM (00 00)	+7
Vladivostok	7:00 PM (19 00)	10:00 PM (22 00)	3:00 AM (03 00*)	+10
Vologda	12:00 M (12 00)	3:00 PM (15 00)	8:00 PM (20 00)	+3
Vostochny	1:00 PM (13 00)	4:00 PM (16 00)	9:00 PM (21 00)	+4
Yakutsk	6:00 PM (18 00)	9:00 PM (21 00)	2:00 AM* (02 00*)	+9
SAUDI ARABIA	12:00 M (12 00)	3:00 PM (15 00)	8:00 PM (20 00)	+3
SINGAPORE	5:00 PM (17 00)	8:00 PM (20 00)	1:00 AM* (01 00*)	+8
SOUTH AFRICA	11:00 AM (11 00)	2:00 PM (14 00)	7:00 PM (19 00)	+2
SPAIN	10:00 AM (10 00)	1:00 PM (13 00)	6:00 PM (18 00)	+1
SWEDEN	10:00 AM (10 00)	1:00 PM (13 00)	6:00 PM (18 00)	+1
SWITZERLAND	10:00 AM (10 00)	1:00 PM (13 00)	6:00 PM (18 00)	+1
TAIWAN	5:00 PM (17 00)	8:00 PM (20 00)	1:00 AM* (01 00*)	+8
TAJIKISTAN	3:00 PM (15 00)	6:00 PM (18 00)	11:00 PM (23 00)	+6
THAILAND	4:00 PM (16 00)	7:00 PM (19 00)	12:00 PM (00 00)	+7
TURKEY	11:00 AM (11 00)	2:00 PM (14 00)	7:00 PM (19 00)	+2
TURKMENISTAN	1:00 PM (13 00)	4:00 PM (16 00)	9:00 PM (21 00)	+4
U.A.E.	1:00 PM (13 00)	4:00 PM (16 00)	9:00 PM (21 00)	+4
UKRAINE	11:00 AM (11 00)	2:00 PM (14 00)	7:00 PM (19 00)	+2
UNITED KINGDOM	9:00 AM (09 00)	12:00 M (12 00)	5:00 PM (17 00)	

(continues)

Greenwich Mean Time—*continued*

(Cities shown only when country observes more than one time.)	9:00 AM (09 00)	12:00 M (12 00)	5:00 PM (17 00)	GMT +/- Hrs
UNITED STATES (See page 142 for additional United States cities.)				
Chicago, IL	3:00 AM (03 00)	6:00 AM (06 00)	11:00 AM (11 00)	-6
Denver, CO	2:00 AM (02 00)	5:00 AM (05 00)	10:00 AM (10 00)	-7
Honolulu, HI	11:00 PM (23 00)	2:00 AM (02 00)	7:00 AM (07 00)	-10
Juneau, AK	12:00 PM (00 00)	3:00 AM (03 00)	8:00 AM (08 00)	-9
Los Angeles, CA	1:00 AM (01 00)	4:00 AM (04 00)	9:00 AM (09 00)	-8
New York, NY	4:00 AM (04 00)	7:00 AM (07 00)	12:00 M (12 00)	-5
UZBEKISTAN	2:00 PM (14 00)	5:00 PM (17 00)	10:00 PM (22 00)	+5
VENEZUELA	5:00 AM (05 00)	8:00 AM (08 00)	1:00 PM (13 00)	-4

Eastern Standard Time (U.S.A.)

(Cities shown only when country observes more than one time.)	9:00 AM (09 00)	12:00 M (12 00)	5:00 PM (17 00)	EST +/- Hrs
ALGERIA	3:00 PM (15 00)	6:00 PM (18 00)	11:00 PM (23 00)	+6
ANGOLA	3:00 PM (15 00)	6:00 PM (18 00)	11:00 PM (23 00)	+6
ARGENTINA	11:00 AM (11 00)	2:00 PM (14 00)	7:00 PM (19 00)	+2
ARMENIA	5:00 PM (17 00)	8:00 PM (20 00)	1:00 AM* (01 00*)	+8
AUSTRALIA				
Adelaide, SA	11:30 PM (23 30)	2:30 AM* (02 30*)	7:30 AM* (07 30*)	+14.5
Perth, WA	10:00 PM (22 00)	1:00 AM* (01 00*)	6:00 AM* (06 00*)	+13
Sydney, NSW	12:00 PM (00 00)	3:00 AM* (03 00*)	8:00 AM* (08 00*)	+15
AUSTRIA	3:00 PM (15 00)	6:00 PM (18 00)	11:00 PM (23 00)	+6
AZERBAIJAN	5:00 PM (17 00)	8:00 PM (20 00)	1:00 AM* (01 00)	+8

12:00 M (12 00) = Noon; 12:00 PM (00 00) = Midnight; * = Next day

Eastern Standard Time (U.S.A.)

(Cities shown only when country observes more than one time.)	9:00 AM (09 00)	12:00 M (12 00)	5:00 PM (17 00)	EST +/- Hrs
BELARUS	4:00 PM (16 00)	7:00 PM (19 00)	12:00 PM (00 00)	+7
BELGIUM	3:00 PM (15 00)	6:00 PM (18 00)	11:00 PM (23 00)	+6
BRAZIL	11:00 AM (11 00)	2:00 PM (14 00)	7:00 PM (19 00)	+2
BULGARIA	4:00 PM (16 00)	7:00 PM (19 00)	12:00 PM (00 00)	+7
CANADA (See page 143 for additional Canadian cities.)				
Edmonton, AB	7:00 AM (07 00)	10:00 AM (10 00)	3:00 PM (15 00)	-2
Halifax, NS	10:00 AM (10 00)	1:00 PM (13 00)	6:00 PM (18 00)	+1
Regina, SK	8:00 AM (08 00)	11:00 AM (11 00)	4:00 PM (16 00)	-1
St. John's, NF	10:30 AM (10 30)	1:30 PM (13 30)	6:30 PM (18 30)	+1.5
Toronto, ON	9:00 AM (09 00)	12:00 M (12 00)	5:00 PM (17 00)	
Vancouver, BC	6:00 AM (06 00)	9:00 AM (09 00)	2:00 PM (14 00)	-3
CHILE	10:00 AM (10 00)	1:00 PM (13 00)	6:00 PM (18 00)	+1
CHINA	10:00 PM (22 00)	1:00 AM* (01 00*)	6:00 AM* (06 00*)	+13
COLOMBIA	9:00 AM (09 00)	12:00 M (12 00)	5:00 PM (17 00)	
COSTA RICA	8:00 AM (08 00)	11:00 AM (11 00)	4:00 PM (16 00)	-1
CZECHOSLOVAKIA	3:00 PM (15 00)	6:00 PM (18 00)	11:00 PM (23 00)	+6
DENMARK	3:00 PM (15 00)	6:00 PM (18 00)	11:00 PM (23 00)	+6
DOMINICAN REPUBLIC	10:00 AM (10 00)	1:00 PM (13 00)	6:00 PM (18 00)	+1
ECUADOR	9:00 AM (09 00)	12:00 M (12 00)	5:00 PM (17 00)	
EGYPT	4:00 PM (16 00)	7:00 PM (19 00)	12:00 PM (00 00)	+7
ESTONIA	4:00 PM (16 00)	7:00 PM (19 00)	12:00 PM (00 00)	+7
FINLAND	4:00 PM (16 00)	7:00 PM (19 00)	12:00 PM (00 00)	+7

(continues)

Eastern Standard Time (U.S.A.)—*continued*

(Cities shown only when country observes more than one time.)	9:00 AM (09 00)	12:00 M (12 00)	5:00 PM (17 00)	EST +/- Hrs
FRANCE	3:00 PM (15 00)	6:00 PM (18 00)	11:00 PM (23 00)	+6
GEORGIA	5:00 PM (17 00)	8:00 PM (20 00)	1:00 AM* (01 00*)	+8
GERMANY	3:00 PM (15 00)	6:00 PM (18 00)	11:00 PM (23 00)	+6
GUATEMALA	8:00 AM (08 00)	11:00 AM (11 00)	4:00 PM (16 00)	-1
HONG KONG	10:00 PM (22 00)	1:00 AM* (01 00*)	6:00 AM* (06 00*)	+13
HUNGARY	3:00 PM (15 00)	6:00 PM (18 00)	11:00 PM (23 00)	+6
INDIA	7:30 PM (19 30)	10:30 PM (22 30)	3:30 AM* (03 30*)	+10.5
INDONESIA				
Jakarta, Java	9:00 PM (21 00)	12:00 PM (00 00)	5:00 AM* (05 00*)	+12
Pontianak, Borneo	10:00 PM (22 00)	1:00 AM* (01 00*)	6:00 AM* (06 00*)	+13
IRELAND	2:00 PM (14 00)	5:00 PM (17 00)	10:00 PM (22 00)	+5
ISRAEL	4:00 PM (16 00)	7:00 PM (19 00)	12:00 PM (00 00)	+7
ITALY	3:00 PM (15 00)	6:00 PM (18 00)	11:00 PM (23 00)	+6
JAPAN	11:00 PM (23 00)	2:00 AM* (02 00*)	7:00 AM* (07 00*)	+14
KAZAKHSTAN				
Alma Ata	8:00 PM (20 00)	11:00 PM (23 00)	4:00 AM* (04 00*)	+11
Atyubinsk	7:00 PM (19 00)	10:00 PM (22 00)	3:00 AM* (03 00*)	+10
KOREA, REPUBLIC OF	11:00 PM (23 00)	2:00 AM* (02 00*)	7:00 AM* (07 00*)	+14
KYRGYZSTAN	7:00 PM (19 00)	10:00 PM (22 00)	3:00 AM* (03 00*)	+10
LATVIA	4:00 PM (16 00)	7:00 PM (19 00)	12:00 PM (00 00)	+7
LITHUANIA	4:00 PM (16 00)	7:00 PM (19 00)	12:00 PM (00 00)	+7
LUXEMBOURG	3:00 PM (15 00)	6:00 PM (18 00)	11:00 PM (23 00)	+6
MALAYSIA	10:00 PM (22 00)	1:00 AM* (01 00*)	6:00 AM* (06 00*)	+13

12:00 M (12 00) = Noon; 12:00 PM (00 00) = Midnight; * = Next day

Eastern Standard Time (U.S.A.)

(Cities shown only when country observes more than one time.)	9:00 AM (09 00)	12:00 M (12 00)	5:00 PM (17 00)	EST +/- Hrs
MEXICO (See page 143 for additional Mexican cities.)				
Hermosillo, SON	7:00 AM (07 00)	10:00 AM (10 00)	3:00 PM (15 00)	-2
Mexico City, D.F.	8:00 AM (08 00)	11:00 AM (11 00)	4:00 PM (16 00)	-1
Tijuana, B.C.N.	6:00 AM (06 00)	9:00 AM (09 00)	2:00 PM (14 00)	-3
MOLDOVA	4:00 PM (16 00)	7:00 PM (19 00)	12:00 PM (00 00)	+7
NETHERLANDS	3:00 PM (15 00)	6:00 PM (18 00)	11:00 PM (23 00)	+6
NEW ZEALAND	2:00 AM* (02 00*)	5:00 AM* (05 00*)	10:00 AM* (10 00*)	+17
NIGERIA	3:00 PM (15 00)	6:00 PM (18 00)	11:00 PM (23 00)	+6
NORWAY	3:00 PM (15 00)	6:00 PM (18 00)	11:00 PM (23 00)	+6
PAKISTAN	7:00 PM (19 00)	10:00 PM (22 00)	3:00 AM* (03 00*)	+10
PERU	9:00 AM (09 00)	12:00 M (12 00)	5:00 PM (17 00)	
PHILIPPINES	10:00 PM (22 00)	1:00 AM* (01 00*)	6:00 AM* (06 00*)	+13
POLAND	3:00 PM (15 00)	6:00 PM (18 00)	11:00 PM (23 00)	+6
PORTUGAL	2:00 PM (14 00)	5:00 PM (17 00)	10: 00 PM (22 00)	+5
ROMANIA	4:00 PM (16 00)	7:00 PM (19 00)	12:00 PM (00 00)	+7
RUSSIA				
Arkhangelsk	5:00 PM (17 00)	8:00 PM (20 00)	1:00 AM* (01 00*)	+8
Irkutsk	9:00 PM (21 00)	12:00 PM (00 00)	5:00 AM* (05 00*)	+12
Kaliningrad	3:00 PM (15 00)	6:00 PM (18 00)	11:00 PM (23 00)	+6
Kazan	5:00 PM (17 00)	8:00 PM (20 00)	1:00 AM* (01 00*)	+8
Khabarovsk	12:00 PM (00 00)	3:00 AM* (03 00*)	8:00 AM* (08 00*)	+15
Magadan	1:00 AM* (01 00*)	4:00 AM* (04 00*)	9:00 AM* (09 00*)	+16
Moscow	5:00 PM (17 00)	8:00 PM (20 00)	1:00 AM* (01 00*)	+8

(continues)

Eastern Standard Time (U.S.A.)—*continued*

(Cities shown only when country observes more than one time.)	9:00 AM (09 00)	12:00 M (12 00)	5:00 PM (17 00)	EST +/- Hrs
Murmansk	5:00 PM (17 00)	8:00 PM (20 00)	1:00 AM* (01 00*)	+8
Nakhodka	12:00 PM (00 00)	3:00 AM* (03 00*)	8:00 AM* (08 00*)	+15
Nizhny Novgorod .... (formerly Gorky)	6:00 PM (18 00)	9:00 PM (21 00)	2:00 AM* (02 00*)	+9
Novorosslisk	5:00 PM (17 00)	8:00 PM (20 00)	1:00 AM* (01 00)	+8
Novosibirsk	9:00 PM (21 00)	12:00 PM (00 00)	5:00 AM* (05 00*)	+12
Omsk	8:00 PM (20 00)	11:00 PM (23 00)	4:00 AM* (04 00*)	+11
St. Petersburg .... (formerly Leningrad)	5:00 PM (17 00)	8:00 PM (20 00)	1:00 AM* (01 00*)	+8
Samara	6:00 PM (18 00)	9:00 PM (21 00)	2:00 AM* (02 00*)	+9
Sverdlovsk	7:00 PM (19 00)	10:00 PM (22 00)	3:00 AM* (03 00*)	+10
Tomsk	9:00 PM (21 00)	12:00 PM (00 00)	5:00 AM* (05 00*)	+12
Vladivostok	12:00 PM (00 00)	3:00 AM* (03 00*)	8:00 AM* (08 00*)	+15
Vologda	5:00 PM (17 00)	8:00 PM (20 00)	1:00 AM* (01 00)	+8
Vostochny	6:00 PM (18 00)	9:00 PM (21 00)	2:00 AM* (02 00*)	+9
Yakutsk	11:00 PM (23 00)	2:00 AM* (02 00*)	7:00 AM* (07 00*)	+14
SAUDI ARABIA	5:00 PM (17 00)	8:00 PM (20 00)	1:00 AM* (01 00*)	+8
SINGAPORE	10:00 PM (22 00)	1:00 AM* (01 00*)	6:00 AM* (06 00*)	+13
SOUTH AFRICA	4:00 PM (16 00)	7:00 PM (19 00)	12:00 PM (00 00)	+7
SPAIN	3:00 PM (15 00)	6:00 PM (18 00)	11:00 PM (23 00)	+6
SWEDEN	3:00 PM (15 00)	6:00 PM (18 00)	11:00 PM (23 00)	+6
SWITZERLAND	3:00 PM (15 00)	6:00 PM (18 00)	11:00 PM (23 00)	+6
TAIWAN	10:00 PM (22 00)	1:00 AM* (01 00*)	6:00 AM* (06 00*)	+13
TAJIKISTAN	8:00 PM (20 00)	11:00 PM (23 00)	4:00 AM* (04 00*)	+11

12:00 M (12 00) = Noon; 12:00 PM (00 00) = Midnight; * = Next day

Eastern Standard Time (U.S.A.)

(Cities shown only when country observes more than one time.)	9:00 AM (09 00)	12:00 M (12 00)	5:00 PM (17 00)	EST +/- Hrs
THAILAND	9:00 PM (21 00)	12:00 PM (00 00)	5:00 AM* (05 00*)	+12
TURKEY	4:00 PM (16 00)	7:00 PM (19 00)	12:00 PM (00 00)	+7
TURKMENISTAN	6:00 PM (18 00)	9:00 PM (21 00)	2:00 AM* (02 00*)	+9
U.A.E.	6:00 PM (18 00)	9:00 PM (21 00)	2:00 AM* (02 00*)	+9
UKRAINE	4:00 PM (16 00)	7:00 PM (19 00)	12:00 PM (00 00)	+7
UNITED KINGDOM	2:00 PM (14 00)	5:00 PM (17 00)	10:00 PM (22 00)	+5
UNITED STATES (See page 142 for additional United States cities.)				
Chicago, IL	8:00 AM (08 00)	11:00 AM (11 00)	4:00 PM (16 00)	-1
Denver, CO	7:00 AM (07 00)	10:00 AM (10 00)	3:00 PM (15 00)	-2
Honolulu, HI	4:00 AM (04 00)	7:00 AM (07 00)	12:00 M (12 00)	-5
Juneau, AK	5:00 AM (05 00)	8:00 AM (08 00)	1:00 PM (13 00)	-4
Los Angeles, CA	6:00 AM (06 00)	9:00 AM (09 00)	2:00 PM (14 00)	-3
New York, NY	9:00 AM (09 00)	12:00 M (12 00)	5:00 PM (17 00)	
UZBEKISTAN	7:00 PM (19 00)	10:00 PM (22 00)	3:00 AM* (03 00*)	+10
VENEZUELA	10:00 AM (10 00)	1:00 PM (13 00)	6:00 PM (18 00)	+1

Central Standard Time (U.S.A.)

(Cities shown only when country observes more than one time.)	9:00 AM (09 00)	12:00 M (12 00)	5:00 PM (17 00)	CST +/- Hrs
ALGERIA	4:00 PM (16 00)	7:00 PM (19 00)	12:00 PM (00 00)	+7
ANGOLA	4:00 PM (16 00)	7:00 PM (19 00)	12:00 PM (00 00)	+7
ARGENTINA	12:00 M (12 00)	3:00 PM (15 00)	8:00 PM (20 00)	+3
ARMENIA	6:00 PM (18 00)	9:00 PM (21 00)	2:00 AM* (02 00*)	+9

(continues)

Central Standard Time (U.S.A.)—*continued*

(Cities shown only when country observes more than one time.)	9:00 AM (09 00)	12:00 M (12 00)	5:00 PM (17 00)	CST +/- Hrs
AUSTRALIA				
Adelaide, SA	12:30 AM* (00 30*)	3:30 AM* (03 30*)	8:30 AM* (08 30*)	+15.5
Perth, WA	11:00 PM (23 00)	2:00 AM* (02 00*)	7:00 AM* (07 00*)	+14
Sydney, NSW	1:00 AM* (01 00*)	4:00 AM* (04 00*)	9:00 AM* (09 00*)	+16
AUSTRIA	4:00 PM (16 00)	7:00 PM (19 00)	12:00 PM (00 00)	+7
AZERBAIJAN	6:00 PM (18 00)	9:00 PM (21 00)	2:00 AM* (02 00*)	+9
BELARUS	5:00 PM (17 00)	8:00 PM (20 00)	1:00 AM* (01 00*)	+8
BELGIUM	4:00 PM (16 00)	7:00 PM (19 00)	12:00 PM (00 00)	+7
BRAZIL	12:00 M (12 00)	3:00 PM (15 00)	8:00 PM (20 00)	+3
BULGARIA	5:00 PM (17 00)	8:00 PM (20 00)	1:00 AM* (01 00*)	+8
CANADA (See page 143 for additional Canadian cities.)				
Edmonton, AB	8:00 AM (08 00)	11:00 AM (11 00)	4:00 PM (16 00)	-1
Halifax, NS	11:00 AM (11 00)	2:00 PM (14 00)	7:00 PM (19 00)	+2
Regina, SK	9:00 AM (09 00)	12:00 M (12 00)	5:00 PM (17 00)	
St. John's, NF	11:30 AM (11 30)	2:30 PM (14 30)	7:30 PM (19 30)	+2.5
Toronto, ON	10:00 AM (10 00)	1:00 PM (13 00)	6:00 PM (18 00)	+1
Vancouver, BC	7:00 AM (07 00)	10:00 AM (10 00)	3:00 PM (15 00)	-2
CHILE	11:00 AM (11 00)	2:00 PM (14 00)	7:00 PM (19 00)	+2
CHINA	11:00 PM (23 00)	2:00 AM* (02 00*)	7:00 AM* (07 00*)	+14
COLOMBIA	10:00 AM (10 00)	1:00 PM (13 00)	6:00 PM (18 00)	+1
COSTA RICA	9:00 AM (09 00)	12:00 M (12 00)	5:00 PM (17 00)	
CZECHOSLOVAKIA	4:00 PM (16 00)	7:00 PM (19 00)	12:00 PM (00 00)	+7
DENMARK	4:00 PM (16 00)	7:00 PM (19 00)	12:00 PM (00 00)	+7

12:00 M (12 00) = Noon; 12:00 PM (00 00) = Midnight; * = Next day

Central Standard Time (U.S.A.)

(Cities shown only when country observes more than one time.)	9:00 AM (09 00)	12:00 M (12 00)	5:00 PM (17 00)	CST +/- Hrs
DOMINICAN REPUBLIC	11:00 AM (11 00)	2:00 PM (14 00)	7:00 PM (19 00)	+2
ECUADOR	10:00 AM (10 00)	1:00 PM (13 00)	6:00 PM (18 00)	+1
EGYPT	5:00 PM (17 00)	8:00 PM (20 00)	1:00 AM* (01 00*)	+8
ESTONIA	5:00 PM (17 00)	8:00 PM (20 00)	1:00 AM* (01 00*)	+8
FINLAND	5:00 PM (17 00)	8:00 PM (20 00)	1:00 AM* (01 00*)	+8
FRANCE	4:00 PM (16 00)	7:00 PM (19 00)	12:00 PM (00 00)	+7
GEORGIA	6:00 PM (18 00)	9:00 PM (21 00)	2:00 AM* (02 00*)	+9
GERMANY	4:00 PM (16 00)	7:00 PM (19 00)	12:00 PM (00 00)	+7
GUATEMALA	9:00 AM (09 00)	12:00 M (12 00)	5:00 PM (17 00)	
HONG KONG	11:00 PM (23 00)	2:00 AM* (02 00*)	7:00 AM* (07 00*)	+14
HUNGARY	4:00 PM (16 00)	7:00 PM (19 00)	12:00 PM (00 00)	+7
INDIA	8:30 PM (20 30)	11:30 PM (23 30)	4:30 AM* (04 30*)	+11.5
INDONESIA				
Jakarta, Java	10:00 PM (22 00)	1:00 AM* (01 00*)	6:00 AM* (06 00*)	+13
Pontianak, Borneo	11:00 PM (23 00)	2:00 AM* (02 00*)	7:00 AM* (07 00*)	+14
IRELAND	3:00 PM (15 00)	6:00 PM (18 00)	11:00 PM (23 00)	+6
ISRAEL	5:00 PM (17 00)	8:00 PM (20 00)	1:00 AM* (01 00*)	+8
ITALY	4:00 PM (16 00)	7:00 PM (19 00)	12:00 PM (00 00)	+7
JAPAN	12:00 PM (00 00)	3:00 AM* (03 00*)	8:00 AM* (08 00*)	+15
KAZAKHSTAN				
Alma Ata	9:00 PM (21 00)	12:00 PM (00 00)	5:00 AM* (05 00*)	+12
Atyubinsk	8:00 PM (20 00)	11:00 PM (23 00)	4:00 AM* (04 00*)	+11
KOREA, REPUBLIC OF	12:00 PM (00 00)	3:00 AM* (03 00*)	8:00 AM* (08 00*)	+15

(continues)

Central Standard Time (U.S.A.)—*continued*

(Cities shown only when country observes more than one time.)	9:00 AM (09 00)	12:00 M (12 00)	5:00 PM (17 00)	CST +/- Hrs
KYRGYZSTAN	8:00 PM (20 00)	11:00 PM (23 00)	4:00 AM* (04 00*)	+11
LATVIA	5:00 PM (17 00)	8:00 PM (20 00)	1:00 AM* (01 00*)	+8
LITHUANIA	5:00 PM (17 00)	8:00 PM (20 00)	1:00 AM* (01 00*)	+8
LUXEMBOURG	4:00 PM (16 00)	7:00 PM (19 00)	12:00 PM (00 00)	+7
MALAYSIA	11:00 PM (23 00)	2:00 AM* (02 00*)	7:00 AM* (07 00*)	+14
MEXICO (See page 143 for additional Mexican cities.)				
Hermosillo, SON	8:00 AM (08 00)	11:00 AM (11 00)	4:00 PM (16 00)	-1
Mexico City, D.F.	9:00 AM (09 00)	12:00 M (12 00)	5:00 PM (17 00)	
Tijuana, B.C.N.	7:00 AM (07 00)	10:00 AM (10 00)	3:00 PM (15 00)	-2
MOLDOVA	5:00 PM (17 00)	8:00 PM (20 00)	1:00 AM* (01 00*)	+8
NETHERLANDS	4:00 PM (16 00)	7:00 PM (19 00)	12:00 PM (00 00)	+7
NEW ZEALAND	3:00 AM* (03 00*)	6:00 AM* (06 00*)	11:00 AM* (11 00*)	+18
NIGERIA	4:00 PM (16 00)	7:00 PM (19 00)	12:00 PM (00 00)	+7
NORWAY	4:00 PM (16 00)	7:00 PM (19 00)	12:00 PM (00 00)	+7
PAKISTAN	8:00 PM (20 00)	11:00 PM (23 00)	4:00 AM* (04 00*)	+11
PERU	10:00 AM (10 00)	1:00 PM (13 00)	6:00 PM (18 00)	+1
PHILIPPINES	11:00 PM (23 00)	2:00 AM* (02 00*)	7:00 AM* (07 00*)	+14
POLAND	4:00 PM (16 00)	7:00 PM (19 00)	12:00 PM (00 00)	+7
PORTUGAL	3:00 PM (15 00)	6:00 PM (18 00)	11:00 PM (23 00)	+6
ROMANIA	5:00 PM (17 00)	8:00 PM (20 00)	1:00 AM* (01 00*)	+8
RUSSIA				
Arkhangelsk	6:00 PM (18 00)	9:00 PM (21 00)	2:00 AM* (02 00*)	+9
Irkutsk	10:00 PM (22 00)	1:00 AM* (01 00*)	6:00 AM* (06 00*)	+13

12:00 M (12 00) = Noon; 12:00 PM (00 00) = Midnight; * = Next day

Central Standard Time (U.S.A.)

(Cities shown only when country observes more than one time.)	9:00 AM (09 00)	12:00 M (12 00)	5:00 PM (17 00)	CST +/- Hrs
Kaliningrad	4:00 PM (16 00)	7:00 PM (19 00)	12:00 PM (00 00)	+7
Kazan	6:00 PM (18 00)	9:00 PM (21 00)	2:00 AM* (02 00*)	+9
Khabarovsk	1:00 AM* (01 00*)	4:00 AM* (04 00*)	9:00 AM* (09 00*)	+16
Magadan	2:00 AM* (02 00*)	5:00 AM* (05 00*)	10:00 AM* (10 00*)	+17
Moscow	6:00 PM (18 00)	9:00 PM (21 00)	2:00 AM* (02 00*)	+9
Murmansk	6:00 PM (18 00)	9:00 PM (21 00)	2:00 AM* (02 00*)	+9
Nakhodka	1:00 AM* (01 00*)	4:00 AM* (04 00*)	9:00 AM* (09 00*)	+16
Nizhny Novgorod .... (formerly Gorky)	7:00 PM (19 00)	10:00 PM (22 00)	3:00 AM* (03 00*)	+10
Novorosslisk	6:00 PM (18 00)	9:00 PM (21 00)	2:00 AM* (02 00*)	+9
Novosibirsk	10:00 PM (22 00)	1:00 AM* (01 00*)	6:00 AM* (06 00*)	+13
Omsk	9:00 PM (21 00)	12:00 PM (00 00)	5:00 AM* (05 00*)	+12
St. Petersburg .... (formerly Leningrad)	6:00 PM (18 00)	9:00 PM (21 00)	2:00 AM* (02 00*)	+9
Samara	7:00 PM (19 00)	10:00 PM (22 00)	3:00 AM* (03 00*)	+10
Sverdlovsk	8:00 PM (20 00)	11:00 PM (23 00)	4:00 AM* (04 00*)	+11
Tomsk	10:00 PM (22 00)	1:00 AM* (01 00*)	6:00 AM* (06 00*)	+13
Vladivostok	1:00 AM* (01 00*)	4:00 AM* (04 00*)	9:00 AM* (09 00*)	+16
Vologda	6:00 PM (18 00)	9:00 PM (21 00)	2:00 AM* (02 00*)	+9
Vostochny	7:00 PM (19 00)	10:00 PM (22 00)	3:00 AM* (03 00*)	+10
Yakutsk	12:00 PM (00 00)	3:00 AM* (03 00*)	8:00 AM* (08 00*)	+15
SAUDI ARABIA	6:00 PM (18 00)	9:00 PM (21 00)	2:00 AM* (02 00*)	+9
SINGAPORE	11:00 PM (23 00)	2:00 AM* (02 00*)	7:00 AM* (07 00*)	+14
SOUTH AFRICA	5:00 PM (17 00)	8:00 PM (20 00)	1:00 AM* (01 00*)	+8

(continues)

Central Standard Time (U.S.A.)—*continued*

(Cities shown only when country observes more than one time.)	9:00 AM (09 00)	12:00 M (12 00)	5:00 PM (17 00)	CST +/- Hrs
SPAIN	4:00 PM (16 00)	7:00 PM (19 00)	12:00 PM (00 00)	+7
SWEDEN	4:00 PM (16 00)	7:00 PM (19 00)	12:00 PM (00 00)	+7
SWITZERLAND	4:00 PM (16 00)	7:00 PM (19 00)	12:00 PM (00 00)	+7
TAIWAN	11:00 PM (23 00)	2:00 AM* (02 00*)	7:00 AM* (07 00*)	+14
TAJIKISTAN	9:00 PM (21 00)	12:00 PM (00 00)	5:00 AM* (05 00*)	+12
THAILAND	10:00 PM (22 00)	1:00 AM* (01 00*)	6:00 AM* (06 00*)	+13
TURKEY	5:00 PM (17 00)	8:00 PM (20 00)	1:00 AM* (01 00*)	+8
TURKMENISTAN	7:00 PM (19 00)	10:00 PM (22 00)	3:00 AM* (03 00*)	+10
U.A.E.	7:00 PM (19 00)	10:00 PM (22 00)	3:00 AM* (03 00*)	+10
UKRAINE	5:00 PM (17 00)	8:00 PM (20 00)	1:00 AM* (01 00*)	+8
UNITED KINGDOM	3:00 PM (15 00)	6:00 PM (18 00)	11:00 PM (23 00)	+6
UNITED STATES (See page 142 for additional United States cities.)				
Chicago, IL	9:00 AM (09 00)	12:00 M (12 00)	5:00 PM (17 00)	
Denver, CO	8:00 AM (08 00)	11:00 AM (11 00)	4:00 PM (16 00)	-1
Honolulu, HI	5:00 AM (05 00)	8:00 AM (08 00)	1:00 PM (13 00)	-4
Juneau, AK	6:00 AM (06 00)	9:00 AM (09 00)	2:00 PM (14 00)	-3
Los Angeles, CA	7:00 AM (07 00)	10:00 AM (10 00)	3:00 PM (15 00)	-2
New York, NY	10:00 AM (10 00)	1:00 PM (13 00)	6:00 PM (18 00)	+1
UZBEKISTAN	8:00 PM (20 00)	11:00 PM (23 00)	4:00 AM* (04 00*)	+11
VENEZUELA	11:00 AM (11 00)	2:00 PM (14 00)	7:00 PM (19 00)	+2

12:00 M (12 00) = Noon; 12:00 PM (00 00) = Midnight; * = Next day

Mountain Standard Time (U.S.A.)

(Cities shown only when country observes more than one time.)	9:00 AM (09 00)	12:00 M (12 00)	5:00 PM (17 00)	MST +/- Hrs
ALGERIA . . . . •	5:00 PM (17 00)	8:00 PM (20 00)	1:00 AM* (01 00*)	+8
ANGOLA	5:00 PM (17 00)	8:00 PM (20 00)	1:00 AM* (01 00*)	+8
ARGENTINA	1:00 PM (13 00)	4:00 PM (16 00)	9:00 PM (21 00)	+4
ARMENIA	7:00 PM (19 00)	10:00 PM (22 00)	3:00 AM* (03 00*)	+10
AUSTRALIA				
Adelaide, SA	1:30 AM* (01 30*)	4:30 AM* (04 30*)	9:30 AM* (09 30*)	+16.5
Perth, WA	12:00 PM (00 00)	3:00 AM* (03 00*)	8:00 AM* (08 00*)	+15
Sydney, NSW	2:00 AM* (02 00*)	5:00 AM* (05 00*)	10:00 AM* (10 00*)	+17
AUSTRIA	5:00 PM (17 00)	8:00 PM (20 00)	1:00 AM* (01 00*)	+8
AZERBAIJAN	7:00 PM (19 00)	10:00 PM (22 00)	3:00 AM* (03 00*)	+10
BELARUS	6:00 PM (18 00)	9:00 PM (21 00)	2:00 AM* (02 00*)	+9
BELGIUM	5:00 PM (17 00)	8:00 PM (20 00)	1:00 AM* (01 00*)	+8
BRAZIL	1:00 PM (01 00)	4:00 PM (16 00)	9:00 PM (21 00)	+4
BULGARIA	6:00 PM (18 00)	9:00 PM (21 00)	2:00 AM* (02 00*)	+9
CANADA (See page 143 for additional Canadian cities.)				
Edmonton, AB	9:00 AM (09 00)	12:00 M (12 00)	5:00 PM (17 00)	
Halifax, NS	12:00 M (12 00)	3:00 PM (15 00)	8:00 PM (20 00)	+3
Regina, SK	10:00 AM (10 00)	1:00 PM (13 00)	6:00 PM (18 00)	+1
St. John's, NF	12:30 PM (12 30)	3:30 PM (15 30)	8:30 PM (20 30)	+3.5
Toronto, ON	11:00 AM (11 00)	2:00 PM (14 00)	7:00 PM (19 00)	+2
Vancouver, BC	8:00 AM (08 00)	11:00 AM (11 00)	4:00 PM (16 00)	-1
CHILE	12:00 M (12 00)	3:00 PM (15 00)	8:00 PM (20 00)	+3
CHINA	12:00 PM (00 00)	3:00 AM* (03 00*)	8:00 AM* (08 00*)	+15

(continues)

Mountain Standard Time (U.S.A.)—*continued*

(Cities shown only when country observes more than one time.)	9:00 AM (09 00)	12:00 M (12 00)	5:00 PM (17 00)	MST +/- Hrs
COLOMBIA	11:00 AM (11 00)	2:00 PM (14 00)	7:00 PM (19 00)	+2
COSTA RICA	10:00 AM (10 00)	1:00 PM (13 00)	6:00 PM (18 00)	+1
CZECHOSLOVAKIA	5:00 PM (17 00)	8:00 PM (20 00)	1:00 AM* (01 00*)	+8
DENMARK	5:00 PM (17 00)	8:00 PM (20 00)	1:00 AM* (01 00*)	+8
DOMINICAN REPUBLIC	12:00 M (12 00)	3:00 PM (15 00)	8:00 PM (20 00)	+3
ECUADOR	11:00 AM (11 00)	2:00 PM (14 00)	7:00 PM (19 00)	+2
EGYPT	6:00 PM (18 00)	9:00 PM (21 00)	2:00 AM* (02 00*)	+9
ESTONIA	6:00 PM (18 00)	9:00 PM (21 00)	2:00 AM* (02 00*)	+9
FINLAND	6:00 PM (18 00)	9:00 PM (21 00)	2:00 AM* (02 00*)	+9
FRANCE	5:00 PM (17 00)	8:00 PM (20 00)	1:00 AM* (01 00*)	+8
GEORGIA	7:00 PM (19 00)	10:00 PM (22 00)	3:00 AM* (03 00*)	+10
GERMANY	5:00 PM (17 00)	8:00 PM (20 00)	1:00 AM* (01 00*)	+8
GUATEMALA	10:00 AM (10 00)	1:00 PM (13 00)	6:00 PM (18 00)	+1
HONG KONG	12:00 PM (00 00)	3:00 AM* (03 00*)	8:00 AM* (08 00*)	+15
HUNGARY	5:00 PM (17 00)	8:00 PM (20 00)	1:00 AM* (01 00*)	+8
INDIA	9:30 PM (21 30)	12:30 AM* (00 30)	5:30 AM* (05 30*)	+12.5
INDONESIA				
Jakarta, Java	11:00 PM (23 00)	2:00 AM* (02 00*)	7:00 AM* (07 00*)	+14
Pontianak, Borneo	12:00 PM (00 00)	3:00 AM* (03 00*)	8:00 AM* (08 00*)	+15
IRELAND	4:00 PM (16 00)	7:00 PM (19 00)	12:00 PM (00 00)	+7
ISRAEL	6:00 PM (18 00)	9:00 PM (21 00)	2:00 AM* (02 00*)	+9
ITALY	5:00 PM (17 00)	8:00 PM (20 00)	1:00 AM* (01 00*)	+8

12:00 M (12 00) = Noon; 12:00 PM (00 00) = Midnight; * = Next day

Mountain Standard Time (U.S.A.)

(Cities shown only when country observes more than one time.)	9:00 AM (09 00)	12:00 M (12 00)	5:00 PM (17 00)	MST +/- Hrs
JAPAN	1:00 AM* (01 00*)	4:00 AM* (04 00*)	9:00 AM* (09 00*)	+16
KAZAKHSTAN				
Alma Ata	10:00 PM (22 00)	1:00 AM* (01 00*)	6:00 AM* (06 00*)	+13
Atyubinsk	9:00 PM (21 00)	12:00 PM (00 00)	5:00 AM* (05 00*)	+12
KOREA, REPUBLIC OF	1:00 AM* (01 00*)	4:00 AM* (04 00*)	9:00 AM* (09 00*)	+16
KYRGYZSTAN	9:00 PM (21 00)	12:00 PM (00 00)	5:00 AM* (05 00*)	+12
LATVIA	6:00 PM (18 00)	9:00 PM (21 00)	2:00 AM* (02 00*)	+9
LITHUANIA	6:00 PM (18 00)	9:00 PM (21 00)	2:00 AM* (02 00*)	+9
LUXEMBOURG	5:00 PM (17 00)	8:00 PM (20 00)	1:00 AM* (01 00*)	+8
MALAYSIA	12:00 PM (00 00)	3:00 AM* (03 00*)	8:00 AM* (08 00*)	+15
MEXICO (See page 143 for additional Mexican cities.)				
Hermosillo, SON	9:00 AM (09 00)	12:00 M (12 00)	5:00 PM (17 00)	
Mexico City, D.F.	10:00 AM (10 00)	1:00 PM (13 00)	6:00 PM (18 00)	+1
Tijuana, B.C.N.	8:00 AM (08 00)	11:00 AM (11 00)	4:00 PM (16 00)	-1
MOLDOVA	6:00 PM (18 00)	9:00 PM (21 00)	2:00 AM* (02 00*)	+9
NETHERLANDS	5:00 PM (17 00)	8:00 PM (20 00)	1:00 AM* (01 00*)	+8
NEW ZEALAND	4:00 AM* (04 00*)	7:00 AM* (07 00*)	12:00 M* (12 00*)	+19
NIGERIA	5:00 PM (17 00)	8:00 PM (20 00)	1:00 AM* (01 00*)	+8
NORWAY	5:00 PM (17 00)	8:00 PM (20 00)	1:00 AM* (01 00*)	+8
PAKISTAN	9:00 PM (21 00)	12:00 PM (00 00)	5:00 AM* (05 00*)	+12
PERU	11:00 AM (11 00)	2:00 PM (14 00)	7:00 PM (19 00)	+2
PHILIPPINES	12:00 PM (00 00)	3:00 AM* (03 00*)	8:00 AM* (08 00*)	+15
POLAND	5:00 PM (17 00)	8:00 PM (20 00)	1:00 AM* (01 00*)	+8

(continues)

Mountain Standard Time (U.S.A.)—*continued*

(Cities shown only when country observes more than one time.)	9:00 AM (09 00)	12:00 M (12 00)	5:00 PM (17 00)	MST +/- Hrs
PORTUGAL	4:00 PM (16 00)	7:00 PM (19 00)	12:00 PM (00 00)	+7
ROMANIA	6:00 PM (18 00)	9:00 PM (21 00)	2:00 AM* (02 00*)	+9
RUSSIA				
Arkhangelsk	7:00 PM (19 00)	10:00 PM (22 00)	3:00 AM* (03 00*)	+10
Irkutsk	11:00 PM (23 00)	2:00 AM* (02 00*)	7:00 AM* (07 00*)	+14
Kaliningrad	5:00 PM (17 00)	8:00 PM (20 00)	1:00 AM* (01 00*)	+8
Kazan	7:00 PM (19 00)	10:00 PM (22 00)	3:00 AM* (03 00*)	+10
Khabarovsk	2:00 AM* (02 00*)	5:00 AM* (05 00*)	10:00 AM* (10 00*)	+17
Magadan	3:00 AM* (03 00*)	6:00 AM* (06 00*)	11:00 AM* (11 00*)	+18
Moscow	7:00 PM (19 00)	10:00 PM (22 00)	3:00 AM* (03 00*)	+10
Murmansk	7:00 PM (19 00)	10:00 PM (22 00)	3:00 AM* (03 00*)	+10
Nakhodka	2:00 AM* (02 00*)	5:00 AM* (05 00*)	10:00 AM* (10 00*)	+17
Nizhny Novgorod .... (formerly Gorky)	8:00 PM (20 00)	11:00 PM (23 00)	4:00 AM* (04 00*)	+11
Novorosslisk	7:00 PM (19 00)	10:00 PM (22 00)	3:00 AM* (03 00*)	+10
Novosibirsk	11:00 PM (23 00)	2:00 AM* (02 00*)	7:00 AM* (07 00*)	+14
Omsk	10:00 PM (22 00)	1:00 AM* (01 00*)	6:00 AM* (06 00*)	+13
St. Petersburg .... (formerly Leningrad)	7:00 PM (19 00)	10:00 PM (22 00)	3:00 AM* (03 00*)	+10
Samara	8:00 PM (20 00)	11:00 PM (23 00)	4:00 AM* (04 00*)	+11
Sverdlovsk	9:00 PM (21 00)	12:00 PM (00 00)	5:00 AM* (05 00*)	+12
Tomsk	11:00 PM (23 00)	2:00 AM* (02 00*)	7:00 AM* (07 00*)	+14
Vladivostok	2:00 AM* (02 00*)	5:00 AM* (05 00*)	10:00 AM* (10 00*)	+17
Vologda	7:00 PM (19 00)	10:00 PM (22 00)	3:00 AM* (03 00*)	+10

12:00 M (12 00) = Noon; 12:00 PM (00 00) = Midnight; * = Next day

Mountain Standard Time (U.S.A.)

(Cities shown only when country observes more than one time.)	9:00 AM (09 00)	12:00 M (12 00)	5:00 PM (17 00)	MST +/- Hrs
Vostochny	8:00 PM (20 00)	11:00 PM (23 00)	4:00 AM* (04 00*)	+11
Yakutsk	1:00 AM* (01 00*)	4:00 AM* (04 00*)	9:00 AM* (09 00*)	+16
SAUDI ARABIA	7:00 PM (19 00)	10:00 PM (22 00)	3:00 AM* (03 00*)	+10
SINGAPORE	12:00 PM (00 00)	3:00 AM* (03 00*)	8:00 AM* (08 00*)	+15
SOUTH AFRICA	6:00 PM (18 00)	9:00 PM (21 00)	2:00 AM* (02 00*)	+9
SPAIN	5:00 PM (17 00)	8:00 PM (20 00)	1:00 AM* (01 00*)	+8
SWEDEN	5:00 PM (17 00)	8:00 PM (20 00)	1:00 AM* (01 00*)	+8
SWITZERLAND	5:00 PM (17 00)	8:00 PM (20 00)	1:00 AM* (01 00*)	+8
TAIWAN	12:00 PM (00 00)	3:00 AM* (03 00*)	8:00 AM* (08 00*)	+15
TAJIKISTAN	10:00 PM (22 00)	1:00 AM* (01 00*)	6:00 AM* (06 00*)	+13
THAILAND	11:00 PM (23 00)	2:00 AM* (02 00*)	7:00 AM* (07 00*)	+14
TURKEY	6:00 PM (18 00)	9:00 PM (21 00)	2:00 AM* (02 00*)	+9
TURKMENISTAN	8:00 PM (20 00)	11:00 PM (23 00)	4:00 AM* (04 00*)	+11
U.A.E.	8:00 PM (20 00)	11:00 PM (23 00)	4:00 AM* (04 00*)	+11
UKRAINE	6:00 PM (18 00)	9:00 PM (21 00)	2:00 AM* (02 00*)	+9
UNITED KINGDOM	4:00 PM (16 00)	7:00 PM (19 00)	12:00 PM (00 00)	+7
UNITED STATES (See page 142 for additional United States cities.)				
Chicago, IL	10:00 AM (10 00)	1:00 PM (13 00)	6:00 PM (18 00)	+1
Denver, CO	9:00 AM (09 00)	12:00 M (12 00)	5:00 PM (17 00)	
Honolulu, HI	6:00 AM (06 00)	9:00 AM (09 00)	2:00 PM (14 00)	-3
Juneau, AK	7:00 AM (07 00)	10:00 AM (10 00)	3:00 PM (15 00)	-2
Los Angeles, CA	8:00 AM (08 00)	11:00 AM (11 00)	4:00 PM (16 00)	-1

(continues)

Mountain Standard Time (U.S.A.)—*continued*

(Cities shown only when country observes more than one time.)	9:00 AM (09 00)	12:00 M (12 00)	5:00 PM (17 00)	MST +/- Hrs
New York, NY	11:00 AM (11 00)	2:00 PM (14 00)	7:00 PM (19 00)	+2
UZBEKISTAN	9:00 PM (21 00)	12:00 PM (00 00)	5:00 AM* (05 00*)	+12
VENEZUELA	12:00 M (12 00)	3:00 PM (15 00)	8:00 PM (20 00)	+3

Pacific Standard Time (U.S.A.)

(Cities shown only when country observes more than one time.)	9:00 AM (09 00)	12:00 M (12 00)	5:00 PM (17 00)	PST +/- Hrs
ALGERIA	6:00 PM (18 00)	9:00 PM (21 00)	2:00 AM* (02 00*)	+9
ANGOLA	6:00 PM (18 00)	9:00 PM (21 00)	2:00 AM* (02 00*)	+9
ARGENTINA	2:00 PM (14 00)	5:00 PM (17 00)	10:00 PM (22 00)	+5
ARMENIA	8:00 PM (20 00)	11:00 PM (23 00)	4:00 AM* (04 00*)	+11
AUSTRALIA				
Adelaide, SA	2:30 AM* (02 30*)	5:30 AM* (05 30*)	10:30 AM* (10 30*)	+17.5
Perth, WA	1:00 AM* (01 00*)	4:00 AM* (04 00*)	9:00 AM* (09 00*)	+16
Sydney, NSW	3:00 AM* (03 00*)	6:00 AM* (06 00*)	11:00 AM* (11 00*)	+18
AUSTRIA	6:00 PM (18 00)	9:00 PM (21 00)	2:00 AM* (02 00*)	+9
AZERBAIJAN	8:00 PM (20 00)	11:00 PM (23 00)	4:00 AM* (04 00*)	+11
BELARUS	7:00 PM (19 00)	10:00 PM (22 00)	3:00 AM* (03 00*)	+10
BELGIUM	6:00 PM (18 00)	9:00 PM (21 00)	2:00 AM* (02 00*)	+9
BRAZIL	2:00 PM (02 00)	5:00 PM (17 00)	10:00 PM (22 00)	+5
BULGARIA	7:00 PM (19 00)	10:00 PM (21 00)	3:00 AM* (03 00*)	+10
CANADA (See page 143 for additional Canadian cities.)				
Edmonton, AB	10:00 AM (10 00)	1:00 PM (13 00)	6:00 PM (18 00)	+1

12:00 M (12 00) = Noon; 12:00 PM (00 00) = Midnight; * = Next day

Pacific Standard Time (U.S.A.)

(Cities shown only when country observes more than one time.)	9:00 AM (09 00)	12:00 M (12 00)	5:00 PM (17 00)	PST +/- Hrs
Halifax, NS	1:00 PM (13 00)	4:00 PM (16 00)	9:00 PM (21 00)	+4
Regina, SK	11:00 AM (11 00)	2:00 PM (14 00)	7:00 PM (19 00)	+2
St. John's, NF	1:30 PM (13 30)	4:30 PM (16 30)	9:30 PM (21 30)	+4.5
Toronto, ON	12:00 M (12 00)	3:00 PM (15 00)	8:00 PM (20 00)	+3
Vancouver, BC	9:00 AM (09 00)	12:00 M (12 00)	5:00 PM (17 00)	
CHILE	1:00 PM (13 00)	4:00 PM (16 00)	9:00 PM (21 00)	+4
CHINA	1:00 AM* (01 00*)	4:00 AM* (04 00*)	9:00 AM* (09 00*)	+16
COLOMBIA	12:00 M (12 00)	3:00 PM (15 00)	8:00 PM (20 00)	+3
COSTA RICA	11:00 AM (11 00)	2:00 PM (14 00)	7:00 PM (19 00)	+2
CZECHOSLOVAKIA	6:00 PM (18 00)	9:00 PM (21 00)	2:00 AM* (02 00*)	+9
DENMARK	6:00 PM (18 00)	9:00 PM (21 00)	2:00 AM* (02 00*)	+9
DOMINICAN REPUBLIC	1:00 PM (13 00)	4:00 PM (16 00)	9:00 PM (21 00)	+4
ECUADOR	12:00 M (12 00)	3:00 PM (15 00)	8:00 PM (20 00)	+3
EGYPT	7:00 PM (19 00)	10:00 PM (21 00)	3:00 AM* (03 00*)	+10
ESTONIA	7:00 PM (19 00)	10:00 PM (22 00)	3:00 AM* (03 00*)	+10
FINLAND	7:00 PM (19 00)	10:00 PM (21 00)	3:00 AM* (03 00*)	+10
FRANCE	6:00 PM (18 00)	9:00 PM (21 00)	2:00 AM* (02 00*)	+9
GEORGIA	8:00 PM (20 00)	11:00 PM (23 00)	4:00 AM* (04 00*)	+11
GERMANY	6:00 PM (18 00)	9:00 PM (21 00)	2:00 AM* (02 00*)	+9
GUATEMALA	11:00 AM (11 00)	2:00 PM (14 00)	7:00 PM (19 00)	+2
HONG KONG	1:00 AM* (01 00*)	4:00 AM* (04 00*)	9:00 AM* (09 00*)	+16
HUNGARY	6:00 PM (18 00)	9:00 PM (21 00)	2:00 AM* (02 00*)	+9

(continues)

Pacific Standard Time (U.S.A.)—*continued*

(Cities shown only when country observes more than one time.)	9:00 AM (09 00)	12:00 M (12 00)	5:00 PM (17 00)	PST +/- Hrs
INDIA	10:30 PM (22 30)	1:30 AM* (01 30*)	6:30 AM* (06 30*)	+13.5
INDONESIA				
Jakarta, Java	12:00 PM (00 00)	3:00 AM* (03 00*)	8:00 AM* (08 00*)	+15
Pontianak, Borneo	1:00 AM* (01 00*)	4:00 AM* (04 00*)	9:00 AM* (09 00*)	+16
IRELAND	5:00 PM (17 00)	8:00 PM (20 00)	1:00 AM* (01 00*)	+8
ISRAEL	7:00 PM (19 00)	10:00 PM (21 00)	3:00 AM* (03 00*)	+10
ITALY	6:00 PM (18 00)	9:00 PM (21 00)	2:00 AM* (02 00*)	+9
JAPAN	2:00 AM* (02 00*)	5:00 AM* (05 00*)	10:00 AM* (10 00*)	+17
KAZAKHSTAN				
Alma Ata	11:00 PM (23 00)	2:00 AM* (02 00*)	7:00 AM* (07 00*)	+14
Atyubinsk	10:00 PM (22 00)	1:00 AM* (01 00*)	6:00 AM* (06 00*)	+13
KOREA, REPUBLIC OF	2:00 AM* (02 00*)	5:00 AM* (05 00*)	10:00 AM* (10 00*)	+17
KYRGYZSTAN	10:00 PM (22 00)	1:00 AM* (01 00*)	6:00 AM* (06 00*)	+13
LATVIA	7:00 PM (19 00)	10:00 PM (22 00)	3:00 AM* (03 00*)	+10
LITHUANIA	7:00 PM (19 00)	10:00 PM (22 00)	3:00 AM* (03 00*)	+10
LUXEMBOURG	6:00 PM (18 00)	9:00 PM (21 00)	2:00 AM* (02 00*)	+9
MALAYSIA	1:00 AM* (01 00*)	4:00 AM* (04 00*)	9:00 AM* (09 00*)	+16
MEXICO (See page 143 for additional Mexican cities.)				
Hermosillo, SON	10:00 AM (10 00)	1:00 PM (13 00)	6:00 PM (18 00)	+1
Mexico City, D.F.	11:00 AM (11 00)	2:00 PM (14 00)	7:00 PM (19 00)	+2
Tijuana, B.C.N.	9:00 AM (09 00)	12:00 M (12 00)	5:00 PM (17 00)	
MOLDOVA	7:00 PM (19 00)	10:00 PM (22 00)	3:00 AM* (03 00*)	+10
NETHERLANDS	6:00 PM (18 00)	9:00 PM (21 00)	2:00 AM* (02 00*)	+9

12:00 M (12 00) = Noon; 12:00 PM (00 00) = Midnight; * = Next day

Pacific Standard Time (U.S.A.)

(Cities shown only when country observes more than one time.)	9:00 AM (09 00)	12:00 M (12 00)	5:00 PM (17 00)	PST +/- Hrs
NEW ZEALAND	5:00 AM* (05 00*)	8:00 AM* (08 00*)	1:00 PM* (13 00*)	+20
NIGERIA	6:00 PM (18 00)	9:00 PM (21 00)	2:00 AM* (02 00*)	+9
NORWAY	6:00 PM (18 00)	9:00 PM (21 00)	2:00 AM* (02 00*)	+9
PAKISTAN	10:00 PM (22 00)	1:00 AM* (01 00*)	6:00 AM* (06 00*)	+13
PERU	12:00 M (12 00)	3:00 PM (15 00)	8:00 PM (20 00)	+3
PHILIPPINES	1:00 AM (01 00)	4:00 AM* (04 00*)	9:00 AM* (09 00*)	+16
POLAND	6:00 PM (18 00)	9:00 PM (21 00)	2:00 AM* (02 00*)	+9
PORTUGAL	5:00 PM (17 00)	8:00 PM (20 00)	1:00 AM* (01 00*)	+8
ROMANIA	7:00 PM (19 00)	10:00 PM (21 00)	3:00 AM* (03 00*)	+10
RUSSIA				
Arkhangelsk	8:00 PM (20 00)	11:00 PM (23 00)	4:00 AM* (04 00*)	+11
Irkutsk	12:00 PM (00 00)	3:00 AM* (03 00*)	8:00 AM* (08 00*)	+15
Kaliningrad	6:00 PM (18 00)	9:00 PM (21 00)	2:00 AM* (02 00*)	+9
Kazan	8:00 PM (20 00)	11:00 PM (23 00)	4:00 AM* (04 00*)	+11
Khabarovsk	3:00 AM* (03 00*)	6:00 AM* (06 00*)	11:00 AM* (11 00*)	+18
Magadan	4:00 AM* (04 00*)	7:00 AM* (07 00*)	12:00 M* (12 00*)	+19
Moscow	8:00 PM (20 00)	11:00 PM (23 00)	4:00 AM* (04 00*)	+11
Murmansk	8:00 PM (20 00)	11:00 PM (23 00)	4:00 AM* (04 00*)	+11
Nakhodka	3:00 AM* (03 00*)	6:00 AM* (06 00*)	11:00 AM* (11 00*)	+18
Nizhny Novgorod .... (formerly Gorky)	9:00 PM (21 00)	12:00 PM (00 00)	5:00 AM* (05 00*)	+12
Novorosslisk	8:00 PM (20 00)	11:00 PM (23 00)	4:00 AM* (04 00*)	+11
Novosibirsk	12:00 PM (00 00)	3:00 AM* (03 00*)	8:00 AM* (08 00*)	+15

(continues)

Pacific Standard Time (U.S.A.)—*continued*

(Cities shown only when country observes more than one time.)	9:00 AM (09 00)	12:00 M (12 00)	5:00 PM (17 00)	PST +/- Hrs
Omsk	11:00 PM (23 00)	2:00 AM* (02 00*)	7:00 AM* (07 00*)	+14
St. Petersburg . . . . (formerly Leningrad)	8:00 PM (20 00)	11:00 PM (23 00)	4:00 AM* (04 00*)	+11
Samara	9:00 PM (21 00)	12:00 PM (00 00)	5:00 AM* (05 00*)	+12
Sverdlovsk	10:00 PM (22 00)	1:00 AM* (01 00*)	6:00 AM* (06 00*)	+13
Tomsk	12:00 PM (00 00)	3:00 AM* (03 00*)	8:00 AM* (08 00*)	+15
Vladivostok	3:00 AM* (03 00*)	6:00 AM* (06 00*)	11:00 AM* (11 00*)	+18
Vologda	8:00 PM (20 00)	11:00 PM (23 00)	4:00 AM* (04 00*)	+11
Vostochny	9:00 PM (21 00)	12:00 PM (00 00)	5:00 AM* (05 00*)	+12
Yakutsk	2:00 AM* (02 00*)	5:00 AM* (05 00*)	10:00 AM* (10 00*)	+17
SAUDI ARABIA	8:00 PM (20 00)	11:00 PM (23 00)	4:00 AM* (04 00*)	+11
SINGAPORE	1:00 AM* (01 00*)	4:00 AM* (04 00*)	9:00 AM* (09 00*)	+16
SOUTH AFRICA	7:00 PM (19 00)	10:00 PM (21 00)	3:00 AM* (03 00*)	+10
SPAIN	6:00 PM (18 00)	9:00 PM (21 00)	2:00 AM* (02 00*)	+9
SWEDEN	6:00 PM (18 00)	9:00 PM (21 00)	2:00 AM* (02 00*)	+9
SWITZERLAND	6:00 PM (18 00)	9:00 PM (21 00)	2:00 AM* (02 00*)	+9
TAIWAN	1:00 AM* (01 00*)	4:00 AM* (04 00*)	9:00 AM* (09 00*)	+16
TAJIKISTAN	11:00 PM (23 00)	2:00 AM* (02 00*)	7:00 AM* (07 00*)	+14
THAILAND	12:00 PM (00 00)	3:00 AM* (03 00*)	8:00 AM* (08 00*)	+15
TURKEY	7:00 PM (19 00)	10:00 PM (21 00)	3:00 AM* (03 00*)	+10
TURKMENISTAN	9:00 PM (21 00)	12:00 PM (00 00)	5:00 AM* (05 00	+12
U.A.E.	9:00 PM (21 00)	12:00 PM (00 00)	5:00 AM* (05 00*)	+12
UKRAINE	7:00 PM (19 00)	10:00 PM (22 00)	3:00 AM* (03 00*)	+10

12:00 M (12 00) = Noon; 12:00 PM (00 00) = Midnight; * = Next day

Pacific Standard Time (U.S.A.)

(Cities shown only when country observes more than one time.)	9:00 AM (09 00)	12:00 M (12 00)	5:00 PM (17 00)	PST +/- Hrs
UNITED KINGDOM	5:00 PM (17 00)	8:00 PM (20 00)	1:00 AM* (01 00*)	+8
UNITED STATES (See page 142 for additional United States cities.)				
Chicago, IL	11:00 AM (11 00)	2:00 PM (14 00)	7:00 PM (19 00)	+2
Denver, CO	10:00 AM (10 00)	1:00 PM (13 00)	6:00 PM (18 00)	+1
Honolulu, HI	7:00 AM (07 00)	10:00 AM (10 00)	3:00 PM (15 00)	-2
Juneau, AK	8:00 AM (08 00)	11:00 AM (11 00)	4:00 PM (16 00)	-1
Los Angeles, CA	9:00 AM (09 00)	12:00 M (12 00)	5:00 PM (17 00)	
New York, NY	12:00 M (12 00)	3:00 PM (15 00)	8:00 PM (20 00)	+3
UZBEKISTAN	10:00 PM (22 00)	1:00 AM* (01 00*)	6:00 AM* (06 00*)	+13
VENEZUELA	1:00 PM (13 00)	4:00 PM (16 00)	9:00 PM (21 00)	+4

Alaskan Standard Time (U.S.A.)

(Cities shown only when country observes more than one time.)	9:00 AM (09 00)	12:00 M (12 00)	5:00 PM (17 00)	YKN +/- Hrs
ALGERIA	7:00 PM (19 00)	10:00 PM (22 00)	3:00 AM* (03 00*)	+10
ANGOLA	7:00 PM (19 00)	10:00 PM (22 00)	3:00 AM* (03 00*)	+10
ARGENTINA	3:00 PM (15 00)	6:00 PM (18 00)	11:00 PM (23 00)	+6
ARMENIA	9:00 PM (21 00)	12:00 PM (00 00)	5:00 AM* (05 00*)	+12
AUSTRALIA				
Adelaide, SA	3:30 AM* (03 30*)	6:30 AM* (06 30*)	11:30 AM* (11 30*)	+18.5
Perth, WA	2:00 AM* (02 00*)	5:00 AM* (05 00*)	10:00 AM* (10 00*)	+17
Sydney, NSW	4:00 AM* (04 00*)	7:00 AM* (07 00*)	12:00 M* (12 00*)	+19
AUSTRIA	7:00 PM (19 00)	10:00 PM (22 00)	3:00 AM* (03 00*)	+10

(continues)

Alaskan Standard Time (U.S.A.)—*continued*

(Cities shown only when country observes more than one time.)	9:00 AM (09 00)	12:00 M (12 00)	5:00 PM (17 00)	YKN +/- Hrs
AZERBAIJAN	9:00 PM (21 00)	12:00 PM (00 00)	5:00 AM* (05 00*)	+12
BELARUS	8:00 PM (20 00)	11:00 PM (23 00)	4:00 AM* (04 00*)	+11
BELGIUM	7:00 PM (19 00)	10:00 PM (22 00)	3:00 AM* (03 00*)	+10
BRAZIL	3:00 PM (03 00)	6:00 PM (18 00)	11:00 PM (23 00)	+6
BULGARIA	8:00 PM (20 00)	11:00 PM (23 00)	4:00 AM* (04 00*)	+11
CANADA (See page 143 for additional Canadian cities.)				
Edmonton, AB	11:00 AM (11 00)	2:00 PM (14 00)	7:00 PM (19 00)	+2
Halifax, NS	2:00 PM (14 00)	5:00 PM (17 00)	10:00 PM (22 00)	+5
Regina, SK	12:00 M (12 00)	3:00 PM (15 00)	8:00 PM (20 00)	+3
St. John's, NF	2:30 PM (14 30)	5:30 PM (17 30)	10:30 PM (22 30)	+5.5
Toronto, ON	1:00 PM (13 00)	4:00 PM (16 00)	9:00 PM (21 00)	+4
Vancouver, BC	10:00 AM (10 00)	1:00 PM (13 00)	6:00 PM (18 00)	+1
CHILE	2:00 PM (14 00)	5:00 PM (17 00)	10:00 PM (22 00)	+5
CHINA	2:00 AM* (02 00*)	5:00 AM* (05 00*)	10:00 AM* (10 00*)	+17
COLOMBIA	1:00 PM (13 00)	4:00 PM (16 00)	9:00 PM (21 00)	+4
COSTA RICA	12:00 M (12 00)	3:00 PM (15 00)	8:00 PM (20 00)	+3
CZECHOSLOVAKIA	7:00 PM (19 00)	10:00 PM (22 00)	3:00 AM* (03 00*)	+10
DENMARK	7:00 PM (19 00)	10:00 PM (22 00)	3:00 AM* (03 00*)	+10
DOMINICAN REPUBLIC	2:00 PM (14 00)	5:00 PM (17 00)	10:00 PM (22 00)	+5
ECUADOR	1:00 PM (13 00)	4:00 PM (16 00)	9:00 PM (21 00)	+4
EGYPT	8:00 PM (20 00)	11:00 PM (23 00)	4:00 AM* (04 00*)	+11
ESTONIA	8:00 PM (20 00)	11:00 PM (23 00)	4:00 AM* (04 00*)	+11

12:00 M (12 00) = Noon; 12:00 PM (00 00) = Midnight; * = Next day

Alaskan Standard Time (U.S.A.)

(Cities shown only when country observes more than one time.)	9:00 AM (09 00)	12:00 M (12 00)	5:00 PM (17 00)	YKN +/- Hrs
FINLAND	8:00 PM (20 00)	11:00 PM (23 00)	4:00 AM* (04 00*)	+11
FRANCE	7:00 PM (19 00)	10:00 PM (22 00)	3:00 AM* (03 00*)	+10
GEORGIA	9:00 PM (21 00)	12:00 PM (00 00)	5:00 AM* (05 00*)	+12
GERMANY	7:00 PM (19 00)	10:00 PM (22 00)	3:00 AM* (03 00*)	+10
GUATEMALA	12:00 M (12 00)	3:00 PM (15 00)	8:00 PM (20 00)	+3
HONG KONG	2:00 AM* (02 00*)	5:00 AM* (05 00*)	10:00 AM* (10 00*)	+17
HUNGARY	7:00 PM (19 00)	10:00 PM (22 00)	3:00 AM* (03 00*)	+10
INDIA	11:30 PM (23 30)	2:30 AM* (02 30*)	7:30 AM* (07 30*)	+14.5
INDONESIA				
Jakarta, Java	1:00 AM* (01 00*)	4:00 AM* (04 00*)	9:00 AM* (09 00*)	+16
Pontianak, Borneo	2:00 AM* (02 00*)	5:00 AM* (05 00*)	10:00 AM* (10 00*)	+17
IRELAND	6:00 PM (18 00)	9:00 PM (21 00)	2:00 AM* (02 00*)	+9
ISRAEL	8:00 PM (20 00)	11:00 PM (23 00)	4:00 AM* (04 00*)	+11
ITALY	7:00 PM (19 00)	10:00 PM (22 00)	3:00 AM* (03 00*)	+10
JAPAN	3:00 AM* (03 00*)	6:00 AM* (06 00*)	11:00 AM* (11 00*)	+18
KAZAKHSTAN				
Alma Ata	12:00 PM (00 00)	3:00 AM* (03 00*)	8:00 AM* (08 00*)	+15
Atyubinsk	11:00 PM (23 00)	2:00 AM* (02 00*)	7:00 AM* (07 00*)	+14
KOREA, REPUBLIC OF	3:00 AM* (03 00*)	6:00 AM* (06 00*)	11:00 AM* (11 00*)	+18
KYRGYZSTAN	11:00 PM (23 00)	2:00 AM* (02 00*)	7:00 AM* (07 00*)	+14
LATVIA	8:00 PM (20 00)	11:00 PM (23 00)	4:00 AM* (04 00*)	+11
LITHUANIA	8:00 PM (20 00)	11:00 PM (23 00)	4:00 AM* (04 00*)	+11
LUXEMBOURG	7:00 PM (19 00)	10:00 PM (22 00)	3:00 AM* (03 00*)	+10

(continues)

Alaskan Standard Time (U.S.A.)—continued

(Cities shown only when country observes more than one time.)	9:00 AM (09 00)	12:00 M (12 00)	5:00 PM (17 00)	YKN +/- Hrs
MALAYSIA	2:00 AM* (02 00*)	5:00 AM* (05 00*)	10:00 AM* (10 00*)	+17
MEXICO (See page 143 for additional Mexican cities.)				
Hermosillo, SON	11:00 AM (11 00)	2:00 PM (14 00)	7:00 PM (19 00)	+2
Mexico City, D.F.	12:00 M (12 00)	3:00 PM (15 00)	8:00 PM (20 00)	+3
Tijuana, B.C.N.	10:00 AM (10 00)	1:00 PM (13 00)	6:00 PM (18 00)	+1
MOLDOVA	8:00 PM (20 00)	11:00 PM (23 00)	4:00 AM* (04 00*)	+11
NETHERLANDS	7:00 PM (19 00)	10:00 PM (22 00)	3:00 AM* (03 00*)	+10
NEW ZEALAND	6:00 AM* (06 00*)	9:00 AM* (09 00*)	2:00 PM* (14 00*)	+21
NIGERIA	7:00 PM (19 00)	10:00 PM (22 00)	3:00 AM* (03 00*)	+10
NORWAY	7:00 PM (19 00)	10:00 PM (22 00)	3:00 AM* (03 00*)	+10
PAKISTAN	11:00 PM (23 00)	2:00 AM* (02 00*)	7:00 AM* (07 00*)	+14
PERU	1:00 PM (13 00)	4:00 PM (16 00)	9:00 PM (21 00)	+4
PHILIPPINES	2:00 AM* (02 00*)	5:00 AM* (05 00*)	10:00 AM* (10 00*)	+17
POLAND	7:00 PM (19 00)	10:00 PM (22 00)	3:00 AM* (03 00*)	+10
PORTUGAL	6:00 PM (18 00)	9:00 PM (21 00)	2:00 AM* (02 00*)	+9
ROMANIA	8:00 PM (20 00)	11:00 PM (23 00)	4:00 AM* (04 00*)	+11
RUSSIA				
Arkhangelsk	9:00 PM (21 00)	12:00 PM (00 00)	5:00 AM* (05 00*)	+12
Irkutsk	1:00 AM* (01 00*)	4:00 AM* (04 00*)	9:00 AM* (09 00*)	+16
Kaliningrad	7:00 PM (19 00)	10:00 PM (22 00)	3:00 AM* (03 00*)	+10
Kazan	9:00 PM (21 00)	12:00 PM (00 00)	5:00 AM* (05 00*)	+12
Khabarovsk	4:00 AM* (04 00*)	7:00 AM* (07 00*)	12:00 M* (12 00*)	+19
Magadan	5:00 AM* (05 00*)	8:00 AM* (08 00*)	1:00 PM* (13 00*)	+20

12:00 M (12 00) = Noon; 12:00 PM (00 00) = Midnight; * = Next day

Alaskan Standard Time (U.S.A.)

(Cities shown only when country observes more than one time.)	9:00 AM (09 00)	12:00 M (12 00)	5:00 PM (17 00)	YKN +/- Hrs
Moscow	9:00 PM (21 00)	12:00 PM (00 00)	5:00 AM* (05 00*)	+12
Murmansk	9:00 PM (21 00)	12:00 PM (00 00)	5:00 AM* (05 00*)	+12
Nakhodka	4:00 AM* (04 00*)	7:00 AM* (07 00*)	12:00 M* (12 00*)	+19
Nizhny Novgorod .... (formerly Gorky)	10:00 PM (22 00)	1:00 AM* (01 00*)	6:00 AM* (06 00*)	+13
Novorosslisk	9:00 PM (21 00)	12:00 PM (00 00)	5:00 AM* (05 00*)	+12
Novosibirsk	1:00 AM* (01 00*)	4:00 AM* (04 00*)	9:00 AM* (09 00*)	+16
Omsk	12:00 PM (00 00)	3:00 AM* (03 00*)	8:00 AM* (08 00*)	+15
St. Petersburg .... (formerly Leningrad)	9:00 PM (21 00)	12:00 PM (00 00)	5:00 AM* (05 00*)	+12
Samara	10:00 PM (22 00)	1:00 AM* (01 00*)	6:00 AM* (06 00*)	+13
Sverdlovsk	11:00 PM (23 00)	2:00 AM* (02 00*)	7:00 AM* (07 00*)	+14
Tomsk	1:00 AM* (01 00*)	4:00 AM* (04 00*)	9:00 AM* (09 00*)	+16
Vladivostok	4:00 AM* (04 00*)	7:00 AM* (07 00*)	12:00 M* (12 00*)	+19
Vologda	9:00 PM (21 00)	12:00 PM (00 00)	5:00 AM* (05 00*)	+12
Vostochny	10:00 PM (22 00)	1:00 AM* (01 00*)	6:00 AM* (06 00*)	+13
Yakutsk	3:00 AM* (03 00*)	6:00 AM* (06 00*)	11:00 AM* (11 00*)	+18
SAUDI ARABIA	9:00 PM (21 00)	12:00 PM (00 00)	5:00 AM* (05 00*)	+12
SINGAPORE	2:00 AM* (02 00*)	5:00 AM* (05 00*)	10:00 AM* (10 00*)	+17
SOUTH AFRICA	8:00 PM (20 00)	11:00 PM (23 00)	4:00 AM* (04 00*)	+11
SPAIN	7:00 PM (19 00)	10:00 PM (22 00)	3:00 AM* (03 00*)	+10
SWEDEN	7:00 PM (19 00)	10:00 PM (22 00)	3:00 AM* (03 00*)	+10
SWITZERLAND	7:00 PM (19 00)	10:00 PM (22 00)	3:00 AM* (03 00*)	+10
TAIWAN	2:00 AM* (02 00*)	5:00 AM* (05 00*)	10:00 AM* (10 00*)	+17

(continues)

Alaskan Standard Time (U.S.A.)—continued

(Cities shown only when country observes more than one time.)	9:00 AM (09 00)	12:00 M (12 00)	5:00 PM (17 00)	YKN +/- Hrs
TAJIKISTAN	12:00 PM (00 00)	3:00 AM* (03 00*)	8:00 AM* (08 00*)	+15
THAILAND	1:00 AM* (01 00*)	4:00 AM* (04 00*)	9:00 AM* (09 00*)	+16
TURKEY	8:00 PM (20 00)	11:00 PM (23 00)	4:00 AM* (04 00*)	+11
TURKMENISTAN	10:00 PM (22 00)	1:00 AM* (01 00*)	6:00 AM* (06 00*	+13
U.A.E.	10:00 PM (22 00)	1:00 AM* (01 00*)	6:00 AM* (06 00*)	+13
UKRAINE	8:00 PM (20 00)	11:00 PM (23 00)	4:00 AM* (04 00*)	+11
UNITED KINGDOM	6:00 PM (18 00)	9:00 PM (21 00)	2:00 AM* (02 00*)	+9
UNITED STATES (See page 142 for additional United States cities.)				
Chicago, IL	12:00 M (12 00)	3:00 PM (15 00)	8:00 PM (20 00)	+3
Denver, CO	11:00 AM (11 00)	2:00 PM (14 00)	7:00 PM (19 00)	+2
Honolulu, HI	8:00 AM (08 00)	11:00 AM (11 00)	4:00 PM (16 00)	-1
Juneau, AK	9:00 AM (09 00)	12:00 M (12 00)	5:00 PM (17 00)	
Los Angeles, CA	10:00 AM (10 00)	1:00 PM (13 00)	6:00 PM (18 00)	+1
New York, NY	1:00 PM (13 00)	4:00 PM (16 00)	9:00 PM (21 00)	+4
UZBEKISTAN	11:00 PM (23 00)	2:00 AM* (02 00*)	7:00 AM* (07 00*)	+14
VENEZUELA	2:00 PM (14 00)	5:00 PM (17 00)	10:00 PM (22 00)	+5

Hawaiian Standard Time (U.S.A.)

(Cities shown only when country observes more than one time.)	9:00 AM (09 00)	12:00 M (12 00)	5:00 PM (17 00)	HI +/- Hrs
ALGERIA	8:00 PM (20 00)	11:00 PM (23 00)	4:00 AM* (04 00*)	+11
ANGOLA	8:00 PM (20 00)	11:00 PM (23 00)	4:00 AM* (04 00*)	+11
ARGENTINA	4:00 PM (16 00)	7:00 PM (19 00)	12:00 PM (00 00)	+7

12:00 M (12 00) = Noon; 12:00 PM (00 00) = Midnight; * = Next day

Hawaiian Standard Time (U.S.A.)

(Cities shown only when country observes more than one time.)	9:00 AM (09 00)	12:00 M (12 00)	5:00 PM (17 00)	HI +/- Hrs
ARMENIA	10:00 PM (22 00)	1:00 AM* (01 00*)	6:00 AM* (06 00*)	+13
AUSTRALIA				
Adelaide, SA	4:30 AM* (04 30*)	7:30 AM* (07 30*)	12:30 PM* (12 30*)	+19.5
Perth, WA	3:00 AM* (03 00*)	6:00 AM* (06 00*)	11:00 AM* (11 00*)	+18
Sydney, NSW	5:00 AM* (05 00*)	8:00 AM* (08 00*)	1:00 PM* (13 00*)	+20
AUSTRIA	8:00 PM (20 00)	11:00 PM (23 00)	4:00 AM* (04 00*)	+11
AZERBAIJAN	10:00 PM (22 00)	1:00 AM* (01 00*)	6:00 AM* (06 00*)	+13
BELARUS	9:00 PM (21 00)	12:00 PM (00 00)	5:00 AM* (05 00*)	+12
BELGIUM	8:00 PM (20 00)	11:00 PM (23 00)	4:00 AM* (04 00*)	+11
BRAZIL	4:00 PM (16 00)	7:00 PM (19 00)	12:00 PM (00 00)	+7
BULGARIA	9:00 PM (21 00)	12:00 PM (00 00)	5:00 AM* (05 00*)	+12
CANADA (See page 143 for additional Canadian cities.)				
Edmonton, AB	12:00 M (12 00)	3:00 PM (15 00)	8:00 PM (20 00)	+3
Halifax, NS	3:00 PM (15 00)	6:00 PM (18 00)	11:00 PM (23 00)	+6
Regina, SK	1:00 PM (13 00)	4:00 PM (16 00)	9:00 PM (21 00)	+4
St. John's, NF	3:30 PM (15 30)	6:30 PM (18 30)	11:30 PM (23 30)	+6.5
Toronto, ON	2:00 PM (14 00)	5:00 PM (17 00)	10:00 PM (22 00)	+5
Vancouver, BC	11:00 AM (11 00)	2:00 PM (14 00)	7:00 PM (19 00)	+2
CHILE	3:00 PM (15 00)	6:00 PM (18 00)	11:00 PM (23 00)	+6
CHINA	3:00 AM* (03 00*)	6:00 AM* (06 00*)	11:00 AM* (11 00*)	+18
COLOMBIA	2:00 PM (14 00)	5:00 PM (17 00)	10:00 PM (22 00)	+5
COSTA RICA	1:00 PM (13 00)	4:00 PM (16 00)	9:00 PM (21 00)	+4
CZECHOSLOVAKIA	8:00 PM (20 00)	11:00 PM (23 00)	4:00 AM* (04 00*)	+11

(continues)

Hawaiian Standard Time (U.S.A.)—*continued*

(Cities shown only when country observes more than one time.)	9:00 AM (09 00)	12:00 M (12 00)	5:00 PM (17 00)	HI +/- Hrs
DENMARK	8:00 PM (20 00)	11:00 PM (23 00)	4:00 AM* (04 00*)	+11
DOMINICAN REPUBLIC	3:00 PM (15 00)	6:00 PM (18 00)	11:00 PM (23 00)	+6
ECUADOR	2:00 PM (14 00)	5:00 PM (17 00)	10:00 PM (22 00)	+5
EGYPT	9:00 PM (21 00)	12:00 PM (00 00)	5:00 AM* (05 00*)	+12
ESTONIA	9:00 PM (21 00)	12:00 PM (00 00)	5:00 AM* (05 00*)	+12
FINLAND	9:00 PM (21 00)	12:00 PM (00 00)	5:00 AM* (05 00*)	+12
FRANCE	8:00 PM (20 00)	11:00 PM (23 00)	4:00 AM* (04 00*)	+11
GEORGIA	10:00 PM (22 00)	1:00 AM* (01 00*)	6:00 AM* (06 00*)	+13
GERMANY	8:00 PM (20 00)	11:00 PM (23 00)	4:00 AM* (04 00*)	+11
GUATEMALA	1:00 PM (13 00)	4:00 PM (16 00)	9:00 PM (21 00)	+4
HONG KONG	3:00 AM* (03 00*)	6:00 AM* (06 00*)	11:00 AM* (11 00*)	+18
HUNGARY	8:00 PM (20 00)	11:00 PM (23 00)	4:00 AM* (04 00*)	+11
INDIA	12:30 PM (00 30)	3:30 AM* (03 30*)	8:30 AM* (08 30*)	+15.5
INDONESIA				
Jakarta, Java	2:00 AM* (02 00*)	5:00 AM* (05 00)*)	10:00 AM* (10 00*)	+17
Pontianak, Borneo	3:00 AM* (03 00*)	6:00 AM* (06 00*)	11:00 AM* (11 00*)	+18
IRELAND	7:00 PM (19 00)	10:00 PM (22 00)	3:00 AM* (03 00*)	+10
ISRAEL	9:00 PM (21 00)	12:00 PM (00 00)	5:00 AM* (05 00*)	+12
ITALY	8:00 PM (20 00)	11:00 PM (23 00)	4:00 AM* (04 00*)	+11
JAPAN	4:00 AM* (04 00*)	7:00 AM* (07 00*)	12:00 PM* (12 00*)	+19
KAZAKHSTAN				
Alma Ata	1:00 AM* (01 00*)	4:00 AM* (04 00*)	9:00 AM* (09 00*)	+16
Atyubinsk	12:00 PM (00 00)	3:00 AM* (03 00*)	8:00 AM* (08 00*)	+15

12:00 M (12 00) = Noon; 12:00 PM (00 00) = Midnight; * = Next day

Hawaiian Standard Time (U.S.A.)

(Cities shown only when country observes more than one time.)	9:00 AM (09 00)	12:00 M (12 00)	5:00 PM (17 00)	HI +/- Hrs
KOREA, REPUBLIC OF	4:00 AM* (04 00*)	7:00 AM* (07 00*)	12:00 PM* (12 00*)	+19
KYRGYZSTAN	12:00 PM (00 00)	3:00 AM* (03 00*)	8:00 AM* (08 00*)	+15
LATVIA	9:00 PM (21 00)	12:00 PM (00 00)	5:00 AM* (05 00*)	+12
LITHUANIA	9:00 PM (21 00)	12:00 PM (00 00)	5:00 AM* (05 00*)	+12
LUXEMBOURG	8:00 PM (20 00)	11:00 PM (23 00)	4:00 AM* (04 00*)	+11
MALAYSIA	3:00 AM* (03 00*)	6:00 AM* (06 00*)	11:00 AM* (11 00*)	+18
MEXICO (See page 143 for additional Mexican cities.)				
Hermosillo, SON	12:00 M (12 00)	3:00 PM (15 00)	8:00 PM (20 00)	+3
Mexico City, D.F.	1:00 PM (13 00)	4:00 PM (16 00)	9:00 PM (21 00)	+4
Tijuana, B.C.N.	11:00 AM (11 00)	2:00 PM (14 00)	7:00 PM (19 00)	+2
MOLDOVA	9:00 PM (21 00)	12:00 PM (00 00)	5:00 AM* (005 00*)	+12
NETHERLANDS	8:00 PM (20 00)	11:00 PM (23 00)	4:00 AM* (04 00*)	+11
NEW ZEALAND	7:00 AM* (07 00*)	10:00 AM* (10 00*)	3:00 PM* (15 00*)	+22
NIGERIA	8:00 PM (20 00)	11:00 PM (23 00)	4:00 AM* (04 00*)	+11
NORWAY	8:00 PM (20 00)	11:00 PM (23 00)	4:00 AM* (04 00*)	+11
PAKISTAN	12:00 PM (00 00)	3:00 AM* (03 00*)	8:00 AM* (08 00*)	+15
PERU	2:00 PM (14 00)	5:00 PM (17 00)	10:00 PM (22 00)	+5
PHILIPPINES	3:00 AM* (03 00*)	6:00 AM* (06 00*)	11:00 AM* (11 00*)	+18
POLAND	8:00 PM (20 00)	11:00 PM (23 00)	4:00 AM* (04 00*)	+11
PORTUGAL	7:00 PM (19 00)	10:00 PM (22 00)	3:00 AM* (03 00*)	+10
ROMANIA	9:00 PM (21 00)	12:00 PM (00 00)	5:00 AM* (05 00*)	+12
RUSSIA				
Arkhangelsk	10:00 PM (22 00)	1:00 AM* (01 00*)	6:00 AM* (06 00*)	+13

(continues)

Hawaiian Standard Time (U.S.A.)—*continued*

(Cities shown only when country observes more than one time.)	9:00 AM (09 00)	12:00 M (12 00)	5:00 PM (17 00)	HI +/- Hrs
Irkutsk	2:00 AM* (02 00*)	5:00 AM* (05 00*)	10:00 AM* (10 00*)	+17
Kaliningrad	8:00 PM (20 00)	11:00 PM (23 00)	4:00 AM* (04 00*)	+11
Kazan	10:00 PM (22 00)	1:00 AM* (01 00*)	6:00 AM* (06 00*)	+13
Khabarovsk	5:00 AM* (05 00*)	8:00 AM* (08 00*)	1:00 PM* (13 00*)	+20
Magadan	6:00 AM* (06 00*)	9:00 AM* (09 00*)	2:00 PM* (14 00*)	+21
Moscow	10:00 PM (22 00)	1:00 AM* (01 00*)	6:00 AM* (06 00*)	+13
Murmansk	10:00 PM (22 00)	1:00 AM* (01 00*)	6:00 AM* (06 00*)	+13
Nakhodka	5:00 AM* (05 00*)	8:00 AM* (08 00*)	1:00 PM* (13 00*)	+20
Nizhny Novgorod . . . . (formerly Gorky)	11:00 PM (23 00)	2:00 AM* (02 00*)	7:00 AM* (07 00*)	+14
Novorosslisk	10:00 PM (22 00)	1:00 AM* (01 00*)	6:00 AM* (06 00*)	+13
Novosibirsk	2:00 AM* (02 00*)	5:00 AM* (05 00*)	10:00 AM* (10 00*)	+17
Omsk	1:00 AM* (01 00*)	4:00 AM* (04 00*)	9:00 AM* (09 00*)	+16
St. Petersburg . . . . (formerly Leningrad)	10:00 PM (22 00)	1:00 AM* (01 00*)	6:00 AM* (06 00*)	+13
Samara	11:00 PM (23 00)	2:00 AM* (02 00*)	7:00 AM* (07 00*)	+14
Sverdlovsk	12:00 PM (00 00)	3:00 AM* (03 00*)	8:00 AM* (08 00*)	+15
Tomsk	2:00 AM* (02 00*)	5:00 AM* (05 00*)	10:00 AM* (10 00*)	+17
Vladivostok	5:00 AM* (05 00*)	8:00 AM* (08 00*)	1:00 PM* (13 00*)	+20
Vologda	10:00 PM (22 00)	1:00 AM* (01 00*)	6:00 AM* (06 00*)	+13
Vostochny	11:00 PM (23 00)	2:00 AM* (02 00*)	7:00 AM* (07 00*)	+14
Yakutsk	4:00 AM* (04 00*)	7:00 AM* (07 00*)	12:00 PM* (12 00*)	+19
SAUDI ARABIA	10:00 PM (22 00)	1:00 AM* (01 00*)	6:00 AM* (06 00*)	+13
SINGAPORE	3:00 AM* (03 00*)	6:00 AM* (06 00*)	11:00 AM* (11 00*)	+18

12:00 M (12 00) = Noon; 12:00 PM (00 00) = Midnight; * = Next day

Hawaiian Standard Time (U.S.A.)

(Cities shown only when country observes more than one time.)	9:00 AM (09 00)	12:00 M (12 00)	5:00 PM (17 00)	HI +/- Hrs
SOUTH AFRICA	9:00 PM (21 00)	12:00 PM (00 00)	5:00 AM* (05 00*)	+12
SPAIN	8:00 PM (20 00)	11:00 PM (23 00)	4:00 AM* (04 00*)	+11
SWEDEN	8:00 PM (20 00)	11:00 PM (23 00)	4:00 AM* (04 00*)	+11
SWITZERLAND	8:00 PM (20 00)	11:00 PM (23 00)	4:00 AM* (04 00*)	+11
TAIWAN	3:00 AM* (03 00*)	6:00 AM* (06 00*)	11:00 AM* (11 00*)	+18
TAJIKISTAN	1:00 AM* (01 00*)	4:00 AM* (04 00*)	9:00 AM* (09 00*)	+16
THAILAND	2:00 AM* (02 00*)	5:00 AM* (05 00*)	10:00 AM* (10 00*)	+17
TURKEY	9:00 PM (21 00)	12:00 PM (00 00)	5:00 AM* (05 00*)	+12
TURKMENISTAN	11:00 PM (23 00)	2:00 AM* (02 00*)	7:00 AM* (07 00*)	+14
U.A.E.	11:00 PM (23 00)	2:00 AM* (02 00*)	7:00 AM* (07 00*)	+14
UKRAINE	9:00 PM (21 00)	12:00 PM (00 00)	5:00 AM* (05 00*)	+12
UNITED KINGDOM	7:00 PM (19 00)	10:00 PM (22 00)	3:00 AM* (03 00*)	+10
UNITED STATES (See page 142 for additional United States cities.)				
Chicago, IL	1:00 PM (13 00)	4:00 PM (16 00)	9:00 PM (21 00)	+4
Denver, CO	12:00 M (12 00)	3:00 PM (15 00)	8:00 PM (20 00)	+3
Honolulu, HI	9:00 AM (09 00)	12:00 M (12 00)	5:00 PM (17 00)	
Juneau, AK	10:00 AM (10 00)	1:00 PM (13 00)	6:00 PM (18 00)	+1
Los Angeles, CA	11:00 AM (11 00)	2:00 PM (14 00)	7:00 PM (19 00)	+2
New York, NY	2:00 PM (14 00)	5:00 PM (17 00)	10:00 PM (22 00)	+5
UZBEKISTAN	12:00 PM (00 00)	3:00 AM* (03 00*)	8:00 AM* (08 00*)	+15
VENEZUELA	3:00 PM (15 00)	6:00 PM (18 00)	11:00 PM (23 00)	+6

BUSINESS AND BANKING HOURS

Banking and business hours are the generally observed hours when banks and businesses are open. There are, of course, many exceptions and variations. Government office hours are similar.

For information on prayer calls and Ramadan, observed by Muslims in all countries, refer to the entry for Saudi Arabia.

Many countries use the 24-hour time system. The hours are numbered 1 to 24 starting at 1 a.m., not 1 to 12 a.m. and then 1 to 12 p.m. In the 24-hour system, 1 p.m. would be 1300 hours and 8 p.m. would be 2000 hours. For example, a German letterhead might show something like the following.

Burozeiten: Mo.-Fr.8.00 - 12.00 u. 14.00 - 17.00 Uhr

This means office hours (*burozeiten*) are Monday–Friday from 8 a.m. to 12 noon and (*u.*) 2 p.m. to 5 p.m. The office is closed for two hours at lunchtime. See page 141 for more on 12-hour and 24-hour time.

Algeria
Business hours: Sat–Wed, 8:30 a.m. to noon, 2 p.m. to 6 p.m.
Banking hours: Sat–Wed, 8 a.m. to noon, 2 p.m. to 4 p.m.
Angola
Business hours: Mon–Fri, 8 a.m. to noon, 3 p.m. to 7 p.m.; Sat 8 a.m. to noon.
Banking hours: Mon–Fri, 8 a.m. to noon.
Argentina
Business hours: Mon–Fri, 9 a.m. to 7 p.m.
Banking hours: Mon–Fri, 10 a.m. to 4 p.m.
Australia
Business hours: Mon–Fri, 9 a.m. to 5 p.m.
Banking hours: Mon–Thu, 9:30 a.m. to 4 p.m., Fri, 9:30 a.m. to 5 p.m.
Austria
Business hours: 8 a.m. to 4 p.m.
Banking hours: 8 a.m. to 4 p.m.
Belgium
Business hours: Mon–Fri, 9 a.m. to noon, 2 p.m. to 5:30 p.m.; Sat, 9 a.m. to noon
Banking hours: Mon–Fri, 9 a.m. to 3:30 p.m.
Brazil
Business hours: Mon–Fri, 8 a.m. to 6 p.m.
Banking hours: Mon–Fri, 10 a.m. to 4:30 p.m.
Bulgaria
Business hours: Mon–Fri, 8:30 a.m. to noon, 1 p.m. to 4:30 p.m.; Sat, 8:30 a.m. to 1:30 p.m.
Banking hours: Mon–Fri, 8 a.m. to 2:30 p.m.

Canada
Business hours: Mon–Fri, 9 a.m. to 5 p.m.
Banking hours: Mon–Thu, 10 a.m. to 3 p.m.; Fri, 10 a.m. to 6 p.m.
Chile
Business hours: Mon–Fri, 9 a.m. to 6 p.m.
Banking hours: Mon–Fri, 9 a.m. to 2 p.m.
China
Business hours: Mon–Sun, 8:30 a.m. to 6 p.m.
Banking hours: Mon–Sat 9 a.m. to noon, 2 p.m. to 6 p.m.
Colombia
Business hours: Mon–Sat, 9 a.m. to noon, 2 p.m. to 6 p.m.
Banking hours: Mon–Fri, 9 a.m. to 3 p.m. Last day of month, 9 a.m. to noon
Costa Rica
Business hours: Mon–Fri, 8 a.m. to 12:30 p.m., 1:30 to 5:30 p.m.; Sat, 8 a.m. to noon
Banking hours: Mon–Fri, 8 a.m. to 11 a.m., 1:30 p.m. to 3 p.m.; Sat, 8 a.m. to 11 a.m.
Czechoslovakia
Business hours: Mon–Sat, 8 a.m. to 4 p.m.
Banking hours: Mon–Fri, 8 a.m. to 2 p.m.
Denmark
Business hours: 9 a.m. to 4 p.m. Some companies close early on Friday.
Banking hours: Mon–Fri, 10 a.m. to 4 p.m., except Thursday, when open to 6 p.m.
Dominican Republic
Business hours: Mon–Fri, 8 a.m. to noon, 2 p.m. to 6 p.m.
Banking hours: Mon–Fri, 8:30 a.m to 4:30 p.m.
Ecuador
Business hours: Mon–Fri, 8:30 a.m. to 12:30 p.m., 2:30 p.m. to 6:30 p.m.
Banking hours: Mon–Fri, 9 a.m to 1:30 p.m.
Egypt
Business hours: Sun–Thu, 9 a.m. to 2 p.m., 5 p.m. to 8 p.m.
Banking hours: Sun–Thu, 8 a.m. to 2 p.m.
Finland
Business hours: 8 a.m. to 5 p.m. Summer 8 a.m. to 4 p.m.
Banking hours: Mon–Fri, 9 a.m. to 4:30 p.m.
France
Business hours: Mon–Fri, 9 a.m. to noon, 2 p.m. to 6 p.m.
Banking hours: Mon–Fri, 9 a.m. to noon, 1:30 p.m. to 4:30 p.m. Banks close one half day before a public holiday. If Tuesday is a holiday, banks take Monday off also.
Germany
Business hours: 8:30 a.m. to 5 p.m.
Banking hours: Mon–Wed, and Fri, 9 a.m. to 1 p.m., 3 p.m. to 4 p.m.; Thu, 9 a.m. to 1 p.m., 3 p.m. to 5:30 p.m.
Guatemala
Business hours: Mon–Fri, 9 a.m. to 12:30 p.m., 3 p.m. to 7 p.m.; Sat, 9 a.m. to 1 p.m.
Banking hours: Mon–Fri, 9 a.m. to 3 p.m.

Hong Kong
Business hours: Mon–Fri, 8:30 a.m. to 1 p.m., 2 p.m. to 5 p.m.; Sat, 8:30 a.m. to 12:30 p.m.
Banking hours: Mon–Fri, 9 a.m. to 4 p.m.; Sat, 9 a.m. to noon
Many businesses and banks are open longer than the hours given above.

Hungary
Business hours: Mon–Fri, 8 a.m. to 5:30 p.m.
Banking hours: Mon–Fri, 9 a.m. to 1 p.m.; Sat, 9 a.m. to 11 a.m.

India
Business hours: Mon–Fri, 10 a.m. to 5 p.m.
Banking hours: Mon–Fri, 10 a.m. to 2 p.m.; Sat, 10 a.m. to noon

Indonesia
Business hours: Mon–Fri, 8 a.m. to 4 p.m.; Sat, 8 a.m. to 1 p.m.
Banking hours: Mon–Fri, 8 a.m. to 12:30 p.m., 1 p.m. to 4 p.m; Sat, 8 a.m. to 12:30 p.m.

Ireland
Business hours: Mon–Fri, 9 a.m. to 1 p.m., 2 p.m. to 5:30 p.m.
Banking hours: Mon–Fri, 10 a.m. to 12:30 p.m., 1:30 p.m. to 3 p.m.; Thu, 10 a.m. to 12:30 p.m., 1:30 p.m. to 5 p.m.

Israel
Business hours: Sun–Thu, 8 a.m. to 4 p.m. Closed Fri and Sat.
Banking hours: Sun–Thu, 8:30 a.m. to 1:30 p.m. Closed Friday afternoon and all day Saturday.

Italy
Business hours: Mon–Fri, 8 or 9 a.m. to noon or 1 p.m., 3 p.m. to 6 or 7 p.m.
Banking hours: Mon–Fri, 8:30 a.m. to 1:30 p.m., 2:45 p.m to 3:45 p.m.

Japan
Business hours: Mon–Fri, 9 a.m. to 5 p.m.; Sat, 9 a.m. to noon
Banking hours: Mon–Fri, 9 a.m. to 3 p.m.

Korea, Republic of
Business hours: Mon–Fri, 9 a.m. to 6 p.m. or later.
Banking hours: Mon–Fri, 9:30 a.m. to 4:30 p.m.; Sat, 9:30 a.m. to 1:30 p.m.

Luxembourg
Business hours: Mon–Fri, 9 a.m. to noon, 2 p.m. to 6 p.m.
Banking hours: Mon–Fri, 9 a.m. to noon, 3:30 p.m. to 4:30 p.m.

Malaysia
Business hours: Mon–Fri, 8 a.m. to 4:30 p.m.; Sat, 8 a.m. to 12:45 p.m.
Banking hours: Mon–Fri, 10 a.m. to 3 p.m.; Sat, 9:30 a.m. to 11:30 a.m.
In the fasting month of Ramadan, business hours are from 8 a.m. to 2 p.m.

Mexico
Business hours: Mon–Fri, 9 a.m. to 5 p.m. In northern cities the lunch break is likely to be one hour starting at 12:30 p.m. or 1 p.m. as in the United States; further south it may be later, between 2 p.m. and 4 p.m.
Banking hours: 9 a.m. to 1:30 p.m.

Netherlands
Business hours: Mon–Fri, 8:30 a.m. to 5:30 p.m.
Banking hours: Mon–Fri, 9 a.m. to 4 p.m.

New Zealand
Business hours: Mon–Fri, 9 a.m. to 5 p.m.
Banking hours: 9 a.m. to 4 p.m.

Nigeria
Business hours: Mon–Fri, 8 a.m. to 12:30 p.m., 2 p.m. to 4:30 p.m.; Sat, 8 a.m. to 12:30 p.m.
Banking hours: Mon–Thu, 8 a.m. to 1 p.m.; Fri, 8 a.m. to 3 p.m.

Norway
Business hours: Mon–Fri, 8 a.m. to 4 p.m.; Sat, 9 a.m. to 1 p.m.
Banking hours Mon–Fri, 8:45 a.m. to 3:45 p.m.; Thu, 8:15 a.m. to 6 p.m.

Pakistan
Business hours: Sat–Thu, 9 a.m. to 1 p.m., 2 p.m. to 5:30 p.m.
Banking hours: Sat–Thu, 9 a.m. to 1 p.m.

Peru
Business hours: Mon–Fri, 9 a.m. to 3 p.m.; Sat, 8:30 a.m. to noon
Banking hours: Mon–Fri, 9 a.m. to 1 p.m.

Philippines
Business hours: Mon–Fri, 8 a.m. to 5 p.m., or 9 a.m. to 6 p.m. Some companies are open 9 a.m. to noon on Sat.
Banking hours: Mon–Fri, 10 a.m. to 3 p.m.

Poland
Business hours: Mon–Sat, 8:30 a.m. to 3:30 p.m.
Banking hours: Mon–Sat, 8:30 a.m. to 12:30 p.m., 1 p.m. to 4:30 p.m.

Portugal
Business hours: Mon–Fri, 9 a.m. to 1 p.m., 3 p.m. to 7 p.m.
Banking hours: Mon–Fri, 8:30 a.m. to 2:45 p.m.

Romania
Business hours: Mon–Fri, 7:30 a.m. to 4 p.m.; Sat, 8 a.m. to 12:30 p.m.
Banking hours: Mon–Fri, 8:30 a.m. to 1:30 p.m.; Sat, 8 a.m. to 12:30 p.m.

Russia
Business hours: Mon–Fri, 9 a.m. to 6 p.m.
Banking hours: Mon–Fri, 9 a.m. to 1 p.m.

Saudi Arabia
Business hours: Sun–Wed or Thu, 8 a.m. to noon, 3 p.m. to 6 p.m.
Friday is the day of worship.
Banking: Sun–Wed, 8 a.m. to noon, 5 p.m. to 8 p.m.
The fasting month of Ramadan and the season of the Hajj are special religious occasions when businesses and shops may observe different hours, for example, open from 9 a.m. to 3 p.m. and in the evening. Because the months in the Islamic calendar move throughout the years Ramadan occurs in different seasons in different years.
Business is conducted before and after daily prayer calls. Of the five calls, the noon, afternoon, and sunset calls are most likely to fall during working hours. A prayer schedule with exact times for a full year may be obtained from a consulate or other organization if it is important for you to know when these brief moments will occur.

Singapore
Business hours: Mon–Fri, 8 a.m. to 5:30 p.m.
Banking hours: Mon–Fri, 10 a.m. to 3 p.m.; Sat, 9:30 a.m. to 11:30 a.m.

South Africa
Business hours: 8 a.m. to 4:30 p.m. or 9 a.m. to 5:30 p.m.
Banking hours: Mon–Fri, 9 a.m. to 3:30 p.m.; Sat, 8:30 a.m. to 11 a.m.

Spain
Business hours: Mon–Fri, 9 a.m. to 5 p.m., except from the end of June until mid-September when hours are 8 a.m. to 3 p.m.
Banking hours: Mon–Fri, 9 a.m. to 2 p.m.
Sweden
Business hours: Mon–Fri, 9 a.m. to 5 p.m.
Banking hours: Mon–Fri, 9:30 a.m. to 3 p.m.
Switzerland
Business hours: Mon–Fri, 8 a.m. to 6 p.m.
Banking hours: Mon–Fri, 8:30 a.m. to 12:30 p.m., 1:30 p.m. to 5 p.m.
Taiwan
Business hours: Mon–Fri, 9 a.m. to 6 p.m.; Sat, 8:30 a.m. to noon
Banking hours: Mon–Fri, 9 a.m. to 3:30 p.m.; Sat, 9 a.m. to noon
Thailand
Business hours: Mon–Fri, 8 a.m. to 5 p.m.; Sat, 8 a.m. to noon
Banking hours: Mon–Fri, 8:30 a.m. to 3:30 p.m.
Turkey
Business hours: Mon–Fri, 8:30 a.m. to 5:30 p.m. or 9 a.m. to 6 p.m.
Banking hours: Mon–Fri, 8:30 a.m. to noon, 1:30 p.m. to 6 p.m.
United Arab Emirates
Business hours: Sat–Thu, 8 a.m. to 1 p.m., 4 p.m. to 7 p.m. People often take Thursday off.
Banking hours: Sat–Thu, 8 a.m to noon or 2 p.m. (shorter hours during Ramadan)
United Kingdom
Business hours: Mon–Fri, 9 a.m. to 5:30 p.m.
Banking hours: Mon–Fri, 9:30 a.m. to 3:30 or 4 p.m.
United States
Business hours: Mon–Fri, 9 a.m. to 5 p.m.
Banking hours: Mon–Thu, 9 a.m. to 3 p.m.; Fri, 9 a.m. to 6 p.m.; Sat, 9 a.m. to noon
Venezuela
Business hours: Mon–Fri, 8 a.m to noon, 2 p.m. to 6 p.m.
Banking hours: Mon–Fri, 8:30 a.m. to 11:30 a.m., 2 p.m. to 4:30 p.m.

HOLIDAYS

Many holidays are observed around the world for many different purposes: to celebrate religious occasions and historic events of national importance, to promote social welfare, to enjoy nature and life.

Holiday dates may be determined by the moon or the stars; they may be moved to the first or last day of the working week for the convenience of business. Sometimes the exact dates are determined years in advance and other times they are set only a few months in advance. Some holidays are not observed as business holidays every year. Countries undergoing major political change, such as those of the former Soviet

Union and Czechoslovakia, may cease to observe some holidays and start observing new ones. Refer to Part 15 for the predominant religion of each country for an idea of religious holidays that are observed.

Sometimes holidays are known by several different names, such as Memorial Day, also known as Decoration Day, in the United States.

Some countries honor official birthdays of their rulers. Countries in the British Commonwealth observe the Queen's Birthday, in honor of Queen Elizabeth II. The Dutch observe their queen's birthday, the Japanese their emperor's birthday.

For all these reasons it is important to check with a reliable source close to the time you need to know about forthcoming holidays. Embassies, consulates, chambers of commerce, and travel agents are good sources.

Weekly Holiday

Most countries observe one or two nonworking days a week when businesses, banks, and government offices are closed, although shops may be open. In predominantly Christian countries, these days are Saturday and Sunday. In Muslim countries they are Thursday and Friday. In Israel they are Friday and Saturday.

In some countries where the work week is Monday to Friday, some people work Saturday morning as well (in Hong Kong and Japan, for example).

☞ See pages 182–186 for business and banking hours by country.

Fixed and Variable Holidays

Some holidays, like the American Independence Day, or Fourth of July, are fixed—that is, always observed on the same day of the same month from year to year. Others, especially religious ones, are variable; they are observed on different days and sometimes in different months from one year to the next. These include many religious holidays that are determined by the lunar calendar, including the Chinese New Year, the Christian Easter, the Muslim month of Ramadan.

When important fixed holidays fall on normal nonworking days, the next working day may be a holiday. The day after Christmas, December 26, or the next working day, is a holiday in many countries, called Boxing Day in the United Kingdom and Boxing Day or St. Stephen's Day elsewhere.

Optional and Regional Holidays

There are many regional and optional holidays as well that are observed only in certain regions or by some people and not by others. Whether a business is closed for a national or a regional holiday it is still closed and you can be unpleasantly surprised if you are not aware of it ahead of time.

Major Religious Holidays and Festivals

Information is given below on fixed and variable holidays of the Western Christian church. Eastern Christianity includes a number of groups. Eastern Orthodoxy is present in Russia, Romania, Bulgaria, Greece, Georgia, and elsewhere. Eastern Catholicism is present in Ukraine. Still other groups are found through the Middle East eastward to India. Holy days and feasts with the same name as in the Western Church may not be observed on the same day as in the West or as in other Eastern churches.

Western Christian Holidays

Important fixed Western Christian Holidays: Epiphany (Jan.6), Assumption (Aug. 15), All Saints' Day (Nov. 1), All Souls' Day (Nov. 2), Immaculate Conception (Dec. 8), Christmas (Dec. 25), St. Stephen's Day (Dec. 26).

Muslim Holidays

Two of the most important Muslim holidays are Eid al Fitr and Eid al Adha. Eid al Fitr celebrates the breaking of the annual Ramadan fast. It begins on the 25th day of the month of Ramadan and lasts through the 5th day of the following month of Shawal.

Eid al Adha, celebrating the pilgrimage to Mecca, lasts approximately 10 days from the 5th to the 15th of the month of Dhul-Hijjah.

The fasting month of Ramadan and the season Hajj are special religious occasions. During Ramadan, businesses may observe different hours, being open from 9 a.m. to 3 p.m. and in the evening.

The dates of the Muslim religious occasions change each year according to the lunar calendar. The religious day for Muslims begins at sunset of the preceding day.

Chinese Holidays

The Chinese New Year is celebrated by Chinese people throughout the world. The date is fixed to occur with the second new moon after the winter solstice, which is sometime between January 21 and February 19.

Important Jewish Holidays, 1993–1997

	1993	1994	1995	1996	1997
Purim	Mar. 7	Feb. 25	Mar. 16	Mar. 5	n.a.
Passover	Apr. 6	Mar. 27	Apr. 15	Apr. 4	Apr. 22
Shavuot	May 26	May 16	June 4	May 24	June 11
Rosh Hashanah	Sept. 16	Sept. 6	Sept. 25	Sept. 14	Oct. 2
Yom Kippur	Sept. 25	Sept. 15	Oct. 4	Sept. 23	Oct. 11
Succot	Sept. 30	Sept. 20	Oct. 9	Sept. 28	Oct. 16
Simchat Tora	Oct. 7	Sept. 27	Oct. 16	Oct. 5	Oct. 23
Chanukah	Dec. 9	Nov. 28	Dec. 18	Dec. 6	n.a.

Important Western Christian Holidays, 1993–1997

	1993	1994	1995	1996	1997
Ash Wednesday	Feb. 24	Feb. 16	Mar. 1	Feb. 21	Feb. 12
Holy (Maundy) Thursday	Apr. 8	Mar. 31	Apr. 13	Apr. 4	Mar. 27
Good Friday	Apr. 9	Apr. 1	Apr. 14	Apr. 5	Mar. 28
Easter	Apr. 11	Apr. 3	Apr. 16	Apr. 7	Mar. 30
Easter Monday	Apr. 12	Apr. 4	Apr. 17	Apr. 8	Mar. 31
Ascension	May 20	May 12	May 25	May 16	May 9
Whit or Pentecoste Monday	May 31	May 23	June 5	May 27	May 19
Corpus Christi	June 10	June 2	June 15	June 6	May 29

Important Muslim Holidays

	1992/1993	1993/1994	1994/1995
Islamic New Year's Day	July 1, 1992	June 20, 1993	June 9, 1994
Ashoora	July 10, 1992	June 29, 1993	June 18, 1994
Muhammad's Birthday	Sept. 9, 1992	Aug. 29, 1993	Aug. 18, 1994
Lailat Al-Mi'raj	Jan. 20, 1993	Jan. 9, 1994	Dec. 29, 1994
Lailat Al-Bara'a	Feb. 6, 1993	Jan. 26, 1994	Jan. 15, 1995
Ramadan Begins	Feb. 22, 1993	Feb. 11, 1994	Jan. 31, 1995
Lailat Al Qadar	Mar. 20, 1993	Mar. 9, 1994	Feb. 26, 1995
Eid Al Fitr	Mar. 24, 1993	Mar. 13, 1994	Mar. 2, 1995
Pilgrimage Begins	May 22, 1993	May 11, 1994	April 30, 1995
Eid Al Adha	May 31, 1993	May 20, 1994	May 9, 1995

Important Chinese Holidays, 1993–1997

	1993	1994	1995	1996	1997
New Year Day	Jan. 23	Feb. 10	Jan. 31	Feb. 19	Feb. 7
Lantern Festival	Feb. 6	Feb. 24	Feb. 14	Mar. 4	Feb. 21
Ch'ing Ming Day	Apr. 5/6	Apr. 5/6	Apr. 5/6	Apr. 5/6	Apr. 5/6
Dragon Boat Festival	June 24	June 13	June 2	June 20	June 9
Autumn Festival	Sept. 30	Sept. 20	Sept. 9	Sept. 27	Sept. 16

Holidays by Country

Algeria

Jan. 1　New Year's Day
May 1　Labor Day
June 19 Ben Bella's Overthrow
July 5　Independence Day
Nov. 1　Anniversary of the Revolution

Variable: Muslim religious holidays

Angola

Jan. 1　New Year's Day
Feb. 4
May 1　Labor Day
Nov. 2
Nov. 11　National Day
Dec. 10
Dec. 25　Christmas

Argentina

Jan. 1　New Year's Day
May 1　Labor Day
May 25　Revolution Day
June 10 Sovereignty Day
June 20 Flag Day
July 9　Independence Day
Aug. 17　Death of San Martin
Oct. 12　Columbus Day
Dec. 8　Virgin's Day
Dec. 25　Christmas
Dec. 31　New Year's Eve

Variable: Holy Thursday, Good Friday

Armenia

Sept. 21 National Holiday

Australia

Some holidays are not celebrated on the day shown below or in the same season in some parts of Australia.
Jan. 1　New Year's Day
Jan. 26　Australia Day (Or first
　　　　　Monday after)
Apr. 25　Anzac Day
Dec. 25　Christmas

Variable: Good Friday, Easter Saturday, Easter Monday, Queen's Birthday, Labor Day, Boxing Day (Dec.

26 or next working day except South Australia)

Regional: Numerous state holidays

Austria

Jan. 1　New Year's Day
Jan. 6　Epiphany
May 1　Labor Day
Aug. 15　Assumption
Oct. 26　National Holiday
Nov. 1　All Saints' Day
Dec. 8　Immaculate Conception
Dec. 25　Christmas
Dec. 26　St. Stephen's Day

Variable: Easter Monday, Whit Monday, Corpus Christi

Belarus

July 27　National Holiday

Belgium

Jan. 1　New Year's Day
May 1　Labor Day
July 21　Independence Day
Aug. 15　Assumption Day
Nov. 1　All Saints' Day
Nov. 11　Veterans' Day
Dec. 25　Christmas

Variable: Easter Monday, Ascension Day, Whit Monday

Regional: July 11 Flemish Community Day, Sept. 27 French Community Day

Optional: Nov. 15 Dynasty Day

Brazil

Businesspeople in Brazil are most likely to be on vacation in February, the first two weeks in March, July, and the end of December.
Jan. 1　New Year's Day
Apr. 21　Tiradentes Day
May 1　Labor Day
Sept. 7　Independence Day
Nov. 2　All Souls' Day
Nov. 15　Proclamation of the Republic

Dec. 8   Immaculate Conception
Dec. 25   Christmas
Dec. 26   Day after Christmas

Variable: Carnival (two weeks in February or March), Ash Wednesday (half day), Good Friday, Easter Saturday, Easter Monday, Corpus Christi, Our Lady Appeared (October)

Regional: Jan. 20 Founding of Rio de Janeiro (in Rio de Janeiro), Jan. 25 Founding of São Paulo (in São Paulo)

Optional: Holy Thursday; Nov. 1 All Saints' Day

Bulgaria

Jan. 1   New Year's Day
Mar. 3   National Day
May 1   Labor Day
May 24   Education Day
Dec. 25   Christmas

Variable: Easter Monday

Canada

* Observed on nearest Monday.
Jan. 1   New Year's Day
July 1   Canada Day
Nov. 11   Remembrance Day*
Dec. 25   Christmas
Dec. 26   Boxing Day

Variable: Good Friday; Easter Monday; Victoria Day (May 24, 1993; May 23, 1994; May 22, 1995; May 20, 1996); Labor Day (Sept. 6, 1993; Sept. 5, 1994; Sept. 4, 1995; Sept. 2, 1996); Thanksgiving (Oct. 11, 1993; Oct. 10, 1994; Oct. 9, 1995; Oct. 14, 1996)

Regional:
Alberta: 1st Monday in August, Heritage Day
British Columbia: 1st Monday in August, British Columbia Day
Manitoba: 1st Monday in August, Civic Holiday
Newfoundland: 2nd Monday in March, Commonwealth Day; Mar. 17 St. Patrick's Day*; Apr. 24 St.

George's Day*; June 24 Discovery Day*; July 1 Memorial Day*; July 12 Orangemen's Day*
Ontario: 1st Monday in August, Civic Holiday
Quebec: June 24 Fete National
Saskatchewan: 1st Monday in August, Civic Holiday
Yukon Territory: 3rd Monday in August, Discovery Day
Northwest Territory: 1st Monday in August, Civic Holiday

Chile

Jan. 1   New Year's Day
May 1   Labor Day
May 21   Commemoration of the
          Battle of Iquique
Aug. 15   Assumption Day
Sept. 11 National Day
Sept. 18 Independence Day
Sept. 19 Armed Forces Day
Oct. 12   Columbus Day
Nov. 1   All Saints' Day
Dec. 8   Immaculate Conception
Dec. 25   Christmas

Variable: Good Friday, Easter Saturday, Corpus Christi

China

Jan. 1   New Year's Day
Mar. 8   International Women's Day
          (women only)
May 1   Labor Day
Aug. 1   Army Day
Sept. 9   Teachers' Day
Oct. 1–2 China's National Days

Variable: Lunar New Year, three-day business holiday

Colombia

Vacations are taken in December, January, June, and July.
Jan. 1   New Year's Day
Jan. 6   Epiphany
May 1   Labor Day
June 9   Thanksgiving
June 29   SS. Peter and Paul
July 20   Columbia Independence Day

Aug. 7 Battle of Boyaca
Aug. 15 Assumption Day
Oct. 12 Columbus Day
Nov. 1 All Saints' Day
Nov. 11 Independence of Cartagena
Dec. 8 Immaculate Conception
Dec. 25 Christmas

Variable: St. Joseph's Day (March), Holy Thursday, Good Friday, Ascension Thursday, Corpus Christi

Optional: Feast of Sacred Heart and SS. Peter and Paul

Costa Rica

Jan. 1 New Year's Day
Mar. 19 Saint Joseph's Day
Apr. 11 Battle of Rivas
May 1 Labor Day
June 29 SS. Peter and Paul
July 25 Annexation of the Province of Guanacaste
Aug. 2 Festivity of Our Lady of the Angels
Aug. 15 Mother's Day
Sept. 15 Independence Day
Oct. 12 Columbus Day
Dec. 8 Festivity of the Immaculate Conception
Dec. 25 Christmas

Variable: Holy Thursday, Good Friday, Corpus Christi

Czechoslovakia

Jan. 1 New Year's Day
May 1 Labor Day
May 8 National Day, Anniversary of Liberation
July 5 National Day, Day of the Apostles SS. Cyril and Methodius
Oct. 28 Anniversary of Independence
Dec. 25 Christmas
Dec. 26 Day after Christmas
With separation of Czechoslovakia into two nations, holidays may change.

Variable: Easter Monday

Denmark

Jan. 1 New Year's Day
May 15 Common Prayer's Day
June 5 Constitution Day (from noon)
Dec. 25 Christmas
Dec. 26 Boxing Day

Variable: Maundy Thursday, Good Friday, Easter Monday, Common Prayer's Day, Ascension Day, Whit Monday

Dominican Republic

Jan. 1 New Year's Day
Jan. 6 Feast of the Kings
Jan. 21 Our Lady of Altagracia
Jan. 26 Day of Duarte
Feb. 27 Independence Day
May 1 Labor Day
Aug. 16 Restoration of Independence
Sept. 24 Mercedes Day
Oct. 12 Columbus Day
Dec. 25 Christmas

Variable: Good Friday, Corpus Christi

Ecuador

Jan. 1 New Year's Day
May 1 Labor Day
May 24 Battle of Pichincha
July 24 Bolivar's Birthday
Aug. 10 Independence Day
Oct. 9 Independence of Guayaquil
Oct. 12 Columbus Day
Nov. 1 All Saints' Day
Nov. 2 All Souls' Day
Nov. 3 Independence of Cuenca
Dec. 6 Founding of Quito
Dec. 25 Christmas

Variable: Carnival Day, Holy Thursday, Good Friday

Regional: Founding of Guayaquil (in Guayaquil only)

Egypt

Jan. 1 New Year's Day
May 1 Labor Day
June 18 Evacuation Day
July 23 Revolution Day

Oct. 6 Armed Forces Day
Oct. 24 Popular Resistance Day
Dec. 23 Victory Day

Variable: Muslim religious holidays; Coptic Christian holidays; Mouloud, Birth of Muhammad (August)

Optional: Jan. 7 Coptic Christmas

Estonia

Jan. 1 New Year's Day
May 1 Labor Day
June 23 Victory Day
Dec. 25 Christmas
Dec. 26 Day after Christmas
Variable: Good Friday, Midsummer Day (June)

Finland

Jan. 1 New Year's Day
Jan. 6 Epiphany
Apr. 30 May Day Eve
May 1 May Day
Dec. 6 Independence Day
Dec. 24 Christmas Eve
Dec. 25 Christmas
Dec. 26 Boxing Day

Variable: Good Friday, Easter Monday, Ascension Day, Midsummer Eve (June 25, 1993; June 24, 1994; June 23, 1995), Midsummer Day (June 26, 1993; June 25, 1994; June 24, 1995), All Saints' Day (Nov. 6, 1993; Nov. 5, 1994; Nov. 5, 1995)

France

Many people are on vacation between mid-July and mid-September.
Jan. 1 New Year's Day
May 1 Labor Day
May 8 Armistice 1945
July 14 Bastille Day
Aug. 15 Assumption
Nov. 1 All Saints' Day
Nov. 11 Memorial Day
Dec. 25 Christmas

Variable: Easter Monday, Ascension Day, Whitmonday

Germany

Jan. 1 New Year's Day
May 1 Labor Day
Oct. 3 German Unity Day
Nov. 18 Day of Repentance and Prayer
Dec. 25 Christmas
Dec. 26 Boxing Day

Variable: Good Friday, Easter Monday, Ascension Thursday, Whit Monday

Regional: Epiphany (in Baden-Württemberg and Bayern), Corpus Christi (in Baden-Württemberg, Bayern, Hessen, Nordrhein-Westfalen, Rheinland-Pfalz, Saarland), Assumption of the Blessed Virgin (in parts of Bayern, Saarland), Oct. 31 Reformation Day (in Brandenburg, Mecklenburg-Vorppommern, Sachsen, Sachsen-Anhalt, Thüringen), All Saints' Day (in Baden-Württemberg, Bayern, Nordrhein-Westfalen, Rheinland-Pfalz, Saarland, parts of Thüringen)

Guatemala

Jan. 1 New Year's Day
Jan. 6 Epiphany
May 1 Labor Day
June 30 Anniversary of the Revolution
Sept. 15 Independence Day
Oct. 12 Columbus Day
Oct. 20 Revolution Day
Nov. 1 All Saints' Day
Dec. 25 Christmas
Dec. 26 Day after Christmas
Dec. 31 New Year's Eve
Variable: Good Friday, Easter

Regional: Assumption of the Virgin (Guatemala City only), Aug. 15

Hong Kong

Dec. 25 Christmas

Variable: The first weekday in January; Lunar New Year's Day and possibly days before and after; Ching

Ming Festival; Good Friday; Easter Saturday; Easter Monday; Birthday of Her Majesty the Queen, two days in June; Tuen Ng (Dragon Boat) Festival; Saturday preceding the last Monday in August; Liberation Day (last Monday in August); the day following the Chinese Mid-Autumn Festival: Chung Yeung Festival; the first weekday after Christmas Day

Hungary

Jan. 1   New Year's Day
Mar. 15 Anniversary of 1848 Uprising Against Austrian Rule
May 1   Labor Day
Aug. 20 Constitution Day
Oct. 23 Day of Proclamation of the Republic
Dec. 25 Christmas
Dec. 26 Day after Christmas

Variable: Easter Monday

India

Because of the religious and regional diversity of India many holidays are celebrated. Some religious holidays vary according to astronomical observations and are determined at the beginning of the year.
Jan. 26 Republic Day
Aug. 15 Independence Day
Oct. 2   Mahatma Gandhi's Birthday

Indonesia

Jan. 1   New Year's Day
Aug. 17 Indonesian National Day
Dec. 25 Christmas
Variable: Ascension of the Prophet Muhammad (Jan., Feb.), Good Friday, Ascension Day (Christian), Mouloud (Prophet Muhammad's Birthday, Aug., Sept.), Muslim religious holidays

Ireland

Jan. 1   New Year's Day
Mar. 17 St. Patrick's Day
Dec. 25 Christmas

Dec. 26 St. Stephen's Day

Variable: Good Friday; Easter Monday; the First Monday in June, bank holiday; the First Monday in August, bank holiday; the Last Monday in October, bank holiday

Israel

Variable: Independence Day (Apr. 26, 1993; Apr. 14, 1994; May 4, 1995; Apr. 24, 1996; May 12, 1997) plus Jewish religious holidays

Italy

Many people are on vacation between mid-July and mid-September.
Jan. 1   New Year's Day
Jan. 6   Epiphany
Apr. 25   Liberation Day
May 1   Labor Day
Aug.15   Assumption of the Virgin
Nov. 1   All Saints' Day
Dec. 8   Immaculate Conception
Dec. 25   Christmas
Dec. 26   Santo Stefano

Variable: Good Friday, Easter Monday

Regional:
Apr. 25   Venice, St. Mark
June 24   Florence, Genoa, and Turin, St. John the Baptist
June 29   Rome, SS. Peter and Paul
July 15   Palermo, Santa Rosalia
Sept. 19 Naples, San Gennaro
Oct. 4   Bologna, St. Petronio
Oct. 30   Cagliari, St. Saturnino
Nov. 3   Trieste, San Giusto
Dec. 6   Bari, St. Nicola
Dec. 7   Milan, St. Ambrose

Japan

Jan. 1   New Year's Day
Jan. 15   Coming of Age Day
Feb. 11   National Foundation Day
Mar. 21   Vernal Equinox
Apr. 29   Greenery Day
May 3   Constitution Memorial Day
May 4   People's Holiday
May 5   Children's Day

Sept. 15 Respect for the Aged Day
Sept. 23 Autumnal Equinox
Oct. 10 Health-Sports Day
Nov. 3   Cultural Day
Nov. 23 Labor Thanksgiving Day
Dec. 23 Emperor's Birthday

Korea, Republic of

Jan. 1–2 New Year's Observed
Mar. 1   Independence Movement Day
Apr. 5   Arbor Day
May 5   Children's Day
June 6   Memorial Day
July 17 Constitution Day
Aug. 15 Liberation Day
Oct. 1   Armed Forces Day
Oct. 3   National Foundation Day
Oct. 9   Hangul, or Korean
         Alphabet Day
Dec. 25 Christmas

Variable: Lunar New Year's Day or
Solnal; Buddha's Birthday (April,
May); Choo Suk, Korean Thanksgiv-
ing Day (September)

Kyrgyzstan

Aug. 31 National Holiday

Latvia

Nov. 18 National Holiday

Lithuania

Feb. 16 National Holiday

Luxembourg

Jan. 1   New Year's Day
May 1   Labor Day
May 28
Aug. 15 Assumption Day
Nov. 1-2 All Saints' Day
Dec. 25 Christmas
Dec. 26 Day after Christmas

Variable: Carnival, Good Friday,
Easter Monday, Ascension Day,
Whit Monday

Malaysia

Jan. 1   New Year's Day
May 1   Labor Day

Aug. 31 Malaysia National Day
Dec. 25
Variable: Chinese New Year, King's
Birthday (June), Hari Raya Puasa,
Wesak Day, Hari Raya Haji, Awal
Muhurram, Deepavali, Muhammad's
Birthday (October), Chinese and
Muslim religious holidays

Mexico

Mexico does not move holidays to
the beginning or end of the week.
Jan. 1   New Year's Day
Feb. 5   Anniversary of Mexican
         Constitution
Mar. 21 Juarez's Birthday
May 1   Labor Day
May 5   Anniversary of the Battle
         of Puebla
Sept. 1 President's State of the
         Union Address
Sept. 16 Independence Day
Oct. 12 Dia de la Raza–Columbus Day
Nov. 2   Day of the Dead
Nov. 20 Mexican Revolution
Dec. 25 Christmas

Variable: Holy Thursday, Good Friday

Optional: Dec. 12 Our Lady of Gua-
dalupe

Netherlands

Jan. 1   New Year's Day
Apr. 30 Queen's Birthday
May 5   Liberation Day
Dec. 25 Christmas
Dec. 26 Boxing Day

Variable: Good Friday, Easter Monday, Ascension, Whit Monday

New Zealand

Jan. 1   New Year's Day
Feb. 6   New Zealand (Waitangi) Day
Apr. 25 Anzac Day
Oct. 26 Labor Day
Dec. 25 Christmas
Dec. 26 Boxing Day

Variable: Good Friday, Easter Monday, Queen's Official Birthday (June)

Regional:
Jan. 22 in Wellington
Jan. 29 in Auckland, in Northland
Feb. 1   in Nelson
Mar. 23 in Otago and Southland
Mar. 31 in Taranaki
Nov. 1   in Hawke's Bay and
         Marborough
Dec. 1   in Westland
Dec. 16 in Canterbury

Nigeria

Jan. 1   New Year's Day
Oct. 1   National Day
Dec. 25

Variable: Muslim religious holidays,
Second Monday in March, Good Friday, Easter Monday

Norway

Jan. 1   New Year's Day
May 1   Labor Day
May 17   Constitution Day
Dec. 25 Christmas
Dec. 26 Day after Christmas

Variable: Holy Thursday, Good Friday, Easter Monday, Ascension Day, Whit Monday

Pakistan

Mar. 23 National Holiday

Peru

Jan. 1   New Year's Day
May 1   Labor Day
June 29 SS. Peter and Paul
July 28 Independence Day
Aug. 30 St. Rosa of Lima
Oct. 8   Battle of Angamos
Nov. 1   All Saints' Day
Dec. 8   Immaculate Conception
Dec. 25 Christmas

Variable: Maundy Thursday, Good Friday

Philippines

Jan. 1   New Year's Day
Feb. 25 Freedom Day

May 1   Labor Day
May 6   Fall of Bataan
June 12 Independence Day
Aug. 27 National Heroes' Day
Sept. 11 Barangay Day
Sept. 21 Thanksgiving Day
Nov. 1   All Saints' Day
Nov. 30 Bonifacio Day
Dec. 25 Christmas
Dec. 30 Rizal Day
Dec. 31 Usually nonworking holiday

When a legal holiday falls on a Sunday, the following Monday shall not be a holiday unless a proclamation is issued declaring it a public holiday.

Variable: Maundy Thursday, Good Friday, Last Sunday of August National Heroes Day

Poland

Jan. 1   New Year's Day
May 1   Labor Day
May 3   Polish National Day
May 9   Victory Day
Aug. 15 Assumption Day
Nov. 1   All Saints' Day
Dec. 25 Christmas
Dec. 26 Day After Christmas

Variable: Easter Monday, Corpus Christi

Portugal

Jan. 1   New Year's Day
Apr. 25 Liberty Day
May 1   Labor Day
June 10 Portugal Day
Aug. 15 Assumption of the Virgin
Oct. 5   Proclamation of the Republic
Nov. 1   All Saints' Day
Dec. 1   Restoration of Independence
Dec. 8   Immaculate Conception
Dec. 25 Christmas

Variable: Carnival Day, Shrove Tuesday, Good Friday, Corpus Christi

Regional: June 13 St. Anthony (Lisbon only), June 24 St. John the Baptist (Porto only)

Romania

Jan. 1–2 New Year's Day
May 1–2 Labor Day
Dec. 1 National Day
Dec. 25 Christmas

Russia

Nov. 7–8 National Holiday

Saudi Arabia

There are no official holidays except for Eid al Fitr and Eid al Adha.

Variable: Eid al Fitr, celebrating the breaking of Ramadan (businesses and government closed approximately four days). Eid al Adha, celebrating the *Hajj*, or pilgrimage to Mecca (businesses and government closed approximately five days). Other Muslim religious holidays

Singapore

Jan. 1 New Year's Day
May 1 Labor Day
Aug. 9 National Day
Dec. 25 Christmas

Variable: Chinese New Year, Good Friday, Vesak Day, Hari Raya Puasa, Hari Raya Haji, Deepavali

South Africa

Jan. 1 New Year's Day
Apr. 6 Founder's Day
May 1 Workers' Day
May 31 Republic Day
Oct. 10 Kruger Day
Dec. 16 Day of the Vow
Dec. 25 Christmas
Dec. 26 Day of Goodwill

Variable: Good Friday, Family Day, Ascension Day

Regional: Jan. 2 (the Western Cape)

Spain

Jan. 1 New Year's Day
Jan. 6 Epiphany
May 1 St. Joseph the Workman

July 25 St. James of Campostela
Aug. 15 Assumption
Oct. 12 Day of Spain
Nov. 1 All Saints' Day
Dec. 6 Constitution Day
Dec. 8 Immaculate Conception
Dec. 25 Christmas

Variable: Maundy Thursday, Good Friday, Easter Monday, Corpus Christi

Regional: May 15 St. Isidro (Madrid)

Sweden

Jan. 1 New Year's Day
Jan. 6 Epiphany
May 1 Labor Day
Dec. 25 Christmas
Dec. 26 Boxing Day

Variable: Good Friday, Easter Monday, Ascension Day, Whit Monday, Midsummer Eve, Midsummer Day, All Saints' Day

Switzerland

Jan. 1 New Year's Day
Jan. 2 Baerzelis Day
Aug. 1 Swiss National Day
Dec. 25 Christmas
Dec. 26 St. Stephen's Day

Variable: Good Friday, Easter Monday, Ascension Thursday, Whit Monday

Taiwan

Jan. 1–2 Founding Day of the Republic of China
Mar. 29 Youth Day
Apr. 5 Anniversary of President Chiang Kai-shek's Passing
Sept. 28 Teacher's Day, Confucius' Birthday
Oct. 10 National Day
Oct. 25 Taiwan Retrocession Day
Oct. 31 President Chiang Kai-shek's Birthday
Nov. 12 Dr. Sun Yat-sen's Birthday
Dec. 25 Constitution Day

Variable: Lunar New Year, Lantern Festival, Dragon Boat Festival, Mid-Autumn Moon Festival

Thailand

Jan. 1 New Year's Day
Apr. 6 Memorial Day, Chakri Day
Apr. 13 Songkran Day
Aug. 12 Queen's Birthday
Oct. 23 Chulalongkorn Day
Dec. 5 King's Birthday
Dec. 10 Constitution Day
Dec. 31 New Year's Eve

Variable: Chinese New Year, Makhabuja (February), Coronation Day (May), Ploughing Ceremony (May), Visakhabuja (May, June), Asalhabuja (July), Beginning of Buddhist Lent (July)

Turkey

Jan. 1 New Year's Day
Apr. 23 National Sovereignty and Children's Day
May 19 Youth and Sports Day
Aug. 30 Victory Day
Oct. 29 Republic Day

Variable: Seker Bayrami, Kurban Bayrami

Turkmenistan

Oct. 27 National Holiday

Ukraine

Aug. 24 National Holiday

United Arab Emirates

Jan. 1 New Year's Day
Dec. 25
Dec. 31

Variable: Muslim religious holidays

Regional: Aug. 6 Accession, Ruler of Abu Dhabi (Abu Dhabi only); Dec. 2 National Day (Abu Dhabi only)

United Kingdom

Queen's Birthday observed on a Saturday in June. Business not affected.

The spring and summer holidays, often called bank holidays, are observed by all businesses.

England, Wales, Scotland

Jan. 1 New Year's Day
Dec. 25 Christmas

Variable: Good Friday; Easter Monday; May 3, 1993, May Day; May 31, 1993, Spring Holiday or bank holiday; Aug. 30, 1993, Summer Holiday or bank holiday; Dec. 27, 1993, Boxing Day; Dec. 28, 1993, the day after Boxing Day

Northern Ireland

Same as England plus: Mar. 17 St. Patrick's Day; July 12, 1993, Orangemen's Day

Channel Islands

Same holidays as England plus May 5 Liberation Day

Isle of Man

Same holidays as England plus July 5 Tynwald Day

United States

Jan. 1 New Year's Day
July 4 Independence Day
Dec. 25 Christmas

Variable: Presidents' Day (third Monday in February), Memorial Day (last Monday in May), Labor Day (first Monday in Sept.), Thanksgiving Day (fourth Thursday in Nov).

Optional: Jan. 21 Martin Luther King Day; Feb. 12 Lincoln's Birthday; Good Friday; a working day before or after July 4; Columbus Day (Oct. 12 or 2nd Monday in Oct.); Election Day (first Tuesday after first Monday in Nov.); Nov. 11 Veterans' Day; Friday after Thanksgiving; often a working day before or after Christmas.

Uzbekistan

Sept. 1   National Holiday

Venezuela

Jan. 1   New Year's Day
Apr. 19   Declaration of Independence
May 1   Labor Day
June 24   Battle of Carabobo
July 5   Independence Day
July 24   Simon Bolivar's Birthday,
           Battle of Logo de Maracaibo
Sept. 4   Civil Servants' Day
Oct. 12   Columbus Day

Dec. 24   Christmas
Variable: Carnival, Holy Thursday,
Good Friday

Optional:
Jan. 6   Epiphany
Mar. 19   St. Joseph
June 29   SS. Peter and Paul
Aug. 15   Assumption Day
Nov. 1   All Saints' Day
Dec. 8   Immaculate Conception

Regional: Mar. 10 in La Guiara
only, Oct. 24 in Maracaibo only

Part 11

International Telephone Calls

Placing an International Call

There are various ways to place international calls. The options available to you depend on the phone system you are using, where you are located, and where you want to call.

Many countries have international direct dialing (IDD or DDD), which is the easiest way to place an international call because you dial the number yourself without having to go through an operator.

You may not be able to use international direct dialing in the following situations:

1. If you are in an office building or hotel that requires you to go through the office or hotel operator.
2. If you are using a phone in a system that cannot handle international direct dialing. In the United States AT&T, MCI, and SPRINT all provide international direct dialing. Other systems may require you to dial an AT&T operator first.
3. If the country you are calling is not part of the international direct dialing system.
4. International direct dialing may not be available in your area even though it is available in other parts of the country and in the country you want to call.

When International Direct Dialing Is Available

When this is available, you dial an international prefix or international access code followed by the phone number. Your call will go through without assistance or interference of an operator.

If you recognize the different parts of a telephone number you will be less likely to misdial it. It is possible to dial a country or city code twice if either is included in what you think is only the local number. International telephone numbers usually consist of three elements:

1. the country code
2. an area code (also called city code, trunk code)
3. a local number (also called subscriber number)

Not all countries use area or city codes.

The number of digits in a phone number varies from country to country and often within a country as well. In Mexico area codes have one, two, or three digits and local numbers have five, six, or seven digits. The area code in the United States is always a three-digit number and the local number seven digits.

Also the use of spaces and punctuation in numbers varies. If you have a general idea of the number of digits and the pattern used in a particular country it may help you to avoid misdialing. If the pattern is unfamiliar, you may be able to sort it out if you recognize the country code and the city code. The number of the Johannesburg Chamber of Commerce might be given as (2711) 726-5316, the (2711) being the country code (27) of South Africa and the Johannesburg area code (11).

The country code is usually either a two- or three-digit number. The Commonwealth of Independent States and the United States both have one-digit numbers.

Local numbers are grouped in various patterns. In the United States, it is three digits, then a hyphen, then four digits: 111-2222. In Denmark it is eight digits grouped in four pairs with space between: 11 22 33 44. The first digit is like a city code.

☞ See pages 209–218 for country codes and major area codes within countries.

International Access Code

The international access code connects you with the system for international calling. Although many countries use the same numbers for their international access code (often 00) they are not standardized. The international access code is not the same as the country code. Each country has its own specific country code, much the same as the area or city code for a specific region.

Following are two examples of how to place an international call with direct dialing:

To call from U.S. to Paris, France

011	33	1	11 22 33 44
U.S. int'l access code	French country code	Paris city code	local no.

To call from Finland to Paris, France

990	33	1	11 22 33 44
Finnish int'l access code	French country code	Paris city code	local no.

When International Direct Dialing Is Not Available

Only a few places in the world cannot be reached by direct dialing. In those cases, you will have to use an international operator to help you. You do not dial the international access number to get an operator but a different number listed in the phone book. If you know the country code as well as the rest of the number, the call may cost less than if you have to get the country or city code from the operator.

Operator-Assisted Calls

Of course if you want to make a collect call, a person-to-person call, request time and charges, or other assistance you will need an operator and the call will cost more than direct dialing.

Office Hours and Holidays

Sometimes it may be difficult to find a good time to call someone in another part of the world. If the time difference between your office and the one you want to call is 10 to 15 hours, then it may be difficult to find a good time to talk on the phone during normal business hours (8 a.m. to 5 p.m.).

The custom in some countries is to take a long midday lunch break and in others a short break. In Belgium and Spain people are likely to take long breaks. In parts of Mexico the lunch hour may be both long and late, although in northern border cities the lunch hour may be shorter and early as in the United States.

☞ See pages 182–186 for customary business and banking hours.

☞ See pages 186–199 for legal holidays.

Prefixes

Often a prefix is dialed first when calling within the country to a number outside the immediate area. In the United States, the prefix 1 is dialed when calling from one area to another and also often to call from one exchange to another within the same area code. In Finland and in Spain the prefix 9 is dialed when calling from one area to another.

This prefix, used in national calls, is dropped when making an international call. In other words, within Spain to call from Barcelona to Madrid you would first dial 91 (prefix and city code). To call Madrid from outside of Spain you would drop the 9 and just dial 1, the Madrid city code.

When a prefix is shown as part of the number, as 91 above, not separated, 9-1 for example, it may be difficult to recognize, causing a person to dial the prefix by mistake when making an international call.

Dial Tones

Various dial tones are used by different systems to indicate whether the line is ringing or is busy. For example you could hear a tone and a silence of equal length no longer than a second or a short tone followed by a longer pause to indicate that the line is busy. If you are not sure what the tone means you can always stay on the line long enough to hear if someone answers.

In many countries you simply dial one number after another, but in some places you have to wait for a dial tone after dialing the international access code.

Countries in Same Region

Sometimes a call from one country to another in the same region is dialed as a national not an international call. In these cases do not dial the international access code and country code. To call Canada from the United States or the United States from Canada, dial 1 + area code + local number. A call to Mexico from the United States or Canada, however, is an international call.

Faxes

In most cases you use the same international access code, country code, and area code for sending a fax as for making a phone call. In a few places you dial a different international access code to send a fax. In Hong Kong, for example, the access code for an international phone call is 001 and for an international fax is 002.

☞ See pages 221–224 for more on faxes and telexes.

Telephone Phrases

Placing a call to someone in a country where they do not speak your language can be daunting. However, you will be able to handle this situation well if you remember a few commonsense points.

Unless you are making a cold call where no previous contact exists between you and the person you are calling, there's a good chance the person who answers speaks your language at least a little or recognizes it enough to put someone else on the line who can understand you. Be patient and calm while this is happening. Be confident, keep a friendly tone in your voice, and do not become frustrated. At all costs, avoid sounding impatient or defensive.

Consider learning a few phrases in the other language to get things started. A good one is how to ask for someone who speaks your language. Doing this shows interest and willingness to try to work together. Even if your accent is not very good, people appreciate the effort. Keep in mind that in international business everyone gets used to hearing other languages, not to mention dialects, regional variations, and different accents from their own. See page 66 on pronouncing names.

English is considered the common language of business. However because it is so widely spoken it takes on many variations in pronunciation and usage. British and American English can sound very different, almost unrecognizable as the same language. In places where the English spoken is influenced by local languages, it will be different in yet other ways.

In normal conversation, most people use slang, colloquial expressions, and company jargon. Your international conversations will go more smoothly if you avoid these expressions and stick to basic words and phrases. Speak clearly and not too fast. If someone calls from overseas to talk to your colleague, it would better to say, "She has gone out for lunch but will be back in thirty minutes" rather than "She's gone to grab a quick bite but will be right back."

If you need to talk to someone who does not speak your language you might contact AT&T or another major telephone company about using the services of a translator. Major phone companies can provide translators to translate phone conversations.

If you do not want to take your chances on being able to get through to the person you want, you could place a person-to-person call through an international operator who speaks the necessary language.

Although you do not speak the language of the country you are calling, it is beneficial to recognize a few conversational phrases. You may want to speak them and at the least should know what they mean when hearing them on the other end of the line. The following list includes some of the common ones. It is nice to be able to at least greet the person you are calling in his or her own language before switching over to your own.

In English it is customary to say "hello" rather than "good morning" when first speaking into the phone. In Italy it is customary to say "pronto," which means something like "I am ready" to listen to you. It does not mean "hurry up" as in English. Often people answer the phone saying the company name or their own name.

You should not avoid making a call simply because you do not speak the language of the country you are calling. In international business people are accustomed to coping with various languages. Many people speak more than one language and will recognize a request to talk to someone who speaks yours. A polite request for someone who speaks your language will not be laughed at or ignored.

French
Hello *Allo*
Good morning *Bonjour*
Good evening *Bonsoir*
Good night *Bonne nuit*
Goodbye *Au revoir*
How are you? *Comment allez-vous?*
Very well *Trés bien*
Can you assist me?
 Pouvez-vous m'aider?
Do you speak English?
 Parlez-vous anglais?
I don't understand *Je ne comprends pas*
Yes *Oui*
No *Non*
Please *S'il vous plaît*
Thank you *Merci*
You're welcome *Il n'y a pas de quoi*
Excuse me *Excusez-moi*

German
Good morning *Guten Morgen*
Good evening *Guten Abend*
Good night *Gute Nacht*
Goodbye *Auf Wiedersehen*
How are you? *Wie geht es Ihnen?*
Very well *Sehr gut*
Can you assist me?
 Können Sie mir helfen?
Do you speak English?
 Sprechen Sie Englisch?
I don't understand *Ich verstehe nicht*
Yes *Ja*
No *Nein*
Please *Bitte*
Thank you *Danke*
You're welcome *Gern geschehen*
Excuse me *Entschuldigen Sie*

Italian
Hello or ready, as in I'm ready to talk to you *Pronto*
Good morning *Buon giorno*
Good evening *Buona sera*
Good night *Buona notte*
Goodbye *Arrivederci or ciao*
How are you? *Come sta?*
Very well *Benissimo*
Do you speak English? *Parla inglese?*

I don't understand *Non capisco*
Yes *Si*
No *No*
Please *Per favore*
Thank you *Grazie*
You're welcome *Prego*
Excuse me *Mi scusi*

Japanese
Hello *Moshi Moshi*
Good morning *Ohayo gozaimasu*
Good afternoon *Konnichiwa*
Good evening *Konbanwa*
Good night *Oyasumi nasai*
Goodbye *Sayonara*
How do you do? *Hajime mashite?*
How are you? *Ogenki desu ka?*
How are you? *Ikaga desu ka?*
Very well *Hijoni yoidesu*
Can you assist me?
 Tasukete kudasaimasuka
Do you speak English?
 Anatawa eigo wo hanasemasuka?
I do not understand *Wakarimasen*
Yes *Hai*
No *Iie*
Please *Dozo*
Thank you *Arigato*
Thank you very much *Domo arigato*
You're welcome *Do itashi mashite*
Sorry or Excuse me *Sumimasen*
Just a moment please
 Chotto matte kudasai

Spanish
Good morning *Buenas días*
Good evening *Buenas tardes*
Good night *Buenas noches*
Goodbye *Adiós*
How are you? *¿Como está usted?*
Very well *Muy bien*
Can you assist me? *Puede ayudarme?*
Do you speak English?
 Habla usted inglés?
I don't understand *No entiendo*
Yes *Si*
No *No*
Please *Por favor*
Thank you *Gracias*
You're welcome *De nada*
Excuse me *Dispénseme*

COUNTRY AND CITY CODES

Telephone dialing procedures are rapidly changing. The growing use of cellular phones and faxes results in the need for more telephone numbers. To meet demand, phone companies add prefixes to the beginning of local numbers and area codes, require users to dial the area code even when dialing within the same area, assign new area codes, and so on.

Sometimes the number of digits in the local number and in the area codes varies from town to town; however, the combination of local number, area code, and prefix will always add up to the same number.

The following information serves as a guide. Specific procedures may change or be different for the call you are trying to make. Some examples are given of how to dial a number nationally, that is, within the country, as well as internationally, that is, from another country. When you are in the country the local phone directory is the best source of information. You might purchase telephone directories for cities where you plan to do a lot of business. Directories contain much useful information, including all area codes for the country, instructions on calling locally, nationally, and internationally. Even if it is written in a language you do not understand, diagrams will make the point clear.

Look in your telephone directory for a number to call for ordering foreign directories or contact Worldwide Directory Products Sales (in St. Louis, MO), 1-800-792-2665. The price may be $50 or higher and your order may take some weeks to fill.

Algeria 213

International: +213 **2** 60-18-63

Algiers	2
Annaba	8
Constantine	4

Argentina 54

International: + 54 **1** 773-1063

Buenos Aires	1
Cordoba	51
La Plata	21
Rosario	41
Tucuman	81

Armenia 7

Yerevan	8852

Australia 61

National: **02** 261-9200
International: + 61 **2** 261-9200
Prefix: To call from one area to another within Australia dial 0 first.

Adelaide	8
Brisbane	7
Canberra	6
Darwin	89
Melbourne	3

In the sample phone numbers, + means to dial international access code first. **Bold** indicates area code (city code, routing code, trunk code, etc.) .

Newcastle	49
Perth	9
Sydney	2

Austria 43

National: **0222** 31-55-11
International: + 43 **1** 31-55-11
Prefix: To call from one area to another within Austria dial 0 first.

Graz		316
Innsbruck		512
Linz		732
Salzburg		662
Vienna	(in Austria)	222
	(from the U.S.)	1

Azerbaijan 7

Baku	8922

Belarus 7

Minsk 0172

Belgium 32

National: **02** 513-6770
International: + 32 **2** 513-6770
Prefix: To call from one area to another within Belgium dial 0 first.

Antwerp	3
Bruges	50
Brussels	2
Charleroi	71
Ghent	91
Liege	41

Brazil 55

National: **061** 321-7272
International: + 55 **61** 321-7272
Prefix: To call from one area to another within Brazil dial 0 first.

Belo Horizonte	31
Brasilia	61
Porto Alegre	512
Recife	81
Rio de Janeiro	21
Salvador	71
São Paulo	11

Bulgaria 359

International: + 359 **2** 884-801

Burgas	56
Plovdir	32
Ruse	82
Sofia	2
Varna	52

Canada 11

National: 1 **613** 238-5353
International: + 11 **613** 238-5353
Prefix: To call from one area to another within Canada dial 1 first.
To call between Canada and the United States dial 1 + area code + local number; do not dial country code.

Calgary, AB	403
Charlottetown, PE	902
Edmonton, AB	403
Fredericton, NB	506
Gander, NF	709
Halifax, NS	902
Hamilton, ON	416
London, ON	519
Ottawa-Hull, ON	613
Québec City, PQ	418
Regina, SK	306
St. Catharines-Niagara, ON	416
St. John's, NF	709
Toronto, ON	416
Vancouver, BC	604
Victoria, BC	604
Whitehorse, YK	403
Winnipeg, MB	204

Chile 56

National: **02** 671-0133
International: + 56 **2** 671-0133
Prefix: To call from one area to another within Chile dial 0 first.

Antofagasta	55
Concepción	41
Santiago	2
Talcahuano	41
Valparaiso	32

In the sample phone numbers, + means to dial international access code first. **Bold** indicates area code (city code, routing code, trunk code, etc.) .

China 86

International: + 86 **1** 532-3831

Beijing	1
Chongqing	811
Guangzhou	20
Harbin	451
Nanjing	25
Shanghai	21
Shenyang	24
Tianjin	22
Wuhan	27

Colombia 57

International: + 57 **1** 232-6550

Barranquilla	58
Bogotá	1
Cali	23
Cartagena	53
Medellín	4

Commonwealth of Independent States (CIS)

All countries of the former Soviet Union can be direct dialed. The country code for all is 7. See each country for capital city area code. Local numbers are usually 6 digits.

Costa Rica 506

International: + 506 20-3939
No city codes are required.

Czech Republic 42

International: +42 **2** 536641

Brno	5
Ostrava	69
Pilsen	19
Prague	2

Denmark 45

National: **31** 42 31 44
International: + 45 **31** 42 31 44
Danish phone numbers have 8 digits, the first of which indicates the city. All 8 digits are dialed whether inside or outside Denmark.

When looking for information in Danish sources be aware that in the Danish alphabet the vowels æ, ø and å are the 27th, 28th, and 29th letters, following the letter z.

In an alphabetic listing the letter Ü, ü is listed with y; Ä, ä, with æ; Ö, ö with ø; Aa is listed with Å, å (as the last letter of the alphabet). In a Danish phone directory, the cities of Aalborg and Aarhus would appear at the end of the listing, not at the beginning as shown below.

Aalborg	8
Aarhus	6
Copenhagen	3
	4 (suburbs)
Odense	7

Dominican Republic 809

International: + 809 563-3151
Other comments: To call from the United States, dial as if 809 is area code (in other words, dial 1 + 809 + local number).
There are no city codes.

Ecuador 593

International: + 593 **2** 561-404

Cuenca	7
Guayaquil	4
Quito	2

Egypt 20

National: 0**2** 354-1583
International: + 20 **2** 354-1583
Prefix: To call from one area to another within Egypt dial 0 first.

Alexandria	3
Cairo	2

Estonia 7

Tallinn	0142

Finland 358

National: 9 **0** 171-931

In the sample phone numbers, + means to dial international access code first. **Bold** indicates area code (city code, routing code, trunk code, etc.) .

International: + 358 **0** 171-931
Prefix: To call from one area to another within Finland dial 9 first.

Helsinki	0
Tampere	31
Turku	21

France 33

National: (from Paris to provinces):
prefix 16 + local 8-digit number
(from province to province):
prefix 16 + local 8-digit number
(from provinces to Paris):
prefix 16 + **1** + local 8-digit number

International:
(to Paris) + 33 **1** 42 96 12 02. To areas outside Paris, dial + 33 and 8-digit local number; no area code is needed. All local calls in France are 8 digits. The first one or two digits indicate the city. Even when calling within an area, say from one building to another in Bordeaux, you dial the city number first followed by six digits.

Georgia 7

Tbilisi	8832

Germany 37 and 49

National: **030** 819-7888
International: + 49 **30** 819-7888
Country code for western Germany is 49 and for eastern Germany is 37. Prefix: Within western Germany, dial 0 before the area code. To call eastern Germany from western Germany, dial as if an international call. For example to call from Frankfurt in western Germany to eastern Berlin, dial 00 + 37 + 2 + local number. The 00 is the international access code in western Germany.

Berlin (East)	**37**	2
Berlin (West)	**49**	30
Bonn	**49**	228

Bremen	**49**	421
Cologne	**49**	221
Dortmund	**49**	231
Dresden	**37**	51
Dusseldorf	**49**	211
Essen	**49**	201
Frankfurt	**49**	69
Hamburg	**49**	40
Leipzig	**37**	41
Munich	**49**	89
Stuttgart	**49**	711

Guatemala 502

International: + 502 **2** 311-541

Guatemala City	2
Other cities	9

Hong Kong 852

National: 526-0165
International: + 852 526-0165
There are no area codes.

India 91

National: **11** 600-651
International: + 91 **11** 600-651

Ahmedabad	272
Bangalore	812
Bombay	22
Calcutta	23
Kanpur	512
Madras	44
New Delhi	11

Indonesia 62

National: **021** 360-360
International: + 62 **21** 360-360
Prefix: To call from one area to another within Indonesia dial 0 first.

Bandung	22
Jakarta	21
Medan	61
Semarang	24
Surabaya	31

Ireland 353

National: **01** 687-122
International: + 353 **1** 687-122

In the sample phone numbers, + means to dial international access code first. **Bold** indicates area code (city code, routing code, trunk code, etc.) .

Prefix: To call from one area to another within Ireland dial 0 first.

Cork	21
Dublin	1
Limerick	61

Israel 972

National: 0**3** 654-338
International: + 972 **3** 654-338
Prefix: To call from one area to another within Israel dial 0 first.

Haifa	4
Jerusalem	2
Tel Aviv/Jaffa	3

Italy 39

National: 0**6** 4674-2202
International: + 39 **6** 4674-2202
Prefix: To call from one area to another within Italy dial 0 first.

Bari	80
Bologna	51
Brindisi	831
Florence (Firenze)	55
Genoa (Genova)	10
Livorno	586
Messina	90
Milan (Milano)	2
Naples (Napoli)	81
Palermo	91
Rome (Roma)	6
Trieste	40
Turin (Torino)	11
Venice (Venezia)	41

Japan 81

National: 0**3** 3224-5050
International: + 81 **3** 3224-5050
Prefix: To call from one area to another within Japan dial 0 first.
Prior to 1991, Tokyo had 7-digit phone numbers. On January 1, 1991, the number 3 was added to the beginning of the number making it an 8-digit number. Thus the number 224-5050 became 3224-5050.

Fukuoka	92
Kawasaki	44
Kobe	78
Kyoto	75
Nagoya	52
Osaka	6
Sapporo	11
Tokyo	3
Yokohama	45

Kazakhstan 7

Alma-Ata	3722

Korea, Republic of 82

National: 0**2** 732-2601
International: + 82 **2** 732-2601
Prefix: To call from one area to another within Korea dial 0 first.

Inchon	32
Pusan	51
Seoul	2
Taegu	53

Kyrgyzstan 7

Bishkek	331

Latvia 7

Riga	0132

Lithuania 7

Vilnius	0122

Luxembourg 352

International: + 352 460-123
There are no area codes.

Malaysia 60

National: 0**3** 248-9011
International: + 60 **3** 248-9011
Prefix: To call from one area to another within Malaysia dial 0 first.

Ipoh	5
Kuala Lumpur	3

Mexico 52

National: 91 **5** 211 0042
International: + 52 **5** 211 0042

In the sample phone numbers, + means to dial international access code first. **Bold** indicates area code (city code, routing code, trunk code, etc.) .

Prefix: To call from one area to another within Mexico, dial 91 first. To call Mexico from the United States, dial as international number using international access code and country code. The local number and area code vary in length but the combination adds up to 8 digits.

Aguascalientes AGS	491
Campeche CAMP	981
Ciudad Victoria TAMPS	131
Colima COL	331
Cuernavaca MOR	73
Culiacán SIN	671
Durango DGO	181
Guadalajara JAL	36
Guanajuato GTO	473
Hermosillo SON	621
Jalapa VER	281
La Paz B.C.S.	682
León GTO	471
Manzanillo COL	333
Matamoros TAMPS	891
Mérida YUC	99
Mexicali B.C.	65
Mexico City D.F.	5
Monterrey N.L.	83
Morelia MICH	451
Oaxaca OAX	951
Pachuca HGO	771
Puebla PUE	22
Querétaro QRO	463
Saltillo COAH	841
San Luis Potosí S.L.P.	481
Tepic NAY	321
Tlaxcala TLAX	246
Toluca MÉX	721
Tuxtla Gutierrez CHIS	961
Villahermosa TAB	931
Zacatecas ZAC	492

Moldova 7

Kishinev	0422

Netherlands 31

National: 070 310-9417
International: + 31 70 310-9417

Prefix: To call from one area to another within the Netherlands dial 0 first.

Amsterdam	20
Eindhoven	40
Rotterdam	10
The Hague	70
Utrecht	30

New Zealand 64

National: 04 722-068
International: + 64 4 722-068
Prefix: To call from one area to another within New Zealand dial 0 first.

Auckland	9
Christchurch	3
Wellington	4

Nigeria 234

International: + 234 1 616-477

Kaduna	62
Lagos	1

Norway 47

National: 02 44-85-50
International: + 47 2 44-85-50
Prefix: To call from one area to another within Norway dial 0 first. When looking for information in Norwegian sources, be aware that in the Norwegian alphabet the vowels æ, ø or ö, and å or aa are the 27th, 28th, and 29th letters, following the letter z.

Bergen	5
Oslo	2
Stavanger	4
Trondheim	7

Pakistan 92

International: + 92 51 826-161

Hyderabad	221
Islamabad	51
Karachi	221
Lahore	42

Peru 51

International: + 51 14 33 0555

Arequipa	54

In the sample phone numbers, + means to dial international access code first. **Bold** indicates area code (city code, routing code, trunk code, etc.) .

Callao	14
Chiclayo	74
Lima	14
Trujillo	44

Philippines 63

National: **2** 818-6674
International: + 63 **2** 818-6674

Cebu	32
Manila	2
Quezon City	2

Poland 48

International: + 48 **22** 21 45 15

Crakow	12
Gdansk	58
Warsaw	22

Portugal 351

National: 0**1** 726-6600
International: + 351 **1** 726-6600
Prefix: To call from one area to another within Portugal dial 0 first.

Lisbon	1
Porto (Oporto)	2

Romania 40

National: **0** 104-040
International: + 40 **0** 104-040

Bucharest (Bucuresti)	0
Cluj-Napoca	51
Constanta	16

Russia 7

International: + 7 **095** 252 24 51

Moscow	095

Saudi Arabia 966

International: + 966 **1** 488-3800

Jeddah	2
Makkah (Mecca)	2
Riyadh	1

Singapore 65

International: + 65 338-9722
There are no city codes.

Slovakia, Republic of 42

Bratislava	7
Kosice	95

South Africa 27

International: + 27 **11** 788-0265

Bloemfontein	51
Cape Town	21
Durban	31
Johannesburg	11
Pretoria	12

Spain 34

National: 9**1** 577-4000
International: + 34 **1** 577-4000
Prefix: To call from one area to another within Spain dial 9 first.
La Coruña would be listed under C not L in a Spanish directory.

Barcelona	3
Madrid	1
Seville	54
Valencia	6

Sweden 46

National: 0**8** 783-5346
International: + 46 **8** 783-5346
Prefix: To call from one area to another within Sweden dial 0 first.
Be aware that in the Swedish alphabet the vowels å, ä, and ö are the 27th, 28th, and 29th letters, following the letter z.

Goteborg	31
Stockholm	8

Switzerland 41

National: 0**31** 437-341
International: + 41 **31** 437-341

Berne	31
Geneva	22
Lausanne	21
Zurich	1

Taiwan 886

National: 0**2** 551-2515

In the sample phone numbers, + means to dial international access code first. **Bold** indicates area code (city code, routing code, trunk code, etc.) .

International: + 886 **2** 551-2515
Prefix: To call from one area to another within Taiwan dial 0 first.

Kaohsiung	7
Keelung	2
Taichung	4
Tainan	6
Taipei	2

Tajikistan 7

Dushanbe	3772

Thailand 66

National: 0**2** 253-4920
International: + 66 **2** 253-4920
Prefix: To call from one area to another within Thailand dial 0 first.

Bangkok	2
Chinag Mai	53
Ubon Ratchanthani	45

Turkey 90

International: + 90 **4** 167-0949

Adana	711
Ankara	4
Bursa	241
Istanbul	1
Izmir	51

Turkmenistan 7

Ashkabad	3632

Ukraine 7

Kiev	044

United Arab Emirates 971

International: + 971 **2** 345545

Abu Dhabi	2
Dubai	3

United Kingdom 44

National: 0**71** 499-9000
International: + 44 **71** 499-9000
Prefix: dial 0 before national code within the U.K.
In the U.K. there are national codes and local codes and three types of calls each involving a slightly different process.

1. Own exchange calls:
To dial numbers within your own exchange no code is required.

2. Local area calls:
Within London, dial 071 or 081 before the subscriber's number if you are calling from one area to another across the 071/081 boundary. Outside London, dial the local area code and the subscriber's number. Refer to the local phone book for the correct local code to use. Exhange names, e.g. Banbury, are often shown in telephone numbers to help determine the correct local code to use for a particular call.

3. National calls:
To call from one local call area to another dial the national code, preceded by 0, and the subscriber's number. The list below shows national numbers which are used in calling from outside the U.K.

Belfast	232
Birmingham	21
Bradford	274
Bristol	272
Cardiff	222
Edinburgh	31
Glasgow	41
Leeds	532
Liverpool	51
London (inner)	71
London (suburbs)	81
Manchester	61
Sheffield	742

United States 1

National: 1 **202** 377-2432
International: + 1 **202** 377-2432
Prefix: To call from one area to another within the United States dial 1 first.

Alabama All points	205
Alaska All points	907
Arizona All points	602

In the sample phone numbers, + means to dial international access code first. **Bold** indicates area code (city code, routing code, trunk code, etc.) .

Arkansas All points   501
California
(Several area codes within state)
Los Angeles   213
Oakland   510
San Diego   619
San Francisco   415
Colorado
(Several area codes within state)
Denver   303
Connecticut All points   203
Delaware All points   302
District of Columbia
    (Washington, D.C.)   202
Florida
(Several area codes within state)
Miami   305
West Palm Beach   407
Georgia
(Several area codes within state)
Atlanta   404
Hawaii All points   808
Idaho All points   208
Illinois
(Several area codes within state)
Chicago   312
Springfield   217
Indiana
(Several area codes within state)
Elkhart   219
South Bend   219
Iowa
(Several area codes within state)
Des Moines   515
Kansas
(Several area codes within state)
Topeka   913
Kentucky
(Several area codes within state)
Louisville   502
Louisiana
(Several area codes within state)
New Orleans   504
Maine All points   207
Maryland
(Several area codes within state)
Baltimore   410

Massachusetts
(Several area codes within state)
Boston   617
Worcester   508
Michigan
(Several area codes within state)
Detroit   313
Grand Rapids   616
Minnesota
(Several area codes within state)
Minneapolis   612
Mississippi All points   601
Missouri
(Several area codes within state)
Kansas City   816
St. Louis   314
Montana All points   406
Nebraska
(Several area codes within state)
Omaha   402
Nevada All points   702
New Hampshire
    All points   603
New Jersey
(Several area codes within state)
Newark   201
Trenton   609
New Mexico All points   505
New York
(Several area codes within state)
Albany   518
Buffalo   716
Kennedy Int'l Airport   718
Long Island   516
New York City:
    Manhattan   212
    Bronx, Brooklyn,
    Queens, Staten Island   718
Rochester   716
Syracuse   315
North Carolina
(Several area codes within state)
Charlotte   704
North Dakota All points   701
Ohio
(Several area codes within state)
Akron   216

In the sample phone numbers, + means to dial international access code first. **Bold** indicates area code (city code, routing code, trunk code, etc.) .

Cincinnati	513	**Vermont** All points	802
Cleveland	216	**Virginia**	
Columbus	614	(Several area codes within state)	
Oklahoma		Alexandria	703
(Several area codes within state)		Newport News	804
Oklahoma City	405	Norfolk	804
Tulsa	918	Richmond	804
Oregon All points	503	Roanoke	703
Pennsylvania		**Washington**	
(Several area codes within state)		(Several area codes within state)	
Erie	814	Seattle	206
Philadelphia	215	Spokane	509
Pittsburgh	412	Tacoma	206
Scranton	717	**Washington, D.C.**	202
Rhode Island All points	401	**West Virginia** All points	304
South Carolina		**Wisconsin**	
All points	803	(Several area codes within state)	
South Dakota All points	605	Madison	608
Tennessee		Milwaukee	414
(Several area codes within state)		**Wyoming** All points	307
Memphis	901		
Nashville	615		

Uzbekistan 7

Tashkent	3712

Texas
(Several area codes within state)

Venezuela 58

Dallas	214	International: + 58 **2** 285-3111	
El Paso	915	Barquisimeto	51
Fort Worth	817	Caracas	2
Galveston	409	Maracaibo	61
Houston	713	Valencia	41
San Antonio	512		
Utah All points	801		

In the sample phone numbers, + means to dial international access code first. **Bold** indicates area code (city code, routing code, trunk code, etc.) .

Part 12

International Telexes and Faxes

Telex and fax communication offer advantages over the telephone, express and regular mail. Both are used in the following situations.

- To send relatively short amounts of printed information within a few minutes
- To send information to an office that is closed at the time but will need the information as soon as it opens (particularly helpful when dealing with a company in a very different time zone)
- To send a one-way message where immediate interaction with the receiver is not required
- To confirm what was said in a phone conversation
- To send a delayed message (after you have left your office for the day)

Possible disadvantages of using telexes and faxes are these:

- Poor quality of copy
- Lack of privacy or security

The heat–sensitive paper that faxes are printed on is not as nice as letterhead stationery. The telex message cannot be sent on letterhead.

If the fax or telex machine is easily accessible, unauthorized people may be able to read incoming messages. Techniques exist and procedures can be put into operation to maintain privacy; however, not every office uses them.

Like telephones, telex and fax machines can be programmed to automatically keep trying to send your message if the line is busy on the first attempt. Faxes can be programmed to send your message automatically at a later time, for example, when you are no longer in your office.

The use of fax machines has increased at a tremendous rate in a short time and in many places has completely replaced the telex. However, until recently the telex was one of the most important ways of communicating in international business. A worldwide telex network is in place and used by more than 190 countries. Some companies only have telex machines, others only have fax machines, others have both, and still others have neither.

How Fax and Telex Differ

You may have more experience with one or the other of these important pieces of office equipment. Here are some ways they are different.

Fax transmission is much faster. Therefore, the cost is less to send the same amount of material by fax than by telex.

Faxes and telexes are sent over different networks. In some countries where the telephone lines cannot handle a rapidly transmitted fax message, the slower telex may be the better or the only way to send a message.

Any image—including drawings, diagrams, logos, letterheads, emblems, and even photographs—can be transmitted by fax. Telex can only transmit letters and numbers. When you want to send a communication on your own letterhead stationery, the fax machine is the way to do it.

Telexes are preferred for some transactions, such as money transfers, because they verify the receiver by name before completing the message. In other words, it is harder to send a message to a wrong number with a telex than with a fax. A telex can be traced more effectively to be sure it was received. Banks use telex for this reason.

To send a fax, you need a piece of paper with your message already printed, typed, or handwritten. To send a telex, you have to type your message into a telecopier or a personal computer, then dial the receiver's telex number to send the message.

USING FAX TECHNOLOGY

To send or receive a fax requires a fax machine. You must know the fax number of the recipient of your message and your message must be in the form of hard copy that can be fed into the fax machine.

You dial the same country code and area code as in making an international telephone call. Usually the local fax number will be different from the local phone number, although in a small business the same number may be used for both fax and telephone.

In a few places, you dial a different international access code to send a fax from the one used to make an international phone call. From Hong Kong, for example, to send a fax, the international access code is 002; to make an international phone call it is 001.

To send a fax from the United States to London, England, dial as follows:

011 (U.S. international access code)
44 (U.K. country code)
71 (London area code)
local fax number

Most businesses leave their fax machines turned on at all times, making it possible to receive messages when no one is there.

It is possible to dial a wrong fax number and not realize it. Your fax will go through but to the wrong place. Or the fax will arrive but not be delivered to the person to whom it is addressed. For these reasons it is advisable to ask for confirmation when sending important information. If setting up an appointment to meet with someone at a specific time, for example, you want to be sure the other person gets your message.

Fax is often the least expensive, as well as the fastest, method for sending messages. Remember that the cost of a fax is charged by the minute. If you have a number of pages of dense copy, transmission will be slow and the cost might be higher than express mail.

Fax machines are purchased from stores or companies that sell copiers, telephone answering machines, and similar kinds of office equipment. You can also send a fax by computer using a fax modem. You probably will want a dedicated phone line installed for your fax machine rather than use the same line as your telephone. The telephone company will do this for you. Once installed your only expenses will be the charge every time you use it. These will be billed as part of your regular telephone bill, just like regular calls.

USING TELEX TECHNOLOGY

To send a telex you need either a telex machine or a personal computer equipped to send telexes. You subscribe to telex service separately from the telephone and fax. The person to receive your telex must also be a telex subscriber and have a teleprinter or computer on which to receive your message.

In the past, companies leased telex equipment and paid a monthly charge as well as a per use fee. Today it is more economical to use your personal computer and avoid the monthly charge.

Because telex uses a different network from the telephone the international access codes and country codes for telexes are different from those for international phone calls and faxes.

WHAT ARE YOUR CHOICES?

Technological developments and a variety of service arrangements make it possible for anyone to send a message using either fax or telex. It is becoming possible for telex machines, fax machines, and personal computers to communicate with each other. If you or your client do not have sophisticated automated electronic equipment you can still get your message through. Various organizations provide these services for moderate fees. Some of the options are:

- You can use an international carrier such as Western Union International (a different company from Western Union, which makes domestic calls within the United States) to send your message by telex. First you deliver your message by phone or in printed form to the carrier.
- Send a fax through a service like INTELPOST, International Electronic Post, of the U.S. Post Office. You either fax or deliver your document to the post office where it is faxed to the post office nearest the addressee. The addressee either picks it up at the post office or it is delivered by mail.
- Send a fax or telex through a local office center, hotel, or message service that provides this service for a fee.
- Send a message through a personal computer to a telex machine.
- Send a message through a fax machine to a personal computer.
- Send a message through a personal computer to a fax machine.

The technology that transmits your message once it has been inputted—over fiber optic cables or by microwave and satellite—is not the subject of this book. The important thing is that telexes and faxes are especially useful in international business because they provide the fastest way to send printed messages long distances and bypass difficulties caused by time differences between sender and receiver.

Translation
and
Interpretation

International business communication is often initiated without the aid of a translator. At this stage, people understand each other well enough to determine that there is interest in becoming business partners. Communication may be mostly spoken, in conversations at trade fairs, at conferences, in the presence of business associates of mutual acquaintance.

WRITTEN TRANSLATION

The next stage requires written communication to start defining the business relationship. Letters may be written in less than grammatically or idiomatically perfect language and still be acceptable and understandable. If the wrong impression is given by mistake, it can be corrected because goodwill has been established between the two parties. If translating is necessary at this stage, a student or instructor at a local university or a bilingual acquaintance might be of help. *But be careful.* Slang and idiomatic expressions change rapidly and may be acceptable to some but not to others; specific phrases and terms familiar in one region may be unknown or carry a different meaning in another. The translator, unless a current native-speaker of the language, may not be aware of these subtleties.

Once beyond the generalities and niceties you should consider using a professional translator, whether for translating printed material or interpreting conversations between speakers at a meeting or on the telephone. The requirements of translating legal or technical documents are different from those of preparing a promotional piece. You may need graphics—drawings, diagrams, photographs, or special symbols, characters, or logos—to accompany the print material. If you have a manual translated, each step must be clearly laid out.

Pay close attention to any translation you have done. Translations are as much a part of good business communication as is writing in your own language. You want your translated material to reflect an understanding of current business and market trends. You will do serious damage to your cause if the tone of your translated material is offensive, disrespectful, outdated, grammatically incorrect, or worse, inaccurate, incomplete, or incomprehensible.

Use a qualified business translator familiar with the technical nature of your work and the culture of the place where your work will appear. It is extremely important to recognize subtle differences between expressions, slang, and meanings of words. Do not assume that speakers of a language in one place use the same colloquial phrases as speakers of the same language in other places. Colloquial expressions used in Germany may be different from those used in Austria or Switzerland. Expressions used in England are different from those used in the United States, Australia, India, Ireland, or Jamaica.

It is important to recognize different styles of writing. A promotional piece may be an appropriate place to use colloquial or slang expressions. You may want a casual, conversational style of writing. However, in formal correspondence, legal documents, user manuals, business reports, leave out the jargon and idiomatic expressions. Use plain language that cannot be misunderstood.

Business translation companies have a variety of qualifications. Some large companies will do market research as well. Depending on the assignment, here are some specific qualifications to consider.

1. Experience in the market you want to reach.
2. Technical knowledge of your field.
3. A translator who is a native speaker of the language and possibly living in the country where your material will be read.
4. Modern communications equipment, including personal computers, modems, fax machines, desktop publishing software, high-quality printers, and graphic arts capabilities.
5. Project managers, proofreaders, editors, and technical consultants for large and complex assignments and for ongoing work.
6. The ability to set up style sheets, glossaries, and other records for your project in case a number of people work on it.
7. Translators for all the languages you expect to need.
8. Interpreters for business conversations.

Your material may not be translated at the office to which you send it. It may be sent by fax or modem to a translator located in the country where it will eventually be used. If the material is extensive, several people, even a large team, may be assembled to work on it.

When having printed material translated, you may expect to take the following steps.

1. Meet with the translation service to explain exactly what you want, determine what the end result should look like, and set up record keeping if you expect to give additional material to the same service in the future.
2. Determine procedures for reviewing the translation. You may want your contact in the other country to review it before you have it printed in large quantities. If the material is technical you need to know that it has been proofread carefully, someone has verified all procedures and confirmed that illustrations and diagrams are placed correctly in the text.
3. Establish a schedule for having it sent to you and to your reviewers.

INTERPRETING SPOKEN WORDS

Interpretation services also are available to translate the spoken word, for example, during a business or legal meeting, a plant tour, or a training session. If you want interpreters at a conference, you should plan to work with a service well ahead of time to determine how many interpreters and what equipment—such as microphones, headsets or wireless equipment, and electrical outlets—will be needed. You may need to alert the hotel or conference center to special needs, such as seating arrangements and booths for the interpreters.

If you need to have a translator for a telephone conversation, you can arrange for this through AT&T and other major telephone carriers.

When you are having your spoken words interpreted, as with written words, avoid slang, jargon, and idiomatic language that will create difficulty for the interpreter.

The costs for translating and interpreting vary depending on the nature of the work and the languages involved. Remember that whatever the material is, it represents you and so should be professional looking or sounding and project the image you want.

Part 14

Sources
of Information

Many directories of business information on individual countries are published by chambers of commerce, trade associations, and government agencies. Many are revised annually or every few years. Often they are expensive but may be available in a good business reference library, such as the Brooklyn Public Libary in New York City.

Useful international shipping information is contained in manuals prepared for their customers by the private shipping companies, such as UPS, Federal Express, Emery Worldwide, and Airborne Express, as well as the postal service.

In the United States, the Department of Commerce and the Small Business Administration are important government agencies for obtaining information on international business. Both have offices throughout the country.

Consulates and embassies, cultural and trade organizations are also sources of information.

The list of publications below is by no means comprehensive but describes a variety of the information sources.

1992 Asia Yearbook, 32nd ed. Hong Kong: National Fair Ltd, Review Publishing Co., 1992. 216 pages.
Information on thirty-one Asian countries, review of political and social affairs, foreign relations, economy, infrastructure; plus regional performance figures, such as consumer price index, debt-service ratio, government expenditures, balance of payments.

A Basic Guide to Exporting. Washington, DC: U.S. Department of Commerce, 1991. 143 pages.
A useful introduction to exporting, updated periodically. Describes government and commercial sources of information, preparing a product for export, service exports, pricing, customs and tax incentives, documentation, financing. Numerous sources for information both in United States and overseas. To purchase, contact the Government Printing Office in Washington, D.C.

Canadian Almanac and Directory, 1992. Toronto: Copp Clark Pitman Limited, 1992.

Chicago Manual of Style, 13th ed. Chicago: University of Chicago Press, 1982. 738 pages.
Widely used by writers and editors for comprehensive coverage of all aspects of manuscript preparation. Some discussion of personal names and style used in other languages, accents marks, and much more.

Do's and Taboos Around the World, 2nd ed. Axtell, Roger E., ed. New York: John Wiley and Sons, 1990.
Humorous, easy reading geared to help Americans feel comfortable and behave well in international settings. Axtell is author of several books on the subject of do's and taboos in international situations.

Do's and Taboos of International Trade: A Small Business Primer. Axtell, Roger E. New York: John Wiley and Sons, 1991. 305 pages.
Topics include how to start, first trip, laws, pricing, shipping, resources, and more.

Economist Business Traveller's Guides. The Economist Publications Ltd and Webster's Business Traveler's Guides. In United States by Prentice Hall Press. Series of guides by country including information on business, cultural awareness, industrial and economic scene, as well as travel.

Encyclopedia of International Commerce. Miller, William J. Centerville, MD: Cornell Maritime Press, 1985.
Definitions of trade terms, tariffs, laws, treaties, and some more generally useful terminology, plus sample forms, appendixes.

Europa World Year Book, 1992. London: Europa Publications, Ltd., 1992. 3267 pages. Published annually.
Descriptions of international organizations and their activities; country listings include statistical surveys of area and population, agriculture, industry, finance, government, and more. Includes all countries, not just Europe.

Exporters' Encyclopaedia. Parsippany, NJ: Dun's Marketing Services. Published annually. More than 1,800 pages.
A comprehensive, extremely useful source. Data on all countries in the world, including profile of population, languages, principal cities, currency, communications, business travel. Also names of key contacts, trade regulations, shipping documentation, postal rates, and more.
Also includes monthly updates and toll-free telephone service. Available in business libraries.

Fast Track Exporting. Renner, Sandra L., and W. Gary Winget. New York: AMACOM, 1991. 275 pages.
Focusing on small and medium size companies, provides advice on conducting a market trial run and on penetrating a foreign market. Uses almost 100 case studies to give pertinent examples of fast-track techniques.

Foreign Commerce Handbook, 17th ed. Maffry, Ann Dwyer. International Division, Chamber of Commerce of the United States, 1981.
Descriptions of agencies, departments, committees, services of U.S. government and United Nations involved in international commerce. Also trade associations, research organizations, chambers of commerce. Also information on international trade documents, finance, and more. Unfortunately not updated recently.

Guide to Incoterms, 1990. New York, NY: International Chamber of Commerce (ICC) Publishing Corporation, 1991. 150 pages.
Detailed comments on the thirteen Incoterms, legal rights of buyer and seller. Intended to help determine which term to use in export/import transactions.

Handbook for Multilingual Business Writing. Lincolnwood, IL: NTC Business Books, a division of National Textbook Co., 1988. 360 pages.
Common phrases in German, English, Spanish, French, Italian. Sample letters. Good for improving understanding of foreign language.

Handbook of Commercial French. Geoghegan, G., and J. Gonthier Geoghegan. Routledge, 1988.
A dictionary of English/French, French/English business terms. Also sample letters in French and English.

Information Please Almanac. New York: Houghton Mifflin Company. Published annually. 1000 pages approximately.

International Mail Manual. U.S. Postal Service. Revised when rates change.
Complete list of U.S. postal rates for all classes of mail to all places in world served by U.S. Postal Service. Available on a subscription basis. See p. 94 on how to order.

International Postal Rates and Fees, U.S. Postal Service. Publication 51, Feb. 1991. 36 pages. Revised when rates change.
Condensed from the *International Mail Manual* (see above), this free booklet from U.S. post office describes classes of mail and services. Also includes select rate tables.

Key Words in International Trade, 2nd rev. ed. International Chamber of Commerce, 1989. 416 pages.
In English, German, Spanish, French, Italian. Predominantly trading, export/import terms.

Kompass Directories. These directories for over twenty countries are published by Kompass Companies Worldwide. Each country directory includes manufacturers, distributors, wholesalers, importers, and exporters. Plus addresses, phone numbers, names of executives, revenue, and more. To obtain the United States Kompass Directory contact Croner, 211-03 Jamaica Ave., Queens Village, NY 11428. Length varies, often over 1,000 pages.

Multilingual Commercial Dictionary. Isaacs, Alan, ed. New York: Facts on File, 1978. 486 pages.
Business terms in English, French, Spanish, Germany, Portuguese, Italian.

National Directory of Addresses and Telephone Numbers. Kirkland, WA: General Information, Inc. Includes foreign corporations and chambers of commerce in United States, U.S. agencies that foster foreign trade, comparisons of rates of postal service and private services and more. Updated annually.

New York Times Atlas of the World, 3rd rev. concise ed. New York: Bartholomew/Times, a division of HarperCollins Publishers, 1992. 243 pages.

OAG Air Cargo Guide. Worldwide Edition. Published monthly by OAG (The Official Airline Guides), 2000 Clearwater Drive, Oak Brook, IL 60521.
Airline flight schedules, city/airport codes, air carrier index, major cargo charter airlines, small package services, air freight forwarder directory, and more. Because published monthly, a good source for current information on currency exchange rates, time chart (including dates for when Daylight Saving starts and ends), bank and public holidays.

Official Export Guide. Philadelphia: North American Publishing Company, 1992. 1,500 pages.
Information for all countries, including required export documentation, trade date, best export prospects, key contacts with addresses, regional maps, and much more.

Profitable Exporting: A Complete Guide to Marketing Your Products Abroad. Gordon, John S., and J.R. Arnold. New York: John Wiley and Sons, 1988. 358 pages.
A general introduction. Topics include organizing your company for export, developing agents/distributors abroad, communications, foreign exchange, and more.

Reference Book for World Traders: A Guide for Exporters and Importers. Queens Village, NY: Croner Publications, 1990. Updated with monthly supplements. In three volumes.

Shipping documents, addresses of government agencies, guide to global import and export controls and tariffs, insurance, information by country, and more.

Statistical Abstract of the US. U.S. Bureau of the Census. Published annually. 1000 pages approximately.

Statistics on U.S. population; labor force, employment, earnings, education, law enforcement, state and local government, banking, finance, insurance, and more.

Talking Business in —. Barron's Business Guides. Hauppauge, NY: Barron's Educational Series, Inc. Approximately 250 pages each.

Series of guides to various languages for English-speakers, with titles like *Talking Business in German.* Each one is combination of dictionary, reference, and travel guide for international business.

Understanding British English. Moore, Margaret E. New York: Citadel, 1989.

Webster's Secretarial Handbook, 2nd ed. Eckersley-Johnson, Anna L., ed. Springfield, MA: Merriam-Webster Inc., Publishers, 1983. 578 pages.

See section on "Travel and the International Character of Modern Business."

What's the Difference? A British-American Dictionary. Moss, Norman. New York: Harper & Row, 1973.

Words Into Type. Skillin, Marjorie E., et al. Englewood Cliffs, NJ.: Prentice-Hall, Inc., 1974. 583 pages.

Style manual widely used by writers and editors, for manuscript preparation, copy editing, typography. Some discussion of personal names and style used in other languages and much more.

World Almanac and Book of Facts. New York: Pharos Books. Published annually. 1000 pages approximately.

Statistics on all countries, on measures and equivalents, recent events, elections, U.S. regional data such as state capitals, major cities, demographics, geographic features, and more.

World Chamber of Commerce Directory. Loveland, CO: World Chamber of Commerce Directory. Published annually in June.

Lists U.S. and Canadian chambers of commerce, boards of tourism (U.S. and foreign), convention and visitors bureaus (U.S.), economic development organizations, American chambers of commerce abroad, foreign chambers of commerce in the United States.

World Is Your Market: An Export Guide for Small Business. Delphos, William A., ed. Washington, DC: Braddock Communications, 1990. 271 pages.

Introduction to the mechanics of exporting, assistance and resources, glossaries.

Write to the Point. Fruehling, Rosemary T., and N.B. Oldham. New York: McGraw-Hill, 1988. 261 pages.

An excellent concise guide to writing effective letters and memos, including examples of good and bad business writing; discussion of various letter formats.

ZIP Code Finder 1992. Chicago: Rand McNally. 646 pages.

ZIP codes for more than 125,000 places in the United States. ZIP maps of thirteen major cities and more.

Part 15

Country Information

The list below provides general information on the countries included in this book. The official name is on the second line. The religion(s) shown are the predominant ones. In most countries other religions are also observed by smaller groups. Also in many countries there are sizeable populations that speak languages other than those shown.

Hong Kong, although not an independent nation, is listed throughout this book as if it were. See sections on addresses, measures, currency, time, holidays, business hours, and telephoning for additional information listed by country. Much of the data below is from *The World Almanac and Book of Facts* and *The Information Please Almanac*.

Algeria

Democratic and Popular Republic of
  Algeria
capital: Algiers
languages: Arabic (official), French
religion: Sunni Muslim
population: 25,714,000
geographic area: 918,497 sq. mi.

Angola

People's Republic of Angola
capital: Luanda
language: Portuguese (official)
religion: Indigenous beliefs, Roman
  Catholic, Protestant
population: 8,802,000
geographic area: 481,353 sq. mi.

Argentina

Argentine Republic
capital: Buenos Aires
language: Spanish
religion: Roman Catholic
population: 32,291,000
geographic area: 1,065,189 sq. mi.

Armenia

Republic of Armenia
capital: Erevan (Yerevan)
language: Armenian
religion: Christian
population: 3,376,000
geographic area: 11,500 sq. mi.

See also Commonwealth of
  Independent States.

Australia

Commonwealth of Australia
capital: Canberra
language: English
religion: Anglican, other Protestant,
  Roman Catholic
population: 16,646,000
geographic area: 2,966,200 sq. mi.

Austria

Republic of Austria
capital: Vienna
language: German
religion: Roman Catholic
population: 7,595,000
geographic area: 32,374 sq. mi.

Azerbaijan

Republic of Azerbaijan
capital: Baku
language: Turkic
religion: Shi'ite Muslim
population: 7,100,000
geographic area: 33,400 sq. mi.

See also Commonwealth of
  Independent States.

Belarus

Republic of Belarus
capital: Minsk
language: Belarusian
religion: Orthodox
population: 10,300,000
geographic area: 80,200 sq. mi.

See also Commonwealth of
  Independent States.

Belgium

Kingdom of Belgium
capital: Brussels
languages: Dutch, French, German, Flemish
religion: Roman Catholic
population: 10,000,000
geographic area: 11,799 sq. mi.

Belgium is divided into three regions: Flanders, Brussels, and Wallonia. Flanders, the northern part of the country, is predominantly Dutch-speaking. Brussels, in the middle, is the capital city of Belgium and principal city of the European Economic Community; the predominant language is French. Wallonia, the southern part of the country, is French speaking.

Brazil

Federative Republic of Brazil
capital: Brasilia
languages: Portuguese (official), English
religion: Roman Catholic
population: 156,275,397
geographic area: 3,286,470 sq. mi.

Bulgaria

Republic of Bulgaria
capital: Sofia
language: Bulgarian
religion: Bulgarian Orthodox
population: 8,900,000
geographic area: 44,365 sq. mi.

Canada

capital: Ottawa
languages: English, French (both official)
religion: Roman Catholic, Protestant
population: 27,400,000
geographic area: 3,558,096 sq. mi.

French is the official language of business in the province of Quebec. English elsewhere.

Chile

Republic of Chile
capital: Santiago
language: Spanish
religion: Roman Catholic
population: 13,600,000
geographic area: 299,257 sq. mi.

China

People's Republic of China
capital: Beijing
language: Mandarin Chinese (official)
religion: Officially atheist. Confucianist, Buddhist, Taoist.
population: 1,165,800,000
geographic area: 3,705,390 sq. mi.

Two southern provinces (Fukien and Guangdong) are among the fastest economically developing regions of Asia. The cities of Shenzhen (a SEZ or Special Economic Zone) and Guangzhou are in Guangdong, a short distance from Hong Kong. Also part of this region of open economics is Hainan Island. Yunnan province is also likely to benefit from free-market economics.

Colombia

Republic of Colombia
capital: Bogotá
language: Spanish
religion: Roman Catholic
population: 34,300,000
geographic area: 439,735 sq. mi.

Commonwealth of Independent States (CIS)

A non-Communist association of states, formed in 1991 by eleven republics of the former Union of Soviet Socialist Republics (USSR). As of early 1993, the members of CIS are Armenia, Azerbaijan, Belarus, Kazakhstan, Kyrgyzstan, Moldova, Russia, Tajikistan, Turkmenistan, Ukraine, Uzebekistan.
Georgia is not part of CIS.

Costa Rica

Republic of Costa Rica
capital: San José
language: Spanish (official)
religion: Roman Catholic
population: 3,200,000
geographic area: 19,575 sq. mi.

Czechoslovakia

Czechoslovakia separated into two
nations at the beginning of 1993.
See Czech Republic and Slovakia,
Republic of.

Czech Republic

capital: Prague. Other large cities:
Brno, Ostrava, Pilsen, Olomouc.
languages: Czech and Slovak
religion: Roman Catholic
population: 10,000,000
geographic area: 30,464 sq. mi.

Denmark

Kingdom of Denmark
capital: Copenhagen
language: Danish
religion: Evangelical Lutheran
population: 5,200,000
geographic area: 16,633 sq. mi.

Dominican Republic

capital: Santo Domingo
language: Spanish
religion: Roman Catholic
population: 7,500,000
geographic area: 18,816 sq. mi.

Ecuador

Republic of Ecuador
capital: Quito
language: Spanish (official)
religion: Roman Catholic
population: 10,300,000
geographic area: 109,483 sq. mi.

Egypt

Arab Republic of Egypt
capital: Cairo
languages: Arabic (official), English
and French frequently used.
religion: Sunni Muslim
population: 57,758,000
geographic area: 386,650 sq. mi.

Estonia

Republic of Estonia
capital: Tallinn
languages: Estonian (official), Russian
religion: Evangelical Lutheran
population: 1,600,000
geographic area: 17,413 sq. mi.

Estonia, Latvia, and Lithuania are
known as the Baltic states.

Finland

Republic of Finland
capital: Helsinki
languages: Finnish, Swedish (both
official)
religion: Lutheran
population: 5,000,000
geographic area: 130,119 sq. mi.

France

French Republic
capital: Paris
language: French
religion: Roman Catholic
population: 56,900,000
geographic area: 220,668 sq. mi.

Georgia

Republic of Georgia
capital: Tbilisi (Tiflis)
language: Georgian
religion: Eastern Orthodox
population: 5,500,000
geographic area: 26,900 sq. mi.

Germany

Federal Republic of Germany
capital: Berlin
seat of government: Bonn
language: German
religion: Protestant,
Roman Catholic
population: 80,600,000

geographic area: 137,838 sq. mi.
On October 3, 1990, East Germany
(German Democratic Republic) and
West Germany (Federal Republic of
Germany) were unified.

Guatemala

Republic of Guatemala
capital: Guatemala City
language: Spanish
religion: Roman Catholic
population: 9,700,000
geographic area: 42,042 sq. mi.

Hong Kong

capital: Victoria
languages: English, Chinese
religion: Confucianist, Buddhist,
Christian
population: 5,700,000
geographic area: 409 sq. mi.
Hong Kong remains a British colony
until 1997, when it becomes a Special Administrative Region of China.

Hungary

Republic of Hungary
capital: Budapest
language: Hungarian (Magyar)
religion: Roman Catholic
population: 10,300,000
geographic area: 35,919 sq. mi.

India

Republic of India
capital: New Delhi
languages: Hindi (official), English
religion: Hindu predominant; also
   Muslim, Christian, Sikh, others
population: 882,600,000
geographic area: 1,266,595 sq. mi.

Indonesia

Republic of Indonesia
capital: Jakarta
languages: Bahasa Indonesian
   (Malay) (official), Javanese
religion: Muslim
population: 184,500,000
geographic area: 735,268 sq. mi.

Ireland

capital: Dublin
language: English, Irish
religion: Roman Catholic
population: 3,500,000
geographic area: 27,137 sq. mi.

Israel

State of Israel
capital: Jerusalem
languages: Hebrew and Arabic (both
   official), English
religion: Jewish
population: 5,200,000
geographic area: 7,847 sq. mi.

The embassies of many countries
are in Tel Aviv.

Italy

Italian Republic
capital: Rome
language: Italian
religion: Roman Catholic
population: 58,000,000
geographic area: 116,303 sq. mi.

Japan

capital: Tokyo
language: Japanese
religion: Buddhist, Shintoism
   shared by majority
population: 124,400,000
geographic area: 145,856 sq. mi.

Kazakhstan

Republic of Kazakhstan
capital: Alma-Ata
language: Kazak
religion: Muslim
population: 16,900,000
geographic area: 1,049,000 sq. mi.

See also Commonwealth of
   Independent States.

Korea, Republic of (South Korea)

capital: Seoul
language: Korean

religion: Buddhist, Confucianist, Christian
population: 44,300,000
geographic area: 38,025 sq. mi.
Democratic People's Republic of Korea (North Korea) is a separate nation. Its capital is Pyongyang.

Kyrgyzstan

Republic of Kyrgyzstan
capital: Bishkek
language: Kyrgyz
religion: Muslim
population: 4,500,000
geographic area: 76,000 sq. mi.

See also Commonwealth of Independent States.

Latvia

Republic of Latvia
capital: Riga
language: Latvian
religion: Lutheran, Catholic, Baptist
population: 2,700,000
geographic area: 24,595 sq. mi.

Estonia, Latvia, and Lithuania are known as the Baltic states.

Lithuania

Republic of Lithuania
capital: Vilnius
language: Lithuanian
religion: Catholic
population: 3,700,000
geographic area: 25,170 sq. mi.

Estonia, Latvia, and Lithuania are known as the Baltic states.

Luxembourg

Grand Duchy of Luxembourg
capital: Luxembourg
languages: French, German, Luxembourgian
religion: Roman Catholic
population: 400,000
geographic area: 998 sq. mi.

Malaysia

capital: Kuala Lumpur
languages: Malay (official), English, Chinese
religion: Muslim, Hindu, Buddhist, Confucianist, Taoist, others
population: 18,700,000
geographic area: 127,316 sq. mi.

Mexico

United Mexican States
capital: Mexico City
language: Spanish
religion: Roman Catholic
population: 87,700,000
geographic area: 761,604 sq. mi.

Moldova

Republic of Moldova
capital: Kishinev
language: Romanian
religion: Eastern Orthodox
population: 4,400,000
geographic area: 13,000 sq. mi.

See also Commonwealth of Independent States.

The Netherlands

Kingdom of the Netherlands
capital: Amsterdam
language: Dutch
religion: Roman Catholic, Dutch Reformed
population: 15,300,000
geographic area: 15,770 sq. mi.

The people are Dutch and the country is often referred to as Holland. In business and official situations the correct way to refer to the country is the Netherlands.

New Zealand

capital: Wellington
language: English (official)
religion: Anglican, Presbyterian, Roman Catholic, others
population: 3,400,000
geographic area: 103,736 sq. mi.

Nigeria

Federal Republic of Nigeria
capital: Lagos (Abuja, designated)
language: English (official)
religion: Muslim, Christian, others
population: 88,500,000
geographic area: 356,667 sq. mi.

Norway

Kingdom of Norway
capital: Oslo
language: Norwegian (official)
religion: Evangelical Lutheran
population: 4,300,000
geographic area: 125,181 sq. mi.

Pakistan

Islamic Republic of Pakistan
capital: Karachi
languages: Urdu, English (official),
  and others
religion: Muslim
population: 121,700,000
geographic area: 310,403 sq. mi.

Peru

Republic of Peru
capital: Lima
language: Spanish, native languages
religion: Roman Catholic
population: 22,500,000
geographic area: 496,222 sq. mi.

Philippines

Republic of the Philippines
capital: Manila
languages: Filipino and English
  (both official), Spanish
religion: Roman Catholic
population: 63,700,000
geographic area: 115,831 sq. mi.

Poland

Republic of Poland
capital: Warsaw
language: Polish
religion: Roman Catholic
population: 38,400,000
geographic area: 120,727 sq. mi.

Portugal

Republic of Portugal
capital: Lisbon
language: Portuguese
religion: Roman Catholic
population: 10,500,000
geographic area: 36,390 sq. mi.

Romania

capital: Bucharest
languages: Romanian,
  Magyar
religion: Orthodox
population: 22,760,449
geographic area: 91,699 sq. mi.

Russia

Russian Federation
capital: Moscow
languages: Russian (official),
  European, Middle Eastern, and
  Asian languages
religion: Eastern Orthodox
population: 148,542,700
geographic area: 6,592,800 sq. mi.

Saudi Arabia

Kingdom of Saudi Arabia
capital: Riyadh
language: Arabic
religion: Muslim
population: 16,100,000
geographic area: 839,996 sq. mi.

Singapore

Republic of Singapore
capital: Singapore
languages: Chinese (Mandarin),
  Malay, Tamil, English (all official)
religion: Buddhist, Taoist,
  Muslim, Christian
population: 2,800,000
geographic area: 224 sq. mi.

Located off the end of the Malay
Peninsula, the republic includes
about forty islets and Singapore Island, on which is located Singapore
City.

Slovakia, Republic of

capital: Bratislava. Other large city: Kosice.
language: Slovak, Czech, Hungarian
religion: Roman Catholic
population: 5,000,000
geographic area: 18,917 sq. mi.

South Africa

Republic of South Africa
capitals: Cape Town (legislative), Pretoria (administrative), Bloemfontein (judicial)
languages: Afrikaans and English (both official), Bantu languages
religion: Christian, Hindu, Muslim, others
population: 41,700,000
geographic area: 472,359 sq. mi.

Spain

capital: Madrid
languages: Castilian Spanish, Catalan (spoken principally in Barcelona, Gerona, Lérida, Tarragona in northeastern Spain), Galician, Basque
religion: Roman Catholic
population: 39,301,000
geographic area: 194,896 sq. mi.

Sweden

Kingdom of Sweden
capital: Stockholm
languages: Swedish, Finnish
religion: Lutheran
population: 8,700,000
geographic area: 173,731 sq. mi.

Switzerland

Swiss Confederation
capital: Bern
languages: German, French, Italian
religion: Roman Catholic, Protestant
population: 6,900,000
geographic area: 15,941 sq. mi.

Taiwan

Republic of China
capital: Taipei
language: Mandarin Chinese (official)
religion: Buddhist, Taoist, Confucianist
population: 20,800,000
geographic area: 13,885 sq. mi.

In 1978 the United States recognized the People's Republic of China and severed diplomatic relations with Taiwan. Officially the United States has no trade relations with Taiwan or trade offices. This has not prevented vigorous trade between the two countries. Taiwan is a top trading partner of the United States. The United States maintains the American Institute in Taiwan and Taiwan maintains the Coordination Council for North American Affairs with offices in Washington, D.C., Chicago, Los Angeles, Houston, and New York. There are many offices maintained by Taiwan throughout the international business world as well as chambers of commerce, trade organizations, and international corporations engaged in international business with Taiwan.

Tajikistan

Republic of Tajikistan
capital: Dushanbe
language: Tajik
religion: Sunni Muslim
population: 5,500,000
geographic area: 55,300 sq. mi.

See also Commonwealth of Independent States.

Thailand

Kingdom of Thailand
capital: Bangkok
language: Thai
religion: Buddhist
population: 56,300,000
geographic area: 198,456 sq. mi.

Turkey

Republic of Turkey
capital: Ankara
languages: Turkish (official),
  Kurdish, Arabic.
religion: Muslim
population: 59,200,000
geographic area: 301,381 sq. mi.

Turkmenistan

Republic of Turkmenistan
capital: Ashkabad
language: Turkic
religion: Sunni Muslim
population: 3,900,000
geographic area: 188,500 sq. mi.

See also Commonwealth of
Independent States.

Ukraine

capital: Kiev
language: Ukrainian
religion: Orthodox, Urkainian Catholic
population: 52,100,000
geographic area: 233,000 sq. mi.

See also Commonwealth of
Independent States.

United Arab Emirates

capital: Abu Dhabi
languages: Arabic (official), Farsi,
  English, Hindi, Urdu
religion: Muslim
population: 2,500,000
geographic area: 32,000 sq. mi.

The seven emirates in the United
Arab Emirates are Abu Dhabi,
Ajman, Dubai, Fujaira, Ras al-
Khaimah, Sharjah, Umm al-
Quaiwain.

United Kingdom

United Kingdom of Great Britain and
  Northern Ireland
capital: London

language: English
religion: Church of England, Roman
  Catholic
population: 57,533,000
geographic area: 94,226 sq. mi.

The main British island includes
England, Scotland, and Wales.
Wales is in the western part, its
area is 8,019 square miles, and its
capital is Cardiff. Scotland is the
northern part, its area is 30,405
square miles, and its capital is Ed-
inburgh. A person from Scotland
is a *Scot*, several are *Scots*. The ad-
jective is *Scottish*, as in *Scottish
company*, and the language is
Scottish. The word *scotch* refers to
the drink.

United States

United States of America (USA)
capital: Washington, D.C.
language: English
religion: Christian, Jewish, many
  others
population: 255,600,000
geographic area: 3,618,770 sq. mi.

Uzbekistan

Republic of Uzbekistan
capital: Tashkent
language: Turkic
religion: Sunni Muslim
population: 21,300,000
geographic area: 172,700 sq. mi.

See also Commonwealth of
Independent States.

Venezuela

Republic of Venezuela
capital: Caracas
language: Spanish (official)
religion: Roman Catholic
population: 18,900,000
geographic area: 352,143 sq. mi.

Index